We are all starving to connect and somehow forgot the basics of how to do it. With *Connect First,* Melanie cracks the code on how to tap into our humanity in order to influence others, be successful, and live a fuller life. Simple and sophisticated tools we all desperately need and didn't even know it. Thank you, Melanie.

—CHRIS MCCARTHY, President, MTV, VH1, CMT, and Logo Media

I found myself mid-chapter, putting this book down and instantly emailing one of my producers to tell her "thank you" for an error she caught on my show yesterday just before I went live! This book is full of brilliant actionable items that we *all* can do to connect, be better employees, be better humans.

—BROOKE BALDWIN, Anchor, *CNN Newsroom with Brooke Baldwin*

In this dynamic, digitalized, and radically changing world, never before has instilling meaning and purpose in our work and deepening connections with others been more important. Drawing on her extensive experience as trusted advisor to senior executives, Melanie offers a wealth of actionable insights which are grounded in neuroscience and psychology and vividly brought to life through case studies. *Connect First* is an invaluable resource.

—NISHA RAO-SCHILLER, Head of Leadership Planning and
Development, Deutsche Bank

Absolutely terrific! In clear prose, Melanie Katzman distills the insights and lessons from over 30 years of studying behavior in the workplace. There is something for everyone: graduates starting their first jobs, newly promoted managers, and veteran CEOs. I only wish I had this wise advice at the beginning of my career.

—PETER ROSE, Senior Advisor, Blackstone and
Vice Chairman, Sard Verbinnen

At a time when we're more connected to our devices than we are to each other, C-suite whisperer Melanie Katzman reminds us that it's the strength of our relationships that lays the foundation for greater success and joy at work. Witty and wise, she gifts us with 52 research-based, easy-to-implement tactics that will unlock connection and foster deep bonds in any workplace.

—CATHERINE STEINER-ADAIR, EdD, author of *The Big Disconnect*

Melanie is a provocateur of innovation. In *Connect First*, she holds up a mirror that allows us to laugh, learn, and alter our behavior. She reconnects us to our most human desire—to experience and spread joy.

—WELLINGTON NOGUEIRA, Founder, Doctors of Joy

CONNECT
FIRST

52 Simple Ways to Ignite Success,
Meaning, and Joy at Work

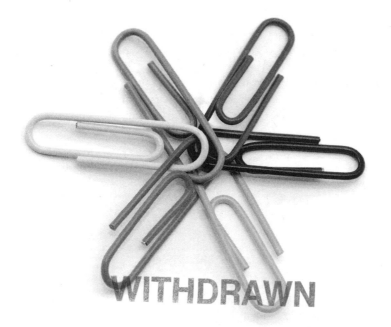

MELANIE A. KATZMAN, PHD

NEW YORK   CHICAGO   SAN FRANCISCO
ATHENS   LONDON   MADRID
MEXICO CITY   MILAN   NEW DELHI
SINGAPORE   SYDNEY   TORONTO

1 2 3 4 5 6 7 8 9   LWI   24 23 22 21 20 19

ISBN: 978-1-260-45783-4
MHID: 1-260-45783-4

e-ISBN: 978-1-260-45784-1
e-MHID: 1-260-45784-2

Design by Lee Fukui and Mauna Eichner

Library of Congress Cataloging in Publication Control Number: 2019026995

McGraw-Hill Education books are available at special quantity discounts to use as premiums and sales promotions or for use in corporate training programs. To contact a representative, please visit the Contact Us pages at www.mhprofessional.com.

For Russell, Wyndam, and Harper

CONTENTS

PART VII
HAVE A BIG IMPACT

PREFACE

Corporate life assumes a convenient fiction: If we assign roles and respon-sibilities, create flowcharts and project plans, and delineate deadlines and deliverables, then somehow magically, coolly, and calmly, the work will get done.

Wrong!

The truth is that organizations are run by people, and people run on emotions. Our feelings supply the energy to fuel our pursuit of profit and purpose. They are formidable and universal. They can't be ignored. Yet, to our great detriment, we have long pretended that emotions have no place in the office.

The future of work demands we recognize that emotions don't make us weak. Instead, they are our power tool, they're processed in the most primal, "animal" part of our brain, and they're critical to our existence. Achieving in business is often falsely equated with being rational, and efforts to be emotionally expressive can seem to make us too vulnerable. What we need is a professional, practical way of establishing quality relationships by connecting first as fellow humans, and then as coworkers and collaborators. From this personal foundation, great teams are formed, and goals are realized.

I've been the psychologist in the corner office, conference room, *and* treatment center for more than 30 years. People seek my counsel when they want to win, and when they need to survive. As a therapist with a private practice, I listen to patients' most private concerns and then—often in the same day—as a corporate consultant, advise on the managerial challenges of the world's biggest brands.

Logging on, swiping in, showing up: Employees and their bosses are crying out for greater respect, inclusion, and meaning at work. CEOs or fresh graduates, office workers or telecommuters—regardless of role, all seek security, cherish praise, and fear shame. We care, and we want to matter.

This shouldn't be surprising news. But what *is* shocking is how often we forget that our colleagues are people just like us. We become so easily enraged by that "other person" whose motives are unclear and whose reactions make no sense. It all gets so complicated, costly, and out of control when egos are bruised. People read each other's minds incorrectly, bad intentions are assumed, and small slights balloon into career-derailing moments. Top performers quit, and even business owners want to leave the companies they built. We often have blinders on when it comes to our own behavior, and a magnifying glass when assessing offenses we have endured. It doesn't have to be this way.

I have helped countless senior executives, middle managers, and entry-level employees become psychologically savvy about themselves and others. My clients succeed because I've increased their motivation and erased the excuses by sharing simple strategies to be a better human (person) at work.

From multinational corporations to mission-driven grassroots organizations, I've witnessed how being "natural" at work just doesn't come naturally. Corporate titles and positions define us. We've lost the ability to really be ourselves. But it can be relearned. I know, because I have successfully taught many of the same lessons over and over and over again.

Connect First: 52 Simple Ways to Ignite Success, Meaning, and Joy at Work is a systematic expression of my three decades of experience as a clinical psychologist and corporate consultant. It's a guide to unleash personal capacity, increase organizational effectiveness, and, for those who dare, drive large-scale change. Most of the suggestions in *Connect First* cost nothing and don't take more than five minutes to implement.

Some of the recommendations may seem quite basic. That's precisely the point! Because too often we get the "basics" wrong, success, meaning, and joy are sucked out of the modern workplace. Today's speed of communication puts unprecedented pressure on personal conduct. The tiniest acts of disrespect can be transmitted broadly. Insensitive behavior can set off an interpersonal storm in your organization and beyond. By attending to the simple but significant moments between people, you will secure your reputation and experience the beauty of how easily and quickly relationships can be improved. We don't stop there. *Connect First* will help you face the future with courage, take delight in the multitude of personalities you encounter, and position you for fruitful partnerships. We will build on the bonds you established to find new market solutions and drive social change. You will grow your personal and organizational influence. *Connect First* will take the mystery out of creating meaning at work, revealing everyday opportunities to make a difference in your immediate world and beyond.

Once you start approaching your job from the inside out, time expands and energy grows. It's addictive and infectious; oxygen fills the room, the mood lightens, and people are drawn to you. You will laugh more and achieve greater results. You will experience joy.

That's why I wrote this book: So you won't need me, or a person like me; so you don't repeat the same work drama over and over again; so your spirited inner self can propel you rather than paralyze you. I wrote this book to show you how work can be imbued with joy and meaning—to empower you to achieve success *and* significance.

THIS BOOK IS FOR YOU

Connect First is for everyone who wakes up in the morning and goes to work. It's for the executive in the corner office and the team crammed in the cubicles. It's for the budding entrepreneur and the aspiring scientist. It's for the proprietor of a small shop on Main Street as well as the CEO of a tech firm in Silicon Valley. Many workplace improvement books are written for company leaders. The underlying assumption is that senior management of the organization is responsible for changing the way we work. I take a different view. We all have the power and responsibility to make a difference. I've written this guide to show you what's possible.

Connect First will teach you how to transform our common human vulnerabilities into the basis of shared trust. We will silence the inner critic that continually questions your competence and will develop an abundant, generous perspective that prompts others to inform and include you more. You will develop the confidence to cut through organizational clutter and conduct conversations that dispel conflict and set shared goals. Start by adopting a winning mindset:

- You have the power to change your world.

- Organizational change starts with the individual and operates from the inside out.

- No matter your role, how *you* show up makes a difference.

- "Impossible" situations are often solved when people speak directly to each other.

- Quality person-to-person moments shift group dynamics and transform organizations.

- By focusing on what you and your coworkers have in common, you can better incorporate and appreciate diversity.

- You can create the community you want to be part of.

- In an increasingly automated, technology-driven world, there is an urgent need to stay connected to our humanity.

- Seemingly "simple" acts can be hugely disruptive.

HOW TO USE THIS BOOK

The step-by-step guidance offered in *Connect First* is by far the cheapest transformation program that any employee, manager, or human resources director will ever come across. There are no costly assessments and no unrealistic expectations. *Connect First* gives you the advice you need—*fast*.

The book is divided into seven parts beginning with Establish Respect and concluding with Have a Big Impact. There are 52 chapters, each accompanied by examples drawn from my three decades of experience, questions to gauge the applicability of the recommendations to your situation, and suggestions on how to apply the concepts effectively. The ideas take just a few moments to implement, yet have a lasting effect. The choice of 52 was intentional, designed to provide the option of experimenting with one new technique each week of the year. Case studies are culled from different countries and from various vantage points along the corporate hierarchy.

Connect First is your personal guide. It can also be read with others. Managers and their direct reports can establish shared expectations by reading *Connect First* together. Participants in staff orientation sessions, team retreats, or executive training programs will all benefit from the methods contained in *Connect First*, which translates broad concepts about culture into actions you can take tomorrow.

My recommendations are supported by compelling research from a variety of disciplines, including neurobiology, management theory, linguistics, and philosophy. There are lessons from farmers, factory workers, financiers, company presidents, and the people who serve them lunch. Sometimes, the best advice comes from surprising sources, and, often, widely disparate vantage points lead to the same profound conclusions.

You can read the chapters in order, or you can jump in where you think you need the most help. Each entry stands on its own. You may find sections validating what you are already doing right. Excellent! Use these affirmations to bravely leverage (and, where appropriate, advertise) your strengths. Each skill you master fortifies you for the sections that pose more of a challenge. There will be chapters that make you smile—or cringe with recognition at yet another way in which you have become *that* person, the one who is less gracious, generous, and approachable than you would like. That's OK—you're here to learn.

Here's a quick orientation. The chapters of *Connect First* are organized into seven sections:

- **Establish Respect.** Messing up the basics is the most common and most easily fixed error. Get them right to set the stage for success.

- **Engage All of Your Senses.** Knowledge is prized organizational currency. To be in the know requires that you do more than talk.

- **Become Popular.** Increase self-awareness, become more interested and interesting, be sought after for opportunities. Learn to be a magnet. You don't want to be left out.

- **Grow Loyalty.** Tap into what matters to the people you work with. Uncork creativity, stimulate cooperation, and make the days fly by.

- **Resolve Conflict.** Work is filled with frustrations: You're angry; they're angry. Clear obstacles and avoid unnecessary complications by naming and resolving differences.

- **Fight Fear.** Manage anxiety and uncertainty by resisting the urge to turn inward. Instead, invite in new perspectives, build bridges, and learn to facilitate innovative discussions.

- **Have a Big Impact.** Changing the world—or your slice of it—is possible when you learn to leverage your platform, no matter its size. Be recognized for *what* you have accomplished and *how* you made things happen. Be successful *and* significant.

A BIT ABOUT ME

Connect First: it's the name of the book and my guiding principle, so I better set a good example and tell you something about myself, given that we will be spending some time together.

I live in New York City with my husband of more than 35 years. I met him the first week of university. He was the cute drummer. He still plays music, though his paying jobs have been in law, finance, and real estate. He's got talent: I can't even sing "Happy Birthday." That's why I am writing this book, not making a musical.

Our children are grown, but they assure me I have yet to mature. When the kids were small, we lived in Hong Kong and London. We all learned to pack light and still use matching carry-on luggage. They indulge me. I can be a bit too organized. Some call it obsessive.

Our home is overflowing with books. I still read on paper. It's also usually filled with people—most of whom we know (but not always). We have twin black cats called Thunder and Lightning.

My grandparents were immigrants. My parents didn't go to college. My sister was in the first class of women to graduate from Yale.

I have a doctorate in clinical psychology. I maintain a private practice in New York City where I see about 20 people a week in my office with corner windows looking south to the Freedom Tower and west to the Empire State Building. It's the visual crossroads of history and the future. That captures my approach to change: be informed by but not beholden to the past, and keep your eye on what you can build tomorrow.

I'm an entrepreneur. I established Katzman Consulting 20 years ago to provide psychological expertise to organizations in transition, recovering from crisis, or seeking to grow impact. Along with a team of professionals (all trained in mental health), we facilitate strategy meetings, consult on corporate culture, and coach executives and the teams they lead. I've worked on six continents advising private and public companies, nonprofit institutions, and governmental agencies. I'm also a founding partner of the social enterprise, Leaders' Quest. Launched in 2001, we convene diverse stakeholders and provide experiential programs for companies and coalitions that allow people from very different backgrounds to see, feel, and touch each other's lives. We work in more than 24 countries and have 16 partners, 50 staff members, and approximately 40 associates. Our offices are in Mumbai, London, Berkeley, and New York. We see business as a force for good.

I'm an academic. I was on the faculty at the Weill Cornell Medical Center and was a senior fellow at Wharton Business School's Center for Leadership and Change Management. When it comes to research, I track the narratives but want to see the numbers. Statistics courses were among my favorites.

I like to talk. I cocreated and cohosted the national radio show *Women@ Work* on SiriusXM Business Radio. I've given more lectures around the world than I can count.

I'm endlessly interested in people and their stories, and I hope you are, too. You will find many case studies in the following chapters. Maintaining confidentiality is critical to my work. When I use a first and last name, that means the individual has given me permission to share their experiences. If you see only a first name, that's an alias. The story is real, but the person's identity has been protected.

Now that I have introduced myself, are you ready to begin? Let's go!

PART I

ESTABLISH
RESPECT

The basics pack an enormous punch, so be sure you perform them brilliantly. You don't have time to smile and say, "Thank you"? Really? I'm not buying it, and neither are your coworkers. These interpersonal niceties aren't superficial, they're essential. They are the quickest and easiest ways to connect first as people. Employee disengagement and turnover are expensive and most frequently linked to feeling disrespected. Whatever your role is in the company, present yourself as the person people want to support because you won't take anyone's efforts for granted, no matter their position. Likely, you know you should say please and offer praise, but efficiency gets in the way of civility. Perhaps you already *are* that considerate colleague. Let's be sure you are getting the dosage right. The volume on your appreciation meter may not be calibrated correctly to what your coworkers need, especially when everyone is under pressure and moving quickly.

Many organizational interactions don't take place in person, either because your colleagues and clients are in remote locations or you have become reliant on technology to "talk" to each other even if you are seated in the same room. Don't let projects become derailed because people assume you have an attitude. Recognize the increased importance placed on how you write to colleagues (even informally). It's your remote handshake; it establishes your personality. Adding an emoticon doesn't replace tuning into the emotions of those around you. In the absence of in-person contact, make coworkers feel valued by providing feedback and giving them the autonomy to manage their own time. Whether you are the CEO or the assistant, the manager or the associate, ignite joy by being your best and helping others do their best.

This Part Is for You If

- You want to feel good going to work.

- You have been described as rough around the edges, arrogant, aloof, or just too busy.

- Your organization is going through a transformation—again.

- Your team is under-resourced and overstressed.

- There are a lot of big shots making demands, and many invisible support staff making things happen.

- Colleagues are rude or "done" trying.

1

SMILE

Activate Immediate Connection

A man without a smiling face must not open a shop.
—Chinese proverb

D o you want to get happy at work *immediately*? Catch my smile. Did you feel it? Quick, toss the smile to the person on your left (or right) and set off a chain reaction of positive feelings. When you smile at people, strangers included, 80 to 90 percent will return the gesture with a grin, even if they don't want to. We are wired from birth to mimic the people around us. Try contaminating your occupational ecosphere with happiness. Even a well-placed, forced smile is a mood enhancer.

Humans are so inherently social that the best predictor of happiness is not gender, religion, health, or income—it's the strength of bonds with family, friends, and coworkers. Frequently occurring positive interactions are powerful. Someone who has a dozen mildly nice things happen each day is likely to be happier than someone who has a single truly amazing experience in his or her life. So why did I start my book off with a smile? Smiling is a great example of a simple act that's powerful, controversial, and often omitted from our daily repertoire, potentially to our own detriment. "Smile more" can seem like a command—I am being asked to grin so that *you* feel comfortable; my needs don't matter. Strangers demanding that you "Smile!" can feel patronizing, but that is not the intent of this chapter. I'm inviting you to make an active choice to smile because it benefits you as well as the recipient of your warmth. Smiling is free and efficient. It asserts your intention to form a mutual, shared, equal connection. In challenging situations your smile can instantaneously and, often unconsciously, relax those around you.

Smiling is the most potent of tools in nature's cooperation workshop. In *Born to Be Good*, Dacher Keltner explains that a smile activates our frontal lobe (the reward center of the brain) and reduces stress for the person smiling, as well as the person on the receiving end of the smile.

A study from Penn State University found that people who smile appear to be more likeable, courteous, and even competent. The Ochsner Health System, a large Louisiana health care provider, implemented what it calls the "10/5 way." Employees are encouraged to make eye contact if they're within 10 feet of someone and say hello if they're within 5 feet. The result? An increase in patient satisfaction and referrals. Senior, junior, or middle manager—make an effort to smile and watch the room (and your mood) brighten. Want to connect first? Be the first to smile.

THIS IS FOR YOU IF

- Spreading instant happiness appeals to you.
- You want to build a rich network of supporters.
- You want to feel like you belong when you arrive at work.
- Staring at your shoes hasn't stopped you from tripping over your own bad attitude.

TAKE ACTION

- Smile as you enter the building, walk the halls, or join a meeting room.
- Put your phone in your pocket and make eye (and smile) contact as you transition from place to place.
- Spread delight. Dare to be the first to turn up the corners of your lips.
- To generate an inner grin that lights up your face, think of something that delights you. If you are desperate, visualize speech bubbles over your co-workers' heads filled with quotes that will make you giggle.
- Learn from a child. Children smile up to 400 times a day.

KEEP IN MIND

- Be careful not to smile when delivering bad news. It can rob you of credibility and generate confusion.

- Find the balance that works for you. Smiling is effective, but being overly cheerful, especially for women, can undermine your authority.

CASE STUDIES

Melt Away Bad Impressions

Jack, a newly minted manager, was meticulously groomed but very reserved. He received feedback that his team saw him as harsh and uncaring. This commentary was at odds with Jack's strong values of empathy and inclusion. Jack appeared stiff but had a flexible approach toward problem-solving. We tried a simple experiment. Smile more. It worked. Although starting a casual conversation did not come naturally to Jack, those receiving his smile often spontaneously started talking, making it easier for him to engage and demonstrate his interest in others.

Smile for Yourself

Jimmie Briggs, journalist and social activist, wasn't going to start grinning because it put someone else at ease. Smile? My suggestion sent Jimmie back in time. As a tall black man growing up in the Midwest in the 1970s, his family coached him to always appear friendly, "You don't want to look menacing. Greet people with a smile." The practice carried over into his professional life. A war reporter in combat zones, Jimmie was still smiling, until he had the confidence to stop.

Jimmie heard me speak about the power of a smile on the same day a photographer asked him if he could try a less somber expression. Jimmie flexed his facial position. He looked at the before and after shots. He felt the effect of his smile, on himself. He left the photo shoot triumphant. "I'm going to start smiling again," Jimmie told me, "but this time I am doing it for myself. It feels good."

2

SAY "PLEASE"

It Implies Freedom to
Comply (or Not)

"Wanna make me?" The absence of "please" can prompt even the best-behaved team members to put their hands on their proverbial hips in adolescent-style protest. In linguists' lingo, "please" is an illocutionary force indicating device, or IFID, which in plain English means that "please" signals a request rather than a demand. Bosses justify the absence of "please," stating that being asked to do one's job is not a request for a favor, but an expectation. That may be true, but it's certainly not a helpful attitude.

Language experts report that the English "please" is short for "if you please" ("if it pleases you to do this"). It is the same in most European languages—the French *s'il vous plait* and the Spanish *por favor*. The literal meaning is "you are under no obligation to do this." Of course, at work this is a polite falsehood. When you ask someone "to set up a meeting with Mary," you are still providing an instruction. It's just that by attaching "please," you are providing at least the illusion of choice, and an implied appreciation for actions taken on your behalf.

As the workplace becomes more technologically complex and culturally diverse, civility matters even more. Yet rudeness is rampant and on the rise. The accumulation of thoughtless actions that leave employees feeling disrespected or publicly belittled should worry every organization. During the past 18 years, Christine Porath, author of *Mastering Civility*, polled thousands of workers worldwide about how they are treated. Nearly half of those surveyed in 1998 reported they were treated rudely at least once a month, a figure that rose to 55 percent in 2011 and 62 percent in 2016.

Top of the list when Porath asked how to improve workplace relationships? Say "please." So please, say "please."

THIS IS FOR YOU IF

- You don't want to take people for granted.
- Work isn't getting done to the highest quality.
- You don't have time for "niceties."
- People put their hands up to help your colleagues, but avoid your gaze.

TAKE ACTION

- ▶ Respect people as more than a head count paid to get things done. Even if someone is obligated to perform, a pleasant "please" prompts more prideful compliance.
- ▶ Turbocharge your "please" by looking the person in the eye and smiling.
- ▶ Try saying "please" in the native language of your coworker for extra impact.
- ▶ Remember that the millennial generation (a large part of the workforce) does not respond well to command-and-control directives.

KEEP IN MIND

- Not all pleases are created equally. Manage the tone of your "please." Especially when interacting with service providers, "please" can make a question sound urgent, blunt, and even downright rude.
- Resist the overuse of "please" to the point of triteness—*please*!

CASE STUDIES

"Please" Was More Powerful Than Botox in Pumping Up This Office

Dr. Suarez's bustling dermatology office is just off Park Avenue. The setting is elegant. The patients are demanding. The nurses, technicians, and receptionist had become increasingly nasty to one another, barking out instructions and not turning to face one another when making a request. The doctor felt the tension among the staff. She didn't look forward to entering her own treatment rooms. The team complained that many patients were rude. It undermined their mood. The irritability was contagious. The doctor posited, "Rather than be contaminated by bad conduct, why don't we inoculate ourselves with really positive behavior?" What if the staff went out of their way to be *super*-polite to each other? They would experience the respect they craved, and perhaps also model for the patients that this office was not only glamorous, it was kind.

Their experiment worked! The technicians and nurses prefaced their requests to each other with a "please." They looked at each other when they asked for and passed an instrument. They felt connected through their positive intentions, and work felt better—for everyone.

End the Day with a "Please"

Corey can read Morgan's mind. He's been his assistant for three years and anticipates Morgan's needs before he even thinks of them. The day flies by and it's filled with jovial banter. It's fun to work for Morgan, but when the sun sets, so does his charm. When Morgan barks, "Get me a car," and grabs his coat to run to yet another *fabulous* client event, Corey isn't feeling all that great. "How about 'please'?" asked the devoted assistant. "It won't change the fact that I'm still chained to my desk, banging out emails while you go to dinner, but it would make me feel a whole lot less like a lackey without a life." "Done!" said Morgan, who had assumed that their easy flow translated into not having to say "please."

3

SAY "THANK YOU"

The People You Neglect Can Undermine Your Success

We all have those crevices in our day. You know, when there isn't enough time to start a project, you're waiting for a meeting, the train is late, you're stuck in line. Rather than check social media, obsess about the calories you shouldn't have eaten, or rewrite your to-do list, try reviewing the past week and take a minute to thank someone who made a difference in your day, your project, or your mood. A sincere thank you is motivational Miracle-Gro, and yet the office ranks dead last among the places people express gratitude.

The London School of Economics reviewed 50 studies illustrating a direct correlation between appreciation and production. Similarly a study by Glassdoor found that 70 percent of workers said they'd feel better about themselves if their boss thanked them more regularly. Saying "thank you" has absolutely no financial cost, yet it generates significant returns for your organization in reputation, employee satisfaction, and output.

Acknowledging our coworkers' efforts has selfish benefits. People who express gratitude daily experience lower levels of stress and boosted immune systems. Facebook founder Mark Zuckerberg sets a personal target each year. On Facebook's tenth anniversary, Zuckerberg challenged himself to write one thank-you note each day. His rationale: "It's important for me because I'm a really critical person." He makes a good point. The harder driving you are, the more impactful those moments of appreciation can be.

Let's face it, who doesn't warm to a well-intended thanks? Sitting in the glittering offices of Hearst Magazines, Jayne Jamison, the SVP, publisher, and Chief Revenue Officer of *The Oprah Magazine*, a seasoned professional, whipped out her phone to reveal a 30-second clip of Oprah singing "Happy Birthday" to her son. Jayne was beaming, and all of us in the room basked in her reflected glory. Oprah provided a unique gift to a valued employee that could be shared with pleasure . . . over and over.

THIS IS FOR YOU IF

- You're an appreciative person.

- You've pushed your team beyond exhaustion, fear some will quit, and are worried about gearing up for the next big push.

- High expectations are the norm, and you often request multiple revisions.

- Your collaborators and/or support team are in remote offices.

- Your boss does a good job advocating for you.

- You manage through influence, but don't have many direct reports.

TAKE ACTION

▶ Get in the habit of thanking someone each day who doesn't expect it. Start creating a list right now of people you are often in contact with and those who are important to your work but are on the periphery. Keep the list on your phone. Scan it over your morning coffee. Start your day by making someone else's.

▶ Connect "thank you" to an existing daily routine. Make a two-minute call to at least one person when you walk to the parking lot, gym, or grocery store.

▶ Plan your "Oprah moment." How can you offer thanks that has your personal stamp? Frame a picture of you and a valued employee at a key event (or just partnering during a mundane day). Sign a copy of the brief your paralegal helped you prepare (and you argued in front of the Supreme Court).

▶ Be genuine and specific. Your appreciation doesn't have to be task-oriented. Sincerely convey the positive emotional impact that someone's actions have had on your own life or on the lives of others. Acknowledge that person's sacrifice.

▶ Look someone in the eye and deliver the thanks in person if possible.

▶ Don't delay. Sometimes we wait to say thanks, intending to do something special, and then the moment passes. You can always thank someone twice. Use the dictation function on your phone. Immediately send a text or quick email saying, "I just left the meeting with X, and there's no way we could have performed at the level we did without you."

▶ Prepare a handwritten message that allows the person to physically reference and touch your appreciation. A Post-it note left on someone's desk or computer "sticks" around for a long time.

▶ Make an appreciation kit, a Ziploc bag containing some stationery and stamps. Tuck it into your work bag or desk drawer. Everything is ready the next time you have an impulse to jot off a note of thanks.

▶ While writing this, I was surprised by a floral delivery thanking me for leading a successful corporate facilitation last week. Even paid "vendors" appreciate the personal touch.

▶ Remember your boss appreciates hearing "thank you" just as much as you do. Be on the lookout for authentic ways in which your superiors have been inspirational or supportive.

▶ It's never too late to say thanks. Be a blast from the past and drop a note to a former professor, mentor, or colleague and let that person know how they have continued to influence you. Don't worry if they will remember you. They will (for sure) after you write.

KEEP IN MIND

• Avoid adding a request to the "thank you." Let the appreciation stand alone.

• A sincere thanks is more meaningful and less open to misinterpretation than an expensive gift.

• Organizing team drinks or events may seem like a good way to show appreciation, but it may also put pressure on people who have long commutes or tight schedules. Be sure the mode of thanks fits the needs of the person you are recognizing.

CASE STUDIES

To Make Your Deadlines, Offer Thanks Rather Than Pushing Requests

The investor capital came in and the crunch was on. It was possible for Deb to make her product's aggressive launch date, but it meant working around the clock. Downing too many coffees and riding high on possibility, Deb set a pace that few could keep up with, and those who tried often made errors. Deb needed a plan. Rather than sending emails lambasting employees' sluggish performance, Deb expressed gratitude for their work. Instead of saying, "What happened to the report you promised to return by this morning at 8:00 a.m.?" she offered appreciation, including phrases such as "I value our partnership." "Your skills are critical to our launch." "Thank you for the continued sacrifices you are making."

Deb's approach had the desired effect. Most of the team responded with, "I'm here to help you. I know this is an insane time. Bring it on." During the two months of almost round-the-clock work, Deb made a point to publicly and privately thank her coworkers in emails and town halls. As she got more bleary-eyed, the calendar reminder she set for each Friday made sure Deb ended the week with a heartfelt thanks connecting the team's efforts to the accomplishment of yet another milestone. Rather than resent Deb's demands, the team was proud of its achievements, and Deb was relieved that she hadn't fallen prey to her previous habits of criticizing, shaming, and at times just doing the work herself.

The Thank You That You Didn't Write
Could Cost You

During Bob's final interviews for an equity analyst position, he met with his future boss, two potential peers, and one junior member of the team. The group got together to compare impressions. His resume ticked all the right boxes, but something wasn't right. Bob seemed too arrogant. It was a feeling; there was nothing to pin it on. The interviewers all received thoughtful thank-you notes from Bob, except . . . Delilah, the junior member of the team. The hiring manager became concerned that this was a "tell," a potential reveal that Bob might be dismissive of subordinates. He called Bob's references and learned that Bob was much more adept at managing up than respecting those reporting to him. Bob didn't get the job.

4

CALL PEOPLE BY THEIR NAMES

Ignite Attention and Recognize Individuality

I am not a number—I am a free man!
—Patrick McGoohan as Number Six, *The Prisoner*

Hearing your own name is a neural ignition key, activating attention and engaging you in the interaction to follow. Names acknowledge existence, provide an identity, and are a passport to services and opportunities. Denying a person his or her name withers humanity. The importance of having a name is so significant that it is delineated as a fundamental right in South Africa's post-Apartheid constitution. Being named confers dignity and shines a light on us uniquely (if only for a brief moment). Learning the names of people at work demonstrates respect and confirms that they have been noticed and are valued as people. If you want to connect first, start by calling people by their names!

In many offices, everyone knows the boss's name but those down the ranks don't enjoy the same level of recognition, particularly support staff working in areas such as maintenance, dining facilities, and, ironically, receptionists—the very people responsible for knowing and announcing visitors' names. Personnel from foreign backgrounds (no matter their seniority) are diminished and reminded of their difference when their given names are modified to align with the phonetic limitations of their colleagues. As Dale Carnegie observed, "A person's name is the sweetest sound in any language."

While working in Beijing, an American client asked my colleague Zhanna if he could call her Natasha because she's Russian and it would be easier for him to remember. To knowingly misremember a name, especially when working in cross-cultural settings, privileges one group's comfort over another's. To learn a name, to truly recognize who's around you, you must invest some intellectual capital. Not caring enough to ask or remember a name is an insidious slight that might not be meant maliciously but nevertheless can inflict insult and lead to interpersonal chasms.

THIS IS FOR YOU IF

- You appreciate the importance of making an immediate personal connection.

- There are lots of people who make your day more efficient, pleasant, or fun and yet . . . you refer to them as the "tall one" and the "guy with red glasses" because you don't know their names.

- There are lots of staff changes and everyone's looking a bit lost.

- You want to convey respect and dignity.

TAKE ACTION

▶ Get up from your desk now and walk for five minutes around the office. Do you know everyone's name? Now's a good time to ask.

▶ When introducing yourself, ask for the other person's name. Always.

▶ Make sure people know each other's names, whether in a meeting or walking a factory floor. When in doubt, make introductions.

▶ Try scribbling down names in a meeting according to where everyone is seated—it aids recall.

▶ Ask your colleague to share any history attached to a name; it will help you remember while providing a peek into his or her family story.

▶ Create contact cards on your phone for the people who provide services for you at work, include the cleaning crew and parking attendants. Until you get these names memorized, put a prompt in your phone that flashes as you are about to enter the office building at the start of the day.

▶ Sometimes a name is exotic for your ear. Enter the phonetic pronunciation into the person's contact card so you can say the name properly.

▶ Make an effort—don't institutionalize a nickname because it makes your life easier. Everyone has the right to a dignified name in the office.

KEEP IN MIND

- There is no way to fake it. You either know a person's name or you don't, and at certain moments this knowledge will be invaluable. If you forget, apologize and ask to be reminded. You might want to describe when you met last, "I recall we had a lovely discussion about the sculpture in the lobby, but I'm afraid I don't remember your name."

- No matter how jovial (or harmless you think you are), terms of endearment like "sweetie," "honey," and "love" are not appropriate for the workplace and should not be used in lieu of a person's given name.

- To avoid adverse reactions, remember that tone is important. You don't want to suggest that you are asking for a name in order to report someone.

CASE STUDIES

Make a Mental Note

Following a successful client meeting, Wayne, the firm's senior partner, singled out Arman to thank him for his contribution and asked his name. It was the fourth time. The first time Arman was flattered. In the second instance he was still basking in the glow of the earlier praise and was sympathetic to how hard Wayne worked, figuring he just had too much on his mind. The third time Arman started to get upset, and by the fourth round Wayne's insensitivity was to be expected. Arman considered starting an office party fund. If everyone put in a dollar when Wayne asked a subordinate their name (for the fifth time) there was sure to be plenty of money for a great dinner. Wayne's perfunctory, distracted interest in Arman undermined any good intention—he didn't pause long enough to lock in the information offered. Don't be like Wayne.

See and Name Everybody

In contrast, Dr. Anthony (Tony) Lechich spreads a special brand of medical magic around ArchCare's Huntington's disease unit. I joined Dr. Lechich on his Saturday morning rounds and listened as he greeted the receptionist by name, called out to the orderly by name, thanked the nurse, of course, by name, and introduced us to patients whose bodies were ravaged by a brutal illness but whose dignity was bolstered by their doctor's personalized attention. When we stopped for a snack, Dr. Lechich asked the kitchen staff about their weekend plans, and yes, also addressed them by name. Around noon, a visiting pianist started playing in the cafeteria, and one had the sense we were witnessing a very special party in which all the wheelchair-bound guests were celebrating their chance to be together. Dr. Lechich's ability to see and name everyone, no matter their role or disability, established a culture of respect, and communicated that the staff were not assembled to carry out tasks but rather to care for one another in this vibrant community.

Don't Just Give Your Name, Ask for Theirs!

Sherice welcomed her guests in the waiting area, shook each person's hand, and asked their names. She led them to the conference room and offered to get drinks. Three of the four potential business partners provided their orders. Upon returning to the room with their coffees she said, "I am Sherice Torres, marketing director of Google Commerce. So glad to meet you. We have about 52 minutes left of our meeting. How shall we prioritize?"

Mouths agape, the professionals in the room apologized for mistaking her for a receptionist and wasting her time, "We had no idea *you* were Sherice!" When recounting the story, Sherice questioned whether the disinterest in a mutual exchange of names was due to her accessibility (she met her guests personally at the door), her gender, or the color of her skin. Whatever the reason, the failure to ask Sherice her name provided a valuable glimpse into the character of the people pitching a future collaboration, and the impression wasn't positive.

5

OFFER PRAISE

Pride Is Rocket Fuel

I can live for two months on a good compliment.
—MARK TWAIN

Pride is a social elixir motivating individuals and groups to do their best. We all have an intrinsic desire to be of use, to contribute to the larger community. Recognition of our efforts enables us to stand taller, work harder, and garner sustenance from a sense of importance, of adding value. Lady Gaga sings, "I live for the applause, applause, applause."

Pride is a form of *investment currency*. Like saying please and thank you, praise is free, effective, and in great demand. Praise can be deployed by people at all rungs of the organizational ladder. Spread it liberally to enhance satisfaction at work, but be sure it's deserved. Weak praise can sound like empty flattery and undermine later efforts that genuinely warrant acknowledgment. Praising successive approximations to a goal is motivating as it recognizes progress rather than perfection and allows for more frequent genuine appreciation (and chances to establish a positive connection).

Robert Cialdini's *Influence: The Psychology of Persuasion* is the salesperson's bible. A key learning is that most people are phenomenal suckers for flattery. We are more willing to cooperate with those who find good in what we do. If you compliment your colleagues, they will behave in ways that validate your assessment. After all, they have a reputation to live up to!

While most bosses believe they dole out praise frequently, I rarely meet an employee who feels that management sufficiently values their achievements. And speaking of the folks in charge, they may have corner offices, upgraded seats on the plane, and bigger bonuses, but the *grande fromage* has feelings, too. Creating a workplace that respects our shared humanity is a mutual responsibility. It's lonely at the top. If your boss is about to take the podium, give them a nod of confidence. If you see your team leader in the halls during performance review period, step outside your own anxiety to ask, "What's it like for you?" and offer appreciation for their efforts. Writing and delivering appraisals is an onerous annual process.

Keep this statistic in mind: it takes five positive comments to counteract the demoralizing impact of one negative remark—so be on the alert for chances to praise generously.

THIS IS FOR YOU IF

- You are confident in what you've accomplished.

- There's a sense that you grab too much of the spotlight (and credit).

- Energy is low; emotions are high.

- Your team is recovering from the effects of a nasty, competitive, or negative influence.

TAKE ACTION

▶ Enhance thank you's by adding praise for a colleague's unique contribution. Start tomorrow. Look over your calendar. Who has amazed or amused you this week? Take a minute to set the context. Tell your coworker why what they did matters to you, and the larger group. It can be something as simple as noticing that the learning specialist was smiling in the cold and rain as she greeted the kids coming off the bus. Let her know that you appreciated how she set a positive tone for the day.

▶ Recognize early wins. Connect your colleague's contribution to the larger, long-term organizational goals. When creating the agenda for progress meetings, set aside five minutes for appreciation. You don't have to be the boss to suggest taking time to recognize your peers.

▶ Don't delay praise. Be specific and genuine.

▶ The most powerful form of praise matches what recipients highly value about themselves. If your coworker holds community service in high esteem, find ways to comment on how their work has benefited the neighborhood where your business is located.

▶ Make time for others to share their accomplishments with you (so you can praise them). During supervisory sessions don't get lost in problem-solving. Inquire about what's gone well.

▶ You can commend your superiors as well as peers and subordinates. You can also compliment your opponents. Act like an ultimate Frisbee player and praise the winning team.

▶ Be generous in your praise of others. Don't fall prey to the misperception that flattering others diminishes your position. It's just the opposite. Offering an evaluative comment indicates authority.

KEEP IN MIND

• Don't focus on your success when praising others.

• If you receive praise in return, say, "Thank you"—don't reject it.

• Separate requests for additional work from moments of praise.

CASE STUDIES

Olympic Skill

Paul Deighton, CEO of the London 2012 Olympic Organizing Committee, felt strongly that he wanted "to use the power of the Games to inspire lasting change." He focused on inclusion, and recruited 70,000 volunteers representing the many faces of the United Kingdom. The people were selected because they saw themselves as being part of a mission, and Paul was going to do his best not to "mess it up by demotivating them." To foster a culture of respect in this diverse group, he drew upon his quarter of a century of experience as a banker at Goldman Sachs. Paul observed that praise was in high demand and in low supply. There was a market solution. Give people what they crave. Paul looked for ways to catch people doing things well and encouraged his staff to do the same. There were many tough moments during the run-up to and delivery of the Games, and yet Paul remains the only CEO in modern summer Olympic history to have lasted a full seven-year tenure. It's a good bet to take a page out of his playbook.

Praise Those Connected to the Star

I started calling my colleague Jayma Pau "speed dial six" as she became my go-to person from the moment we first worked together in Hyderabad, India, in 2008. Jayma literally gave me the clothes from her closet when I arrived hours before a business meeting with no luggage in sight. She was new in her role but completely comfortable in her skin. She had an amazing ability to put everyone at ease as she coordinated who we should meet, what background information was needed, and even what food we would eat. If I had a question, I'd press number 6 to speed dial Jayma, and voila, she had an answer.

Jayma confided in me that her parents' vision for their daughter's professional life did not include working as a program manager for a social business with goals to which they could not readily relate. Jayma's rapid, effective, and creative problem-solving was invaluable to our team. How could I express appreciation? I opted to write a letter to Jayma, praising her many talents and describing why her skills made such a difference to our organization, and how appreciative I was of her career choice. I encouraged Jayma to share the note with her parents since praise of their daughter was also praise for them! A decade later, I am proud to say Jayma is the Co-Managing Partner of Leaders' Quest. Her ability to see around corners and anticipate solutions continues to make all of us more effective.

6

GOT IT? THEN SAY SO!

Help Coworkers Manage Their Time

Cast a spell to keep projects moving and preserve everyone's sanity. Respect. Attention. Reduced anxiety. Wouldn't that be ideal? Do your part to stamp out undue worry and avoid the diminishment people experience when they feel ignored. When colleagues send completed projects, make requests, or share important announcements over email, reply with "Got it." This easy addition to your daily routine provides the psychological assurance that your colleagues have caught your attention—that you have received their message and they don't have to stress. "Got it" is a superfast point of personal connection indicating that there's a human on the other side of the electronic communication. Saying "Got it" shows respect for superiors, subordinates, and peers. Use it with clients, vendors, and current job applicants. No one wants to send notes into the ether.

While some might argue that "Got it" responses stuff inboxes with unnecessary mail, take up too much slack time, or clog iPhone arteries, a lack of acknowledgment can erode trust, spur negative thinking, and prompt overly dramatic and escalating inner dialogues:

"Why won't she respond? She must not care about me."

"Maybe I offended her somehow?" (Cue the time-wasting activity of going back over past emails looking for offending messages.)

"If I don't get the information I need, this project will never get done. Why am I always the one left waiting?" (Frustration mounts.)

"If we don't make the deadline, it's all her fault." (Now you're angry.)

And you bring these feelings home with you, where you stew on them even more. A straightforward request can blow up into an emotional catastrophe. You're unhappy. And if you confront the other person, they'll soon be unhappy, too. A simple "Got it" could have prevented all these time-consuming reactions. Don't be *that* colleague, someone who is so focused on your own to-do list that you forget that there are people out there wondering if and when they can get the information they need. Similarly, nothing feels worse than grinding away for weeks on a report, sending it over to your boss, and then . . . silence. Don't be the manager who devalues staff by not recognizing that work was completed and received. No, electronic read receipts are not good enough. Yes, it's their job, but don't be a jerk. Let your team know promptly that their efforts are valuable enough to warrant the two reassuring words, "Got it."

In addition to responding with "Got it," if the message contains a request that you can't immediately act on, add an estimate of when you will be able to complete the task. The ability to manage our own time is a form of workplace power. The person who makes us wait is asserting control. By providing an indication of when the requested information will be available, you allow your coworker to plan accordingly. Have junior associates sent you their presentations for edits and then stayed late at the office waiting to do revisions (while you were out at a client dinner with no intention of providing feedback until the morning)? Trust me, your team is not happy.

Well-intentioned people sometimes wait to respond until they have the answers—even if it takes days. We've all been there. Tending to a customer, presenting at a meeting, focusing on another priority—in essence, doing your job—may mean you are delaying or disappointing someone else. Dave in procurement asks you what you paid for plane tickets during the past three years. This will take you some time to compile. You don't write back to Dave, even though you are working on his request. Meanwhile, Dave is left wondering if you received the message, whether you've forgotten about it, and what's taking so long. Your reality? You're a hardworking team player. His perception? You're a bottleneck, holding up the report he has to generate to determine whether he should change corporate travel agents. "Got it" takes seconds to write and saves hours of agitation.

THIS IS FOR YOU IF

- People come to your office after their requests go unanswered.

- You assume that it's the person's job, and therefore don't acknowledge when someone sends material you asked for.

- You weigh less than the number of unread emails in your inbox.

- You put on your headphones and really *focus* when a deadline looms . . . and pray that no one pings you with an off-topic request.

- "It must have gone into the spam folder" is your go-to response when someone chases you for the fifth time.

TAKE ACTION

▶ Respond with "Got it" as soon as you receive a request, special announcement, or finished project.

▶ Don't wait until you have read through lengthy documents or completed time-consuming tasks. First acknowledge receipt.

Managing Requests

▶ Scan your inbox daily and perform email "triage." Respond to any emails you missed earlier that merit a "Got it." If a request is inappropriate or unreasonable, write back right away and explain the issue. Not answering at all often exacerbates potential conflict.

Making Requests

▶ Let people know that an action is required by stating that in the subject line. If you need a response immediately, write "URGENT."

▶ Include expected actions at the start of the message. If you don't need it until next week, then write that, too. Everyone appreciates a chance to breathe and balance their deadlines.

▶ Help your team help you. If you are prone to brainstorms in the middle of the night and generate requests while in your jammies, try filing your notes in a draft email folder. Send them out in the morning when your colleagues are awake enough to acknowledge receipt.

KEEP IN MIND

- "Got it" does not replace a full and reasoned response, so when possible, offer a projected response date. Then put a reminder on your calendar to follow up.

- If you fear that a simple "Got it" will suggest a premature agreement, respond with "received."

CASE STUDIES

It's Not Just Your Questions That Matter

The person you can depend on, the no-nonsense dealmaker, the colleague you want to grab a beer with—that's Wendy. A senior executive at a clothing company, Wendy prides herself on reading the room and being sensitive to others' needs. Wendy received unexpected feedback during her year-end review. Colleagues reported that she often took "forever" to respond to their requests (we're talking weeks compared to minutes), even though they were fast to act when Wendy asked for information. Wendy's initial reaction was to explain the discrepancy away. The answers she needs should be at the fingertips of the finance department, "That's what they're there for." Then she caught herself. "That's not right, is it? It's just that the analyses the accountants ask me for relate to future projects. It can take me weeks to get the projections I need to even start writing the report." It was an aha moment, as Wendy realized that her behavior and desired reputation were not aligned. While she might not be any faster in generating answers, Wendy recognized that she could at least acknowledge requests, explain the necessary steps, and (ideally) provide an anticipated timeline for completion.

Cultural Reveal

When Yasmin was headhunted for a board-level position at a major fashion house, she was asked to respond to four in-depth questions as part of the final selection procedure. The hiring manager asked for responses within 48 hours. Yasmin dropped everything and submitted her answers within a day. She didn't receive any confirmation that her materials had been received or were being reviewed. No "thank you"; no "got it." Two weeks later the designers asked her to return for more interviews, but she was hesitant to do so. Yasmin learned a lot about the corporate culture when no one took the time to acknowledge the receipt of materials the company had deemed so time sensitive.

7

PROVIDE FEEDBACK

It Benefits Everyone

Did I do a good job? Did I do a *great* job? Did I mess up as badly as I think I did? Why won't anyone tell me? Insecurity undermines success. We need to know how we are doing. Giving (or receiving) corrective commentary cements relationships and deepens connections. Illuminating a colleague's blind spot can bring meaning to your job. It's very gratifying to observe the immediate, positive impact of well-placed feedback.

Direct feedback doesn't come our way often, and, in its absence, we scan the faces of our peers, analyze the nuances in a note, and monitor whether we are included in the "right" meetings for clues about our performance. You've seen the glances when you enter the office. You surmise something is amiss, but no one is saying anything.

As a coach, I conduct interviews to obtain insights about the executive I am working with. Without fail, board members, managers, peers, and subordinates provide thoughtful commentary. Yet, when I ask, "Have you told the person directly?" the answer is "no." Fear of conflict, limited time, and the concern that one's perspective might not be valued jams the corporate GPS. Feeling lost? Wondering how you're doing? You don't have to hire an outside consultant. Make time with your colleagues and *just ask*!

Sometimes the fix to embarrassing behavior is easy. Security signs instruct us, "If you see something, say something." If you applied this advice at the office, I would likely lose a lot of work. CEOs can negotiate multinational mergers, yet ask me to tell their subordinates to stop carrying legal briefs in a yellow knapsack.

THIS IS FOR YOU IF

- Supporting professional development is a daily goal.

- You are a keen observer of behavior, but a shy commentator.

- Gossiping is more comfortable than direct discussion.

- You ask other people to inform your direct reports about problematic activities.

- Annual performance reviews are the main times you share feedback.

TAKE ACTION

▶ Provide feedback early and in private if possible. Well-timed feedback, presented as a potential hypothesis, can be more valuable than information offered too late because you were gathering all the evidence "to be sure."

▶ Assume the best intentions of the other person. Focus on the behavior and give specific suggestions for improvement.

▶ Ask for feedback. Don't be the last person to find out how you are doing. Ask others what words they use to describe you when speaking to peers.

▶ Offer criticism sandwiches: begin with a compliment, layer in some suggestions, and end on a positive note.

▶ Remember that those in esteemed positions will value your feedback if provided appropriately. As one of my clients shared, "Once I became famous, I could no longer touch my world. I spoke mostly to the eight people in my executive suite (that became an echo chamber)."

▶ Try to "feed forward." Provide information on how to do better next time instead of focusing on what was done wrong in the past.

KEEP IN MIND

- Remember that making others feel "less than" is a motivation killer. Don't refer to your success when sharing commentary on someone else's performance.

- Give as well as receive feedback with grace. If someone offers feedback, it's valid to them. Say "thank you" even if you don't agree.

Lose the Red Suit

"You are quite different than the British male bankers attending your workshops," observed the head of training at UBS. "You are a woman, an American, a psychologist, and very brightly dressed. The only thing we can change is your suit." True, my audience's wardrobe ran the gamut from grey to dark blue, but I always enjoyed expressing myself with color. Upon receiving the unsolicited fashion consult, my face was as red as my outfit. Once I metabolized my fury, I realized that I wasn't being insulted. I wasn't being fired. I wasn't losing my contract. I was being coached for success. The ruby suit story has become my mental moniker, reminding me to be sensitive to the ways I can connect to (or distance) myself from a group. Aspiring to be *our self at work* may be the goal, but we can't be too absolutist. It's always important to adjust to the audience.

Don't Be Afraid of the Detractors

"How'm I doing?!" was a favorite catchphrase of former New York City Mayor Ed Koch. Early in his career, while running for office, he would hand out flyers at subway stations on Friday mornings. The unexpected question got busy commuters to stop. Over time it defined his brand. Koch paused that half-second to ask the question, and then lingered a second more to hear the answer. He got credit just for asking. Engaging others to offer commentary signals respect and invites people to be partners in your future success. Mayor Koch anticipated the current online craze of rating customer experience. The truth might hurt, but not knowing can be even more dangerous. When conducting feedback interviews on behalf of my clients I always ask to meet with their greatest detractors. Not surprisingly, asking for their opinions often transforms opponents into supporters.

It's Not About the Hair

Jo was making snide remarks in public and at staff meetings, which infuriated her boss, Lida, who ran a successful recruiting firm where autonomy was a proud part of the company culture. Despite the flexible work hours, Lida believed that Jo was taking advantage. She would leave midday and return with perfectly coiffed hair. "How dare she get a blow-dry on my time?" Lida stewed, but didn't say anything as she didn't want to create conflict. Instead, Lida made not-so-subtle faces when Jo left the office and she started to "oops, forget to include Jo on client calls." Lida and Jo were engaged in a passive-aggressive dance that wasn't entertaining anyone.

With some coaching Lida came clean and offered constructive feedback to Jo. Leaving work for personal reasons was taking advantage of the company policy, and her negative comments about the boss were further eroding trust. Jo wasn't pleased initially. She hit her targets, so what's the issue? Lida persisted. Time in the office *was* important. Leaving to meet with candidates was one thing, but midday beauty rituals were not aligned with the hardworking values the company prized. More importantly Lida was deeply disappointed (and hurt) that she couldn't count on a senior staff member to be a role model. Ultimately, it wasn't really about the hair. It was about feeling disrespected, and that was the essential feedback. Once the direct conversation took place, the hidden daggers were dropped, and Jo, Lida, and the team breathed a sigh of relief.

PART II

ENGAGE
ALL OF YOUR
SENSES

K nowledge is your competitive edge. What you don't know *can* hurt you. Hiding behind roles and computer screens won't cut it. Your colleagues convey critical (though at times indirect) messages that elude you daily as you endeavor to "just get the job done." In the moment, the faces they made, the changes in their gait, or the way they shifted in their chairs may seem insignificant or too distracting to address. These seemingly idiosyncratic behaviors may reflect larger, more important patterns. What are you missing?

You can't rely on words alone; they offer up the world in black and white. To really excel, to deeply connect, you want office dynamics to unfold in Technicolor and surround sound. Invest a few minutes to shift your senses from automatic to manual and learn how to *be with* the people around you. What is really driving your colleagues' actions? Listen. Don't be afraid to be quiet—together. Watch. See *everybody*. Experiment with eating as a group. Your colleagues tell me their secrets, and they will share essential information with you, too, if only you would slow down, express interest, and make time for nontransactional, non-goal-directed experiences. Pausing to pay attention to nonverbal clues propels you to your goals. Finding meaning at work does not have to be elusive. You cocreate it in the small moments of shared experience.

This Part Is for You If

- You want to feel more alive at the office.

- Morale is down.

- Conflict is brewing beneath the surface.

- You can't quite figure out what's going on.

- There have been a lot of changes in roles or expectations.

- Your workplace is highly dependent on technology, and people talk through electronic devices and not to each other.

- The team isn't often in the same place, and you have a chance to bring them together.

8

SEE EVERYBODY

Those on the Margins Often
Have Greater Perspective

Attention is an unapologetic discriminator. To avert one's gaze from a fellow human being erases that person's existence. To lock eyes, even briefly, creates a connection, a validation that in this instance, we are here together. We turn our eyes away from what we think we *shouldn't* see because it will embarrass us—or the other person. Opting to look into the distance when approaching another individual communicates "you don't matter." In contrast, looking/seeing and making eye contact with a colleague confers respect. Unfortunately, the privilege of being seen is not equally distributed in organizational life. Failing to acknowledge the presence of the people we work with reinforces a destructive hierarchy. In today's digitally connected world, many workers are out of sight, yet we recognize their contributions and value them as team members. But the flesh-and-blood janitors polishing your floor and cleaning your lavatory mirrors may remain invisible. They see you, but do you see them?

When the printer runs out of toner, the toilet backs up, the heat isn't on, and the windows won't open, you feel the discomfort. When you are locked out of the office and no one's answering your call to get in and suddenly the after-hours security guard appears, the imperceptible ultimately makes itself felt. This is how the cosmos works. An invisible mass alters the orbit of a comet; dark energy accelerates a supernova; the earth's magnetic field tugs on birds, sea turtles, and the compasses of mariners. The whole realm of the visible is compelled by the invisible. Make sure the fullness of your vocational universe stays in focus. To connect first, open your eyes to all that surrounds you.

THIS IS FOR YOU IF

- Everyone matters, and you want to let them know.

- You can be dismissive or rude.

- Support staff deliver incomplete materials or are slow to fulfill your requests.

- Walking around the office is a chance for you to get lost in your own head.

- When you attend meetings with people you don't recognize, you look past them because you are either busy or shy.

TAKE ACTION

▶ As you enter and exit your building, take a second to catch the gaze of the people opening your door, sorting the mail, or cleaning the floor. Tell me right now, can you describe the design of their uniforms or recall what color their shirts were? Go back and reenter. Pretend you forgot something in the car.

▶ Before you begin a meeting, scan the room. Have you made eye contact with everyone? Yes, *everyone*.

▶ Be intentional with your focus. Ask yourself if you would be proud if a secret camera in your retina played back what you have been watching.

▶ Watch the tendency to become overly focused on one person to the exclusion of others. The competition gets an edge when you restrict the definition of who's important. We've all done it: caring too much about one person's opinion can make the rest of the world evaporate. Ask your spouse or roommate if you say one person's name more than any other when you talk about work.

▶ Put your phone in your pocket while walking. Reducing multitasking enhances your vision.

▶ Take a walk with someone different than yourself and open yourself up to focusing on (and being introduced to) the people they know.

▶ Remember, what you choose to see is the foundation of change.

KEEP IN MIND

• Look, don't stare! This is about making eye contact, not being creepy.

• If eyes are the window to the soul, wearing sunglasses pulls down the blinds and blocks the personal connection. Put your shades away.

CASE STUDIES

Why Can't You Look at Me?

After strenuous negotiating, Carol's boss, Sean, finally made sure that the legal department sent her a new contract (five months late). That stung. Carol brought the forms to Sean's office to sign, which he did in a perfunctory way and tossed them back at her across the desk. The money wasn't what she'd hoped for. The delay made her wonder why she worked so hard for him. The indifferent attitude when she asked for his signature made Carol want to quit. "Why couldn't he at least look me in the eye and say, 'I look forward to working with you over the next two years'?" Carol went back to her desk and started updating her resume.

Really See, Don't Just Be, with People

Rain was pelting down as I slipped on mud on the unpaved path leading up to Miguel's home in one of the *favelas* outside of Sao Paulo. I had met Miguel previously through a Brazilian NGO called Instituto Rukha, which connected impoverished families to potential social services. My travel companions were partners in a well-respected international firm, and they wanted to meet representatives of the prospective workforce for the Brazilian-based World Cup and Olympic Games. Miguel had agreed to host a conversation in his home, which would expose the realities of life in a community that lacks basic services and receives limited public investment.

The executives sloshing up the hill put their hands (without asking permission) on the shoulders of the people walking beside them in hopes of steadying their step. They tossed their coats and umbrellas into the willing hands of our volunteer interpreters. The *favela* visit ended, and over lunch at my urging, the executives finally asked the interpreters to say something about themselves. Much to their surprise, our casually dressed, very helpful "assistants" were the heads of family offices, a large consultancy, and a major construction firm. They had volunteered their services in exchange for visiting communities they had only seen from a distance. In many instances our volunteers were leaders of the very companies the executive team was in town to pitch! "I am so sorry. If only I had known, I never would have treated you like that." Our site visit taught the corporate team about Brazil, but more importantly, it revealed a great deal about themselves.

Although the executives prided themselves on being well-mannered and self-aware, they realized that they easily ignored people standing right beside them, or more accurately, failed to "see" and engage with them. The next day I noticed the corporate team members going out of their way to say hello to the hotel chambermaids and talking to the porters as they loaded luggage into the cars. When they entered our meeting rooms there was a concerted effort to look at and acknowledge all the members of our team (and theirs).

9

LISTEN TO INSPIRE

Deepen the Conversation by Responding Without Words

I love listening. It's one of the only spaces where you can be still. And be moved at the same time.
—NAYYIRAH WAHEED

Listening isn't a time to space out while waiting your turn to speak. It's a full-body sport. Good listeners, those who really learn the truth of what's going on, deploy all of their senses and engage their hearts. The experiments in *Mindwise* by Nicholas Epley illustrate that when people are asked to judge the thoughts of strangers, they are highly confident in their ability to see things as others do, but their attempts are typically barely better than chance. We think we know what's going on, but we don't. Too often *we listen autobiographically*, scanning our interior experience library demonstrating empathy by sharing our own story—a process that actually interferes with attention. At times we are more committed to engaging in conversation to *promote understanding of our own position* than in making a true connection.

Stephen Covey found that highly effective people seek first to understand, then to be understood. Once your conversational partner feels you are really listening, they are more likely to ask your opinion, and you are in a better position to provide valuable commentary. "It's about maturity," says Bob Bakish, CEO of Viacom. "You don't have to follow the suggestions offered to you, but since you asked, be sure you demonstrate that you listened."

THIS IS FOR YOU IF

- Your voice is music to your ears.

- You sense there are errors, but no one is taking responsibility.

- The team has come together quickly to deliver immediately, yet no one really knows each other.

- The group is so comfortable with each other they speak in shorthand—to the point of making inaccurate assumptions.

TAKE ACTION

▶ Whether you use your words, your smile, or your eyes, practice saying, "Tell me more."

▶ Demonstrate that you are listening because you want to, not because you have to. Mute your phone. Close your computer. Swivel your chair to face the speaker.

▶ When you ask a question, pause to let the other person answer. Count to five slowly (in your head and do not tap your fingers on the desk).

▶ Be patient. Don't immediately let other people know whether you agree or disagree. Take in what they're saying and try to find common ground between your ideas and theirs.

▶ Be a generous listener. While traveling with a colleague or standing in line at the cafeteria, encourage others to talk about themselves. They will tell you a lot and like you more as a result.

KEEP IN MIND

- Don't make it about you. Resist reloading your verbal gun. Focus on what the other person is saying.

- In *Quiet: The Power of Introverts in a World That Can't Stop Talking*, Susan Cain reminds us that if you talk less, you are likely to hear more. The introverted team member may be the person holding the keenest insights, but you will have to control your own mouth to hear what's on his or her mind.

CASE STUDIES

To Learn More, Listen (Quietly) for a Long Time

"Listen to inspire" was the guidance offered by my South African colleague, Marian Goodman, faculty at the Presencing Institute. Marian recommends that listeners stay silent and rely on other senses to encourage the speaker to express what's on their mind.

I applied this technique during a workshop held in Bermuda for the tight-knit community of insurance industry executives. The topic was "Learning from Fabulous Failures." Although the attendees worked for competing companies, all were motivated to move beyond mutually damaging missteps. In pairs, people took turns being the mouth (the person sharing a story) or the ears (the listener) for five minutes at a time. Do you know what happens when someone listens attentively while a partner shares personal mistakes—for five whole minutes? Across the board the pattern was remarkably similar. Telling the "facts" took a minute or two and felt like a long time—but not as long as the awkward silence for the next 30–60 seconds. The fourth minute was when the feelings came out, and in the fifth more details were revealed along with a deeper sense of personal remorse. The mouths surprised themselves with their candor. They were far more open in sharing than they had initially intended or expected to be. The group observed that in the course of a typical workday, it's rare to give a colleague five minutes of uninterrupted listening. We all agreed that novel ideas would emerge and mistakes would surface (and be addressed) if we periodically shut up and listen!

A Great Leader Listens

Logan performs verbal pyrotechnics. He walks through the audience, makes timely references, cracks jokes, has a story or a slide for every instance. He seems to see into the future. Each year, since he has been CEO, Logan holds a global team meeting. He paints his vision, and everyone is excited. And then they return to their offices and have no clue how to enact the plan. When Logan visits the company offices during the year, he's busy meeting clients and talking to the regional heads. He's featured in the newspaper and meets with local politicians. What he isn't doing is listening to the people "struggling to do the work."

As his coach, I heard it over and over from his direct reports and the staff who reported to them. Logan and I agreed he would go on a one-month listening tour. He met with small groups in the regions. Employees from all levels. No microphones to amplify his messages; only his ears to receive the comments made by employees. At the conclusion of the tour, Logan held a video town hall in which he shared what he had learned and provided practical direction for the upcoming year. He left plenty of room to go off script and to respond to questions that the audience sent in real time over text. Logan boosted morale by naming people who provided inspiration during his interviews. He instilled a greater sense of meaning for the organization, as the staff could better understand how their actions were tied to a big vision. And Logan found that eating in the staff cafeteria could be a lot more fun than dining in fancy restaurants with dignitaries.

10

SILENCE

Be Quiet Together

One cannot fill a cup which is already full.
—CHINESE PROVERB

Here's a surefire way to improve the quality of your meetings. *Don't say anything for five minutes.* Really. You can employ this technique to center colleagues at the start of a session, or at the end of a meeting to ensure that you reach a productive conclusion.

There is a provocative Buddhist concept called *radical emptiness* that in its simplest form encourages us to empty our minds of inflexible "facts" governed by ego and instead open ourselves to whatever is happening in the moment. We are all like cups, so full of preconceived ideas that there's seldom room to fit in new knowledge. Entering a meeting, you peruse the room to assess who is sitting where. You check out which coworkers defined business casual as jeans and a nice shirt. Are your two assumed adversaries whispering to each other? Is it true there are layoffs looming? Your mind wonders until you yank it back to the agenda at hand, and then your thoughts really take flight. If the company proceeds with the expansion plan, you will have more work and no additional staff to deliver it, you won't get any credit, and you're still pissed off about not being adequately recognized for organizing this whole strategy event. Your mind is everywhere but in the present, and as a result, your ability to read the mood in the room—to connect to your colleagues—flits away as fast as the distractions are racing through your head. You're disconnected, and the ensuing group discussion will suffer because there are 6 to 18 other people who, like you, have arrived with the necessary papers but not the requisite mindset.

During the past few years, meditation masters have been welcomed into the corporate world to train staff on techniques to quiet their inner chatter and become more mindful (attentive to the moment). Companies such as Apple, Google, Nike, Deutsche Bank, and HBO not only offer classes; in some cases, they have even built meditation rooms. While a full-blown initiative for brain clearing may not fit your budget or be to your taste, take a chance on shared silence. Help your group clear their thoughts and bond as they begin to breathe as one. At the start of a meeting, try welcoming everyone in, and then invite participants to join you in reflective silence. Offer your colleagues the opportunity to empty their minds, fill their chests with fresh oxygen, and tune in to the people around them. You can't do this too often or it will seem trite, and the cynics will start arriving to your meetings a few minutes late. Used periodically, it is a very powerful tool to infuse fresh air into stale, tense, and unfocused office gatherings.

Studies show that inserting a few seconds of mental space between an event or stimulus and our response to it is the difference between an automatic aggressive reaction and a more considered and often collaborative solution. As a result, inserting silence at the end can be equally effective. If your meeting is run efficiently, the chair will ask the assembled to agree on next steps. If the past hour has been spent arguing your point, sneaking a peek at your incoming messages, or fuming silently about being cut off by the loudmouth to your left, the chance to take a few minutes of calm reflection will allow you to respond with more considered commitments. And for those who were listening in on conference calls with their phones muted while double tasking, the sudden silence will snap them to attention.

THIS IS FOR YOU IF

- It's exciting for you to experiment with new approaches.

- You are leading high-performance teams brimming with ideas . . . and tension.

- Meetings are frustratingly ineffective.

- Everyone's rushing into the conference room breathless, distracted, and ready to slip out early.

TAKE ACTION

▶ Don't advertise that you will be starting the meeting in silence. Welcome the group into the room (as usual), and then say, "To get fully ready for today's discussion we will be doing something a bit different. We will be taking five minutes to be quiet together, to center ourselves as a group and make space for new ideas. Please put down your pens, mute your phones, and get comfortable in your seats. If you would like, you may close your eyes. Here's a chance to breathe together and release tension with each exhale. Let any thoughts that come into your mind go in one ear and out the other. Practice focusing on your breathing." After three minutes you can prompt participants to note how they are feeling, to tune in to the mood in the room. You can then offer another two minutes of additional quiet. Encourage your colleagues to sync their breathing with that of their surrounding coworkers.

▶ Once the exercise is complete, invite any reactions. Don't be surprised if some people express discomfort. That's OK. Not everyone's a buyer at first. Remain confident that some colleagues will express a sense of connection, a release of anxiety, and a readiness to work. Don't push anyone; be patient and avoid judgment. Ask how the group feels now and inquire how they want to feel at the end of the meeting. These prompts will focus the group on *how* they will work together, not just *what* they will accomplish. Then proceed with the agenda.

▶ If you flip the placement of the silence, inserting it just before wrapping up the meeting, be clear that this is not an indication that participants are free to leave. The value of the silence will be revealed once they have taken a breath and then moved on to agreeing to next steps. Unlike silence at the start, which invites a reflection, silence at the conclusion should lead directly into the wrap-up. Let your colleagues experience (not talk about) the effect.

KEEP IN MIND

• Resist making promises about the technique. Just do it.

• If you are in a group that is being invited into silence for the first time, keep from giggling (if you can help it).

- Meet another's gaze with warmth. Don't force people to close their eyes.

- You don't have to be a senior executive to suggest a new approach to a meeting. Sometimes it's easier to challenge the norm when you are the new kid in town.

CASE STUDIES

Silence at Dusk

Our company held its retreat in Somerset, England. Dozens of us. We had spent the day in a lovely British country house . . . working. Expansive fields unfolded out the window, a luscious landscape remained untouched by our boots. Attention was waning. No one was saying it out loud, but we were done. It was the end of day one with two more to go. As the sun was slipping into the west, Hendrik-Jan Laseur gathered our group in a circle and gave us the overview for our next session (it was the seventh meeting of the day, and just before a dinner that promised to include more presentations). Our assignment? Take 10 minutes, in silence, to walk outside and enjoy dusk. Think, feel, and watch the sky. Leave our phones on our seats. When we returned, we would resume our work. What a gift!! Ten minutes of private reflection in the middle of an intensive series of strategic meetings. The overachievers in the group had no choice. Our assignment was to be quiet. And it was delicious.

When we reconvened, a relaxed, alert mood blanketed the previously weary group. There was more capacity for conversation. The chance to connect to nature produced a greater connection between our team, and our work product improved as a result.

Silence Your Ego and Make Space to Listen

The room was filled with bright minds, big egos, lots of power players, and noise. The leadership of this growing conglomerate of avia-
tion companies was gathered to establish a five-year plan that would
create greater value by cooperating rather than functioning as separate entities. We had three days together. By the end of day one, lots
of creative ideas had surfaced. The turf war began on day two. Imple-
mentation would require sharing resources and reducing the size of
some of the service centers. No one was listening to one another. It
was 4 p.m. I took a chance. I asked the group to take five minutes. At
their seats. No phones, no writing instruments. Feet on the floor, eyes
closed if they wanted. I suggested they tune in to their breathing and
let their thoughts flow . . . out of their head. I spoke softly, offering a few
instructions. I encouraged them to try to feel the room by tuning in to
the breath of those around them. I fought through my own discomfort
that this high-powered bunch would scoff at me. I fell silent. I joined
the breathing.

At the five-minute mark, I brought the group back into conversation by asking how they felt. They enjoyed the calm, the connection.
I then asked how they wanted to feel at 7 p.m. when the day's work
would be done. No surprise. Serenity had greater appeal over intensity. To maintain the calm, they agreed that for the next two and a half
hours they would actively stop each other from talking over one another. They would create the space to listen. The ensuing conversation was richer as a result. The group didn't exercise perfect impulse
control, but the experience of silence gave them a starting point and a
reason to police each other when things got too contentious.

11

TOUCH

It Transforms an Interaction

What am I doing telling people to touch each other at work?! This is the twenty-first century, and the #metoo movement is in full force. Am I out of my mind suggesting any kind of physical contact? I thought hard about this chapter. It would be easier to just leave it out. It would also be wrong. Touch is too important in establishing the human connection to ignore just because it's complicated. And because it's complicated, there are men who may opt to avoid any kind of touch at the office. I'm in full agreement. If you have any doubt, any niggling suspicion that your behavior might be misinterpreted or offensive, don't do it! Reading this book doesn't replace the importance of reading your situation.

Before we get started, take out your highlighter and swipe it over the word "appropriate." There is a huge expanse between illegal, disrespectful touching and a quick, gentle tap. Our skin is our largest organ, weighing in at six pounds and covering 18 feet. It's the protective seal that keeps the bad stuff out and the good stuff in. Tactile language is intoxicating.

The orbitofrontal cortex (our brain's decision-making center) is activated by touch, triggering a release of oxytocin, the biological basis of connection. Neuroscientist Matthew Hertenstein and his colleagues consider skin an underrated, sophisticated, differential signaling system. Their research reveals that people who were touched by individuals they could not see accurately identified anger, fear, disgust, love, gratitude, and sympathy. To put it in context, that's as good an emotional reading as when we scan someone's face.

A simple (nonsexual) touch *on the arm* can increase compliance. For example, studies have found that lightly tapping a person just above the elbow before asking them to sign a petition increased participation from 55 to 81 percent.

Want to increase your approval ratings? Take a second. To touch. *Respectfully*. Researchers Damien Erceau and Nicolas Gueguen approached random men at a secondhand car market. Half were touched lightly on the arm for one second; the other half weren't. Afterward, those who had been touched rated the seller as more sincere, friendly, honest, agreeable, and kind. Pats on the back, resting a hand on one's shoulder, and playful nudges all provide the "personal touch." *But be careful*. Even very benign contact can have quite different meanings, depending on one's situation, culture, and gender. Generally, a light touch on the upper arm between the shoulder and elbow is the safest. Pushing and picking someone up are physical contacts of a different order and not recommended at work. Hugging can also get you into trouble. In 2017 in the United States, the 9th Circuit Court of Appeals ruled that hugging at work can create a hostile work environment if the embrace is unwelcome and pervasive.

THIS IS FOR YOU IF

- The office feels inhuman.

- You want to warm up your icy reputation and you are supersensitive to situational clues that inform you as to whether a light touch on the arm or an outstretched hand will be welcome.

- Your colleague seems to be suffering, is having a terrible day, or is lost in their own world and you want to quickly communicate that you care.

TAKE ACTION

- ▶ Increase compliance and connection with a light touch on the arm.

- ▶ Use a quick pat on the arm between the shoulder and elbow to communicate, "It's good to see you."

KEEP IN MIND

- Respect boundaries! Inappropriate touching can get you in trouble and really aggravate the person you laid hands on. When in doubt about even tapping, *don't*.

- If someone pulls away from even a brief, light touch, take the hint. Don't do it again, and don't tease your coworker for having a negative reaction.

- Touching someone to get their attention when one's back is turned can cause a fright. Calling the person's name is more effective.

- Slaps on the back confer friendship in some situations and flaunt power in others. Don't take the chance. Resist showing your might.

CASE STUDIES

Reach Out to the Untouchable

To literally touch another person fosters an immediate connection. To see someone as untouchable communicates a great deal. The word "untouchable" references two contradictory extremes: belonging to the lowest caste in Hindu society or having unrivaled talent. In both instances, those who cannot be touched are distanced from the group and experienced as "other."

One of the longest-serving female professors at the University of Pennsylvania was about to receive a career recognition award. She was a renowned powerhouse who oozed independence. I didn't know her well, yet, standing beside her, I could feel her nervousness as she was about to take the stage. I noticed her collar was crooked. I asked if I could smooth it. It was a simple move and a remarkably (appropriate) intimate moment. Her body seemed to unfold as the crease relaxed into place. In that instance the university icon was just another woman with a penchant for perfection who would be disturbed if the event photos memorialized a messy shirt. Although we were only cursory friends, the professor took the stage knowing she had a pal standing by.

> ### *Who Are You Afraid to Touch?*
>
> My partner, Kenzie Kwong, was asked why she devotes so much time to Leaders' Quest, our organization that facilitates exchanges between people of very different worlds. She told a story about visiting an AIDS clinic where she pulled her hand away when a patient reached out to grasp it. Her unconscious action shocked her. She knew better. You can't catch AIDS from a handshake, and yet she had resisted. Her body had rebelled against her morals. From that moment Kenzie knew that countering our own unconscious bias required in-person interaction—and an ease with communicating respect by not being afraid to shake someone's hand.

12

EAT TOGETHER

Food Is Bait for Conversation and Creates Connection

We all have to eat! Let your belly be the prompt and food the excuse to build trust, reduce isolation, and liberate you from your desk. Office life can be a lonely experience. Many of us are interpersonally hungry. Even though we're surrounded by colleagues, we're often too busy staring at our screens to actually see each other. Copying someone on an email or inviting them into a meeting doesn't ensure you are truly working together. Moving fast, we succumb to shorthand, even before we have established a sense of our colleagues. Opportunities to get to know the people you work with lay the foundation for future success and are the reason companies spend fortunes on team-building exercises to promote collaboration. These can help, but we all know they are often artificial and temporary solutions. It's just too easy to get caught up in immediate pressures. The deadlines loom, and your inbox has 122 unread messages.

Having a decent meal often takes a back seat to productivity. "The way people eat at work is pretty sad," reports ethnographer June Jo Lee, who has spent nearly a dozen years studying dining habits in the office. Despite the image of the "top performer" who "powers through lunch" and thrives on "caffeine and stress," effective workers take a midday break and return more energized and focused. Makes sense. So why, according to a Gallup poll in 2017, do 67 percent of American office workers eat at their desks more than once a week? This (often futile) effort at efficiency leads to greater dissatisfaction and sucks the enjoyment out of working in an office—with living, breathing (and potentially really interesting) coworkers.

The three-martini lunch may be a symbol of corporate indulgence, but it includes essential ingredients for career success, such as creating a space for candid conversation devoid of constraining conference room etiquette as well as an opportunity to move beyond data—to delve into the subtext of office interactions. What new pressure is the CEO putting on the COO? Will the older team members actually use the new client management system? Are Cecil and Sammy really acting as cochairs and sharing the burden? What's said in the hallway can undermine the targets set in the boardroom, but you won't be privy to these conversations unless you make the effort to insert a pause and listen.

Breaking bread together is a time-honored tradition, demonstrating positive intentions to further a relationship. Carving out time to share a coffee, snack, or meal with coworkers is an obvious yet often missed chance to get information, expand networks, and resolve tensions.

Kevin Kniffin and his colleagues at Cornell's Food and Brand Lab have demonstrated the positive effect of eating as a unit. For example, cooperation among firefighters was almost twice as high among team members who ate with one another than among those who didn't. The behaviors underlying the firefighters' meal practices—collecting money, planning, talking, cleaning, and, of course, eating—all enhanced group performance on the job. Nutritional sustenance increased appreciation of the people you work with *and* a chance to get the inside scoop on unofficial information—why wouldn't you ask a colleague to lunch? It's a great way to connect!

THIS IS FOR YOU IF

- You use an app to order your food and then eat at your desk, listening to music on your headphones.

- You try to avoid eye contact with your colleagues during your precious lunch break, so you don't have to "waste time" talking to others. Instead, you ramp up your FOMO (fear of missing out), flipping through your friends' Instagram accounts. Or worse, you are following your coworkers on social media but not talking to them in person.

- You can't recall the last time you shared a laugh with the person at the workstation adjacent to you.

- You feel like a document-generating, phone call–answering machine, rather than a living being with a pulsing heart.

- You wonder what the guy with the cool hair eats for lunch (or watches on his phone during breaks that makes him smile so much)—but you don't know how to ask.

TAKE ACTION

▶ Food is an equalizer. The foods we crave (and those we avoid) are as personal as our names. Food choices capture our culture, express our values, and reveal bits of our world beyond the office. Every member of your organization has a story associated with their favorite fare. If you or other colleagues work remotely, bring the team together for a meal at the office or at someone's home. Don't procrastinate. Send a note to your colleagues right now and see if you can find a convenient moment for a potluck lunch. The goal is to create a connection, not enforce a burden. Avoid requiring people to give up personal time for team bonding. Emphasize that expensive ingredients are not encouraged. If cooking is too time-consuming, tell your colleagues to sign up for dessert and bring a package of their favorite cookies.

▶ Encourage your coworkers to bring a beloved dish—perhaps a comfort food from their childhood (this is especially valuable when working with multicultural groups). Tempt the team with your culinary skills. Aren't you known for making awesome lasagna? Get the person in the next cubicle to commit to making mom's fried chicken (they always talk about eating too much of it on Sundays). Ask the receptionist to make that one dish everyone loves. Get others excited by advertising the upcoming delicacies. The anticipation and planning can immediately provide material for light-hearted teasing and good-natured competition.

▶ Providing food is a form of caring. Tonight, while you binge-watch your Netflix favorites, why not bake some brownies? If you're not up for turning on the oven, grab some sweets in the morning when you stop to pick up your coffee. Showing up with unexpected treats can't transform an incompetent colleague into a superstar, but they can humanize standoffish executives. When tempers are flaring and nerves are frayed, your efforts to bring a "gift" demonstrate that you are paying attention. The actual exchange of food is a reason to look each other in the eye, to say thanks, and to share a moment that is not defined by role or dominated by the to-do list.

► Meals seal relationships. Are you thinking, *I'm a CEO. I'm not about to bake for my office!* That's OK (even though you might enjoy getting out the mixing bowls). How about lunch? Many top executives build client relationships over meals, yet forget to invite junior team members. Or they restrict invitations to a small, familiar group rather than extending it to relevant community leaders, interesting innovators, or academics working in related fields. Restaurant dining comes with a natural rhythm. There's the small talk before the order is taken, the meal to dig into along with the business conversation, and a natural end. Shared meals are a great forum for bringing together people who might not otherwise meet.

► Try being strategic with your invitations. Set aside a day each week to dine with someone at your company that you don't know well. Make the list now. Send out a batch of invites. Create a permanent note on your phone with the names of all the people you want to get to know inside and outside of the company. Keep tossing names on the list, and each month send out lunch requests for the weeks ahead. Invite people of all ages and levels and from different departments.

► Snacks bring access. When people stop by for the midafternoon chocolate you stock in your top drawer, they're likely to share a few spontaneous insights into what's happening on the trading floor. Admit it—everyone knows who has the supply of good snacks. Why not be that person? Hand out the candy and get the informal updates that will help you do your job better.

► Coffee cuts through barriers. Does the staff wish they could ask you questions, but instead try to get information from your assistant (or worse, guess what's going on and often get it wrong)? Many companies claim to have a transparent culture, yet having a conversation with decision-makers is often difficult. Instituting "Coffee with Kelly" every Wednesday at 10 a.m. is a chance for people who don't report to you (and perhaps some who do) to ask questions and share what they have achieved. If you're lucky, the junior staff may even dare to pitch you some of their novel ideas.

► When you meet colleagues overseas at conferences or at their offices, bring some traditional snacks from your country. Nioki always gets a smile out of the staff in Knoxville when he shows up with a box of beautifully wrapped red bean candies from Tokyo (not everyone appreciates the taste, but they love feeling worldly). If you travel often, keep a stash of nonperishable goodies ready to be tossed into your luggage. If you lack imagination, arriving with a canister of jelly beans placed in the middle of the conference room table gets everyone grabbing and laughing as they "fight" for their favorite flavor.

KEEP IN MIND

- Avoid making meals mandatory. Shared eating should be fun. Some companies have been criticized for providing meals as a way of "trapping" people at work.

- Be aware of, but not constrained by, coworkers' food restrictions. Try to have some neutral snacks. Vegetables and fruit can be shared by most, and they look pretty in a bowl.

- No picking! Don't eat the food off your subordinate's plate. One of the executives I worked with had to be told not to snag french fries from coworkers' plates. She thought she was being friendly, but her employees found it too familiar and intrusive.

- Stick around to help clean up the conference room after the team has shared cake celebrating someone's birthday that month. Too often, this falls to the women in the office. Gentlemen, you are not invisible, and the walls (and your colleagues) will talk if you are too focused on feeding and fleeing.

- Male or female, baking is a bridge to relationships, not a replacement. Even if you set up plates of yummy brownies, you still have the responsibility of establishing respect through the many other ways described in this book.

CASE STUDIES

Every Office Needs a Sylvia

The staff of a Brazilian news agency confided in me that office morale was low. They even had someone to blame. "It was Sylvia!" Who was Sylvia? She was the administrator's mother who sold homemade empanadas from the back of her truck. On Wednesdays, Sylvia brought savory specialties to her daughter's office. Everyone loved Wednesdays. They loved Sylvia. When Sylvia died, the reporters no longer engaged in their weekly lunch ritual. The group stopped making time to just be together. Sylvia's delicacies had gotten everyone up from their desks. Sylvia asked each person how they were doing. She got the group talking to each other.

The answer to reviving office morale? The agency reinstated "Sylvia's snack time." On Wednesdays, the team now takes turns ordering in lunch. While they munch, they tell funny stories from the week. The reporters once again make a point to all be in the same place at the same time. Being together reinforces the importance of their work and provides a chance to ask for advice and show off recent triumphs. The group started taking pictures of their weekly ritual to share with reporters in the field (and with Sylvia's family). The return of their shared meal reminded the team how much they enjoy each other's company. No surprise—the office spirit has been revitalized.

An Ancient Ritual Finds Modern Relevance

At a management meeting for the executives overseeing a German truck company, my colleague, Kenzie Kwong, had the engineers don aprons and prepare a meal. While chopping and stirring, the team learned about key concepts from Chinese philosophy. They came to appreciate how the concept of yin and yang infuses Chinese cuisine—how each dish needs a balance of color, flavors, and textures. Every ingredient must exist in harmony with the other elements; nothing can overpower or disappear. With Kenzie by their side, the group discovered that Chinese recipes are not simply instructions for cooking, they are directives for life. The team arrived the next morning for the formal strategy sessions equipped with useful metaphors to inspire their thinking (and some great pictures to share with their families and colleagues).

Uniting Around Food as a Pathway to Peace

Antwan (a Palestinian now living in the West Bank) stood in front of the barrier wall between Israel and Palestine. He's devoted the last decade to increasing the communication between Israelis and Arabs through his work with the Holy Land Trust. This Palestinian nongovernmental organization focuses on "radical peace building" through workshops promoting personal forgiveness and nonviolent community empowerment.

When asked how he got started, Antwan explained that his family ran a tourist shop near Rachel's Tomb, a Jewish holy site in Bethlehem on the way to Jerusalem. At his family's shop, Antwan encountered tour guides and bus drivers who were Mizrachi Jews—people who immigrated to Israel from Arab neighboring countries post 1948. Mizrachi Jews spoke Arabic to him. They brought food to heat in the office kitchen. It smelled and tasted like his mother's food. His body felt at home amidst these Jewish community members, even though politics suggested he be on his guard. "How can a kitchen that smells like my mom's produce people who aren't my relatives?" Antwan's nose didn't lie—there was more in common between the families than was popularly discussed. And so, his career as a community organizer began.

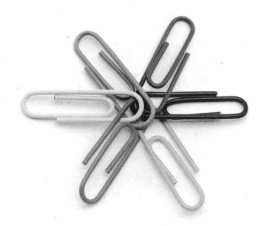

PART III

BECOME
POPULAR

It's about *me*! You are the ultimate change-maker. Don't let your role or title define you. Make a difference by being your most likeable, enchanting self— in all situations. The "work me" and "real me" tributaries are merging. Social media doesn't let us hide. The modern workplace values transparency. Like it or not, our personalities are our brands. Take charge of your reputation.

Recognize how your presence can determine if it's going to be a good day at the office or a rush to the closing bell. In a rapidly changing world, the requisite skills for success are in constant flux; yet self-awareness (an appreciation of your impact on others) continues to predict career advancement. The earlier parts helped you gain respect, nonverbally tune in to others, and refine your perspectives. This part builds on those competencies by showing you how to be the person others want to connect with first. It's time to work on your personal narrative, tell stories, and learn to thrive in possibility, imperfection, confusion, and tension. You want to develop a point of view to increase your value while at the same time knowing when to admit you are wrong. When you are the person people want to be with, opportunities multiply and you are happier and more successful.

This Part Is for You If

- You want to be included and influential.

- You'd like to help your colleagues shine.

- Being wrong—or scared—has some appeal.

- You've been promoted and are concerned about developing your executive presence.

- Your emails are going unanswered.

- It's hard to connect to people you don't know.

- You have access to information and assume (incorrectly) that everyone else does, too.

- Your internal voice is torturing you.

13

BE PRESENT

Showing Up Is Just the Start

The most precious gift we can offer others is our presence.
—THICH NHAT HANH

"He breaks down a brick wall with his mind." That's how my client was described by his peers. When I shared this feedback with the 32-year-old computer programmer, his response was, "I'm just doing my job." It shocked Nick to learn that his participation on a project gave it instant credibility. We forget, or don't even realize that those around us are often deeply impacted by our presence (or lack of it).

Showing up matters. Remote workers make their presence known by their contributions and have pre-arranged expectations for on-site participation. Let's not confuse them with the person who should be at the office but then calls in at the last minute to join a meeting because they hit snooze on the alarm or didn't want to tackle rush-hour traffic.

How many times have you been at a conference table when the colleague who isn't in the room becomes the focus of attention? "Why didn't they make the effort? Are we not important enough?" The team showed up but they're not looking at each other; they're talking *to the speaker phone*! If you're expected to be the human in the room, don't opt to be the voice in the box.

And certainly, avoid being that colleague who only appears at regularly scheduled meetings if they need something. If you are an invited lecturer, spend time with your audience. I have attended many conferences where the keynote speakers, the experts whom everyone wants to learn from and impress, are seen only on stage. That's terribly disappointing to eager participants who plunked down a chunk of change with the hope of having an informal conversation with a famous influencer in their field.

I'm often asked to coach clients on "executive presence." It's a misconception that executive presence is about commanding a room. It's not about you being the star. Power results from your ability to tune in to the needs of the people around you. It seems pretty obvious, but it's worth stating: attending to others is impossible if you are not actually in the right place!

OK. You showed up. Now what? Here's a chance to implement the suggestions we discussed in earlier chapters. Make eye contact, silence your internal chatter, listen deeply, and relax into the moment. Daniel Ludevig, a former dancer who teaches embodied leadership, reminds us that "Your body is not just a brain taxi, transporting it from one meeting to the next." Whether you are entering a conference room, walking the hall, or grabbing a sandwich, you are demonstrating an approachability and interest through all of your nonverbal behaviors.

The more senior your position, the greater likelihood your every move is read and interpreted (often incorrectly) by those around you. Are you the boss, but lost in thought about your sister's disdain for your current beau? Watch out. If you walk down the hall with a frown, the default for your team won't be, "Oh, I see she has a sibling as exasperating as mine," but more likely, "What did I do wrong? My manager seems really annoyed."

It may seem unfair. "Do I always have to monitor myself and my expressions?" you may ask. You may elect not to care, but then don't be surprised if you aren't seen as approachable (or likable). Here's the good news: When one person becomes fully present, it's an almost irresistible force. The connection happens. If you, freed from distractions, sit with a colleague and actively pay attention with all your senses, if you convey that what's happening between you at that moment is all that matters, then your presence can bring others in, inviting them to sit up, take notice, and take action.

THIS IS FOR YOU IF

- You want to be taken seriously.
- Information doesn't readily come your way.
- Modesty is your mantra, and you forget how you affect others.

TAKE ACTION

- Manage your mood, facial expressions, and body language to send the right signals.
- Be intentional with your attention. Identify colleagues and constituents who need face time.

▶ Consider taking handwritten notes in meetings so it's clear you aren't cheating and checking your emails on your electronic device.

▶ Follow my colleague Max Metcalfe's advice if you have a big personality: "manage your muchness." Be careful not to overpower a room.

▶ Assess your personal power meter. If you think you are a 7 on a scale of 1–10 of impact, you are more likely an 11.

▶ Remember to show up when you are expected or when your surprise appearance would motivate and validate others.

KEEP IN MIND

• A Google Hangout or company hashtag does not replace in-person conversations.

• Uncontrollable noise generates stress; remove unnecessary email and text alerts. We all know you are popular. Assume something is coming into your inbox regularly. You don't need a beep or a buzz to announce incoming messages.

CASE STUDIES

Go Ahead, Toss a Ball at Your Boss

Amy is a very effusive manager, constantly making jokes and interacting with her staff—which is why she was taken aback to find out that the team sent each other texts to go, avoid, or delay depending on her mood. True, she was going through a tough divorce and custody battle, but she thought she was a pretty good actress. Clearly not. Given her style and comfort with the team, Amy got a bucket, filled it with sponge balls, and placed it on her desk after receiving the feedback. "Toss them at me when I am sour," she instructed. "I don't want you talking about me behind my back." Her ability to offer up the props and the comic relief they provided turned some cloudy days into a shared good time. This wasn't simply about managing the boss's mood. The goal was to cue Amy to resume her winning style of truly being *with* her team.

Are You a Snubber?

Jason, the head of commodities, received negative feedback during his performance review. People on the trading floor experienced him as self-involved, dismissive, and arrogant. He seemed truly shocked. Digging deeper into the disconnect between his self-appraisal and how others viewed him, Jason related that he was actually very shy. He wasn't comfortable initiating conversation. Being very efficient, he also underestimated the value of a little small talk. I asked Jason if I could follow him as he left his corner office to go to the restroom. He thought my request quite odd.

Relax, I didn't go into the restroom with him! I did, however, see that as Jason walked, he looked at his phone, made no eye contact, and completely missed the efforts those around him were making to catch his attention. The team read his oblivion as a personal snub. We tested it. Biology became the cue. Trips to the bathroom became opportunities to have chats, to actually see, speak to, and be present with others on the return journey. To help prompt conversation, Jason encouraged people to decorate their work stations. Equipped with a reminder to speak and hints at each desk as to what people cared about, Jason's natural humor (once you got to know him) shone through. Now, when asked about their manager, the folks on the trading room floor describe him as a modest, trusted ally.

14

SHARE INFORMATION

News Is a Virtual Valium

Corporate cultures often reveal splits between those "in the know" from the mere mortals awaiting instructions and some indication of what the heck is going on. Access to information enhances one's organizational status. Knowledge is power. Knowledge is also a virtual Valium, a relaxant. Information can motivate and ameliorate stress, yet this interpersonal salve is often sequestered by leaders who incorrectly believe that before they address their teams, they must have all the answers or at least near-perfect responses to challenging questions. Worse, managers forget or don't make time to exchange data, and as a result, demotivate eager employees. Does one person at work report to you? Great! You're a manager. Are you the lowest worker on the totem pole? I bet you have a perspective on what's working on the ground. Remember to share what you know. Here's a common complaint from my clients:

> I'm angry. My bosses know I go crazy without information, that I feel disrespected when I have to sneak around trying to figure out what's really happening and yet they do it over and over. Is it that hard? They pay for me to see you to round out my rough edges. I come in here and spin my wheels trying to figure out if it's me or if it's them. I wish my manager would periodically bring me under the tent. Imagine if all I had to do was focus on my job. I'd knock it out of the park.

Information vacuums create toxic work environments, which are intensified during periods of rapid change. Many managers think they can keep important decisions under wraps. Rather than opening their doors, they batten down the hatches. Hot news inevitably escapes, and a tense situation becomes more complicated as leaders have to undo misinformation and mend relationships with previously loyal colleagues. This is a common pattern: he heard from a colleague who used to work at the firm; she heard from her father-in-law; they heard in the hallways. You are the only one who thinks the merger/sale/closing is a secret.

Especially for those in subordinate positions, the combination of not being able to control the proceedings and not having any sight lines on what might happen next deteriorates mental and physical health.

When people have no way to impact the events around them, they learn to give up. They stop trying because their actions don't matter. Psychologist Martin Seligman termed this "learned helplessness." We can't miraculously make everyone the masters of their own destiny. What can be done to reduce this environmentally induced passivity? Provide information! Research repeatedly shows that the ability to predict when things might happen, even if there's no control over those events, enables individuals to remain active and reduces despair. Have you ever been on the New York City subway or the London Tube? Most stations now post status updates indicating how long it will be before your train will arrive. While you can't get the Northern line to move faster or to arrive just when you want it, you can at least make the decision to wait, walk, or hail a taxi. Providing a choice attenuates feelings of powerlessness; it contributes to success.

THIS IS FOR YOU IF

- The company you started has grown from 3 to 30 people, and you are used to filling people in when you see them.

- You prefer having the answers (and being able to anticipate the questions) before you speak.

- When things get tense, you get quiet.

- You would like colleagues to share information with you.

- Gossip is on the rise.

- You may not have a fancy title, but you know stuff.

TAKE ACTION

On a Regular Basis

▶ Start the day with a five-minute standing meeting. Standing ensures that the time together is crisp and focused. Each member of the team should share at least one important piece of information that will help everyone do their job better *today*. It could be news from outside the company and may be tactical (e.g., there's construction on the highway leading to the mall and workers and customers may be late, or snow is anticipated in the southern part of the state this afternoon, so those with big commutes should leave early). If the team is not collocated, pick a time when everyone can hop on the phone for a quick daily touch base and ask, "What do you need to know today, so your day will run more smoothly?"

▶ Include an information update on your team's weekly meeting agenda. Whiz around the room and have each participant offer something new that they learned from a meeting in the past week that the others did not attend.

▶ If you are out of the office attending a sales meeting, corporate training, or strategy session, compose a brief note to your team each night with a few bullets capturing what you learned. It will help you synthesize the material and will reinforce your value to the group. When you return to the office after having been away at a management offsite, don't get lost in your emails. First, call your group together and share the meeting highlights. Sure, some topics may be confidential, which is why it's important for the management team to agree, before everyone leaves the offsite, that they will (1) establish what is classified, and (2) communicate with their teams on the first day back. If you are running the offsite, make time before it ends to let everyone gather their thoughts and agree to the key messages that will be relayed to the staff.

▶ If you just left a meeting that offered important insights for your team, don't delay. Shoot a quick message out using whatever form of office chat you have established for immediately actionable information. Don't confuse mechanisms to communicate *nice to know* from *need to know* information. Agree in advance when to use email/voicemail/Slack/text/etc.

▶ Set up "surprise me" sessions at which you gather employees from different backgrounds and ages and ask them to share something from their less traditional/nonwork networks. With the advent of social media, many younger employees are accessing data from outside the company that is gold dust for their senior colleagues.

During Times of Massive Change

▶ When corporate reorganizations or potential mergers are afoot, it's unrealistic to inform everyone immediately of their future roles. Often these decisions aren't clear to those in charge until the final hour. However, indicating the date that layoffs will be announced and the process by which people can apply for alternative positions within the company allows employees to plan and arrive at work each day without fear that "today is the day that I lose my job."

▶ Remember, just because you know it, doesn't mean others do. Resist waiting for the perfect, complete answer. Think hard about what you can share and provide as much information as possible.

▶ The more unpredictable the setting, the more anxious people get. The more fearful they are, the less able they are to retain information. Communicate often. Deliver your message verbally and in writing. It's better to repeat yourself than have people spiral in the unknown.

▶ Saying, "I don't know" (if this is true) counts as information. In the absence of real knowledge, people sometimes make inferences, which can be far worse than the truth and fan the fires of anxiety. It's better to indicate that certain decisions have not been made than to let people speculate.

▶ Allow discussions. Don't do what one pharmaceutical company recently did—rather than holding an interactive meeting, the company showed employees a video announcing an upcoming merger and associated downsizing. No questions could be asked.

▶ Sometimes employees don't feel safe asking questions out loud. Include anonymous mechanisms, such as submitting a question on paper or employing technology that enables audience members to text a question to the screen.

▶ There are individuals in a system who have the authority to make a decision and others who need to be informed about ongoing activity. Find out who needs to be copied on communications.

KEEP IN MIND

- Remember, sometimes your boss needs *your* information. Come bearing gifts.
- Don't spread gossip. If you are guessing, say so.

CASE STUDIES

When?!

"I don't know if I will have a job come April, or if I do, what my role will be. It's possible I may have to move to Atlanta if the company consolidates the back offices. I'm taking care of my mom here in Boston, and I have to apply to kindergarten for my twins. I'm jumping out of my skin." Belle was not alone. Her boss and her boss's boss were in the dark. Rumors quenched the thirst for information. The Human Resources Department asked me to conduct a session on coping with uncertainty. It was oversold. Members of the senior management team attended. Although they felt legally constrained from sharing too much about the impending deal, they realized that there was information that could be communicated. Offering time lines reduced some anxiety. For example, staff in support functions would be part of transition teams, should the deal go through, and that translated into job security for at least a year. The deal might be challenged, and if a court battle ensued, nothing would change for anyone for at least six months. There would be no layoffs for at least half a year. The company was reviewing an option for voluntary early retirement and would make an announcement in four weeks.

The administration provided some predictability that enabled employees to experience control over their lives. The leadership agreed to have a question-and-answer session each Thursday at 10 a.m. that was recorded, so everyone could access the latest news. Staff could submit questions, and the executive team would do their best to provide updates on emerging developments. At the very least, they could squash gossip. It wasn't a perfect solution. People still wanted to know *when*, but at least they could plan for the immediate.

Tell Us Before It Hits the Press

"I shouldn't find out in *Variety*!" Tijo was enraged. How could his media company acquire a new channel and not tell him in advance? He's part of the sales team, out there pitching business, meant to be the man in the know. And now he feels foolish. What else has Kane (his boss) been keeping from him?! I did my best to calm Tijo down. It's not unusual for these kinds of transactions to be kept quiet until the final moments. I encouraged Tijo to inquire about Kane's choice not to say *anything*, even at the final hour when it was clear the deal would close. Perhaps there was a reason. When asked, Kane was gracious and self-reflective. He confirmed that *his* boss can be very punishing if there are leaks and had asked the senior leadership team to refrain from sharing information about the potential deal. Kane appreciated the awkward situation this put Tijo in. Kane shared the feedback with his boss who said that going forward she would be more specific about who could receive information along with guidelines about how and when to share it rather than saying, "Let's keep this among ourselves."

15

BE A MAGNET

Become the Person
People Want to Be With

I coach my clients to become magnets—the colleagues everyone wants to work with, the people it feels good to be around. When you are a magnet, your comrades are walking *toward* you at corporate gatherings. When teams are assembled and new opportunities explored, your name is at the top of the list. Impromptu office outings? You get an invite. Being magnetic doesn't mean you are always extroverted, constantly lauded, or never alone. But it does mean that in your presence, people relax, feel safe, and know that you are on their side. Magnets show up with something interesting to say, eagerly engage others in discussion, are professional, reliable, *and* dare to have some fun.

People in my practice complain that their bosses "make their brains shut down." A spelling error gets a reaction, but working overtime covering for three team members out on holiday during the same week doesn't generate one compliment. Self-absorbed or tragically goal-oriented colleagues darken the rooms they inhabit. "I'm not learning anything." "They don't respect my experience." "I can do much more than this basic work." "Why don't they recognize my worth?" "My reputation on the street is diminishing." You may have been promoted, but you still feel like a peon. You aspire to a seat at the table, but the door to the conference room appears firmly shut. You're frustrated with those above and you are driving the people who report to you that much harder. We've all been there. Your pores ooze with negativity and it's *their* fault. My office is frequented by people who arrive wanting to change how others behave, but, as the old joke goes, "How many consultants (therapists, coaches) does it take to change a light bulb?" The answer is, "None. The light bulb must want to change itself." And that's what we focus on: how to be the person you want to be, not the person you are being made to feel like by others.

Magnetism isn't just a term of art. Our nervous systems transmit information through electromagnetic waves that are influenced by the people around us. We survive by mimicking others from the moment we're born through a process called "limbic resonance." It's so important for a newborn baby to match its mother's heartbeat and breathing rate that orphaned children are given teddy bears that simulate these cues. This unconscious process opens the door to communal connection. We are drawn to people who provide a safe, reliable rhythm. Whether you own the company or answer the phones for the executives on the fourth floor, make biology work for you.

Astrologist Rob Brezsny coined the term "pronoia" to capture the importance of continually surveying your environment for opportunity, rather than attending to problems. Magnetic employees are curious about others, attentive to the impact their presence generates, and ready to step into a conflict—not necessarily to solve it, but to demonstrate that disagreements aren't to be feared. They challenge negativity (inside their own heads) and counter pessimism when expressed by others.

To ignite joy at work, radiate wonder, a readiness to engage, and a comfort with whatever the day brings and observe how individuals (and their limbic systems) are drawn to you.

THIS IS FOR YOU IF

- You wish you could be charming, but instead you just feel awkward.

- You can't seem to get the notice you crave.

- "Networking" and "relationship-building" are buzzwords that make you break into hives. You feel more comfortable playing video games at your desk when no one is watching.

- You've mistaken being the boss for being respected, and now you need to reboot your reputation.

- When the caller ID indicates it's you, your colleagues don't pick up.

- You're continually told you are not quite ready for new opportunities, yet the reasons offered as an explanation aren't holding your peers back.

TAKE ACTION

► Lean back. I often find myself in the uncomfortable position of coaching people to care less. The most passionate and committed are often the ones identified as generating too much heat in the organization. Be a surge protector—capture the negative energy by leaning *back* and holding the space for exploration. Let others speak. Listen. Don't focus on promoting your idea or finding a fix. Add value by creating a nonjudgmental place for discussion.

► Prepare conversational gifts. Don't just race to the next meeting. Stop and think about your audience. How can you catalyze a quality discussion? What thought-provoking questions might you ask to ensure the conversation is keeping up with current events? Do you have some relevant (but not obvious) information to share that could make the interaction more interesting and memorable for everyone? Tuck a story or two in your pocket, something from your recent travels or perhaps a behind-the-scenes insight you have from a recent political or media event. Be careful your story isn't too involved, self-aggrandizing, or diminishing of others. Your goal is to offer up a little entertainment—and some new knowledge.

► Don't "own" the things you do well. Delegating the jobs that we don't do well and don't enjoy—that's easy. It's harder to train someone to take over a task that you find pleasurable, but it won't help your reputation (or growth) in the long run. Pick a task. Let's say presenting the monthly profit and loss report to the management committee. We know it's great exposure to senior leadership and you are determined to get the numbers right, down to the last decimal point. Use the chart below to do a quick assessment. Indicate whether only you can perform this responsibility and whether you enjoy having this as part of your job.

TASK:	Only I can do this!	I enjoy this responsibility
Yes		
No		

► Be sure to think expansively about who might be trained to perform tasks that you really enjoy doing. Have you convinced yourself that you are singularly qualified? Sharing opportunities that may have established your reputation is a powerful way of communicating that you are secure in your role and committed to the development of your coworkers. Having completed the chart, note the suggested next steps. Review your to-do list. What plum assignments are you hogging? Can you identify opportunities to develop others by delegating your beloved responsibilities?

TASK:	Only I can do this!	I enjoy this responsibility
Yes	Do it for now	Train others
No	*Don't hog*	Delegate (if you can)

▶ Joy is contagious. From funny paper glasses that turn light bulbs into stars to notepads made to look like napkins, Douglas Gray, an entertainment and cruise line consultant, has an endless supply of humorous props that break the ice, draw smiles, and make him the guy you want to hang out with. Cara opts to leave small puzzles on her desk—they start conversations and instill a welcome sense of whimsy. Sometimes images help—Jenna framed a photo of her hands-free holiday on a zip line. As the company comptroller, she's always monitoring expenses and chasing financial reports, so she wanted people to know that after hours she was up for adventure and has the ability to literally let go.

▶ Delight others by noticing what is important to them. Ask your colleague about the picture on his or her desk (Jenna hung the photo of herself on the zip line for a reason). Did your coworker just finish her graduate degree at night? What was her favorite course? The woman next to you started carrying a bike helmet. Find out how her commute has changed.

▶ Make an extra effort to initiate conversation with shy colleagues. Just because someone is senior to you in the organization doesn't mean that person has your interpersonal skills. Don't be afraid to say hello.

▶ Manage odors. I can see you rolling your eyes, but really, to be a magnet, don't smell. Over the years I have had to tell clients that their colleagues are put off by foot odor when they remove their shoes and rest their feet on the desk. Eating yummy spicy food at your cubicle is usually more fun for you than your neighbor. And don't forget the breath mints. You will thank me.

KEEP IN MIND

- Being magnetic takes preparation, but don't flaunt your efforts. The whole point is to "naturally" infuse interactions with appreciation and opportunity.

- A grumpy day or two is natural (just keep them at a minimum). Feeling particularly out of sorts? If you can, postpone making requests until you can be a bit more charming.

CASE STUDY

Speak to Me; Don't Scare Me

Kori can be found at his computer or the gym. He's quiet. When he speaks, people listen because he often makes insightful contributions. Some of his colleagues experience his reluctance to chime in as distant, even selfish. He's shy. When he walks down the hall, he tends not to make eye contact. Kori's muscles are barely contained by his shirt, and when he's stressed, his veins pop above his eyes. "I fear he will throw a phone at me when he's mad," observed a peer at Kori's tech firm.

Kori had recently been passed over for promotion, and when I shared these perceptions with him, he was surprised and saddened. "I'm working hard. Why isn't that good enough?" No question, performance matters, but Kori's intensity was working against him. Being taller, quieter, more reserved, and possibly stronger than most was experienced by others as intimidating. Kori made an effort to get up from his desk, seek opinions, and share his. He smiled, made eye contact, and contributed more to group conversations. His veins stopped twitching, and he felt more appreciated. The following year he was named the COO of his company.

Care Less to Achieve More

Avery is paid well, gets good reviews, and was relentlessly dissatisfied with her job. She complained she was not being taken seriously, and when her manager investigated her complaints, colleagues were annoyed. "Avery is always looking for evidence that people speak over her. It's a fast-paced department, why does she get so frustrated and shut down?" She was referred for coaching to become more of a leader and less of a victim. Success, her manager said, would be for Avery to talk about something other than herself, to take the initiative to mentor, and to participate in firm-wide initiatives. There was no question that Avery had a bright future, if only she wasn't so . . . "repellent."

Avery experienced the situation quite differently. The primary breadwinner in her family, with two small children and a long commute, Avery was plagued with anxiety about not doing enough, advancing fast enough, and making enough money. She ground her teeth until two had cracked. She felt used up and angry—at home and at work. She was trying so hard she had nothing left to give. If she didn't advocate for herself, who would?

And so, our work began: We explored the misery she experienced and projected onto others, much of it related to unrealistic expectations she had, first and foremost, of herself.

During our meetings Avery's humor was apparent, as was her appreciation that she was in a unique position as a female: a trader and an excellent sector commentator with an impressive following. She recognized that she was sabotaging her success with her intensity. My suggestion? "Care less." Counterintuitive for sure, but she was willing to try—for two weeks. Avery experimented with relinquishing the pressure to advance at rocket pace. Her work product didn't diminish, but her obsessive thoughts did. Suddenly, taking the time to talk to, kid around with, and even advise others didn't seem so onerous. She took half a month off from worrying about her salary (which was already quite competitive). She liked how she felt. Her family and team noticed. Her husband wanted to take the train home with her; she was good company (again).

For the next four weeks, Avery started seeking out ways to compliment others, to partner across the divisions, and to remain calm when the traders' tempers flared in response to the market. Taking everything less personally got consistently easier. After a few months with her new approach Avery declared, "I'm done being angry." Realistically, I don't expect Avery to be free of fury forever. However, we jettisoned the cloak of negativity and exposed her smarts, wit, and deep commitment to everyone's success, not just her own.

16

KNOW HOW TO ENTER

First Impressions Stick

For years, I've slid (and screamed) in despair behind my friend Catrin Bois-sonnas as she careened down ski slopes. During a recent beach adventure, I was surprised to see my agile pal lingering at the water's edge. "I don't know how to enter the ocean. I haven't experienced the rhythm of the waves," she pronounced, jumping back from the crashing surf. It took me a minute to re-alize Catrin's athletic prowess was why she *wasn't* moving. It's counterintuitive to dive into, not run away from, a wave rising above your head. You must make a commitment to the water and run toward the sea as the tide is going out. Ob-serving the cadence and joining the rhythm of existing activity is a skill. Just ask any jazz musician. The belt of Louis Armstrong's horn announces his ar-rival, but only once "Satchmo" has connected with the contours of the melody does his instrument start introducing an improvisation that leads the band in another direction.

Genetically, we are hardwired to make quick decisions. Scientists have identified an unconscious process called rapid cognition or thin slicing, the ability to gauge what is important from a very quick experience. Nobel Prize–winning psychologist Daniel Kahneman explains that there are times when our mind takes mental shortcuts and deals only in "known knowns"—largely ignoring facts that might make a decision more complex. Unfortunately, our efficient but sometimes flawed internal computer can inaccurately affirm pre-determined beliefs rather than attend to more nuanced information. As you seek to connect, be careful about what your behavior is telegraphing.

THIS IS FOR YOU IF

- You never stopped to consider "How *do* I enter?"

- You barrel into a room ready for action and are then surprised when conversation is stalled.

- Praying for an instant invisibility potion is preferable to being noticed when you enter a new situation.

- Tag, you're it! You're the person who is sent out into the community to establish good relationships.

- You are the new kid at the office.

- You are the old geezer at the office.

TAKE ACTION

▶ Seek ways to sync up with, not overpower, a new situation. This can be as simple as going over and standing by someone's desk—waiting for them to be ready to receive you—rather than assuming you are welcome, or listening to and watching a group perform before offering a suggested improvement.

▶ Remember that just as you are assessing the action, you, too, are being observed. Your facial expressions and nonverbal behaviors have a huge impact. This is especially true if you are a person in authority as your entry will likely be experienced with a volume and intensity beyond your imagination (and awareness). Psychologist Nalina Ambady found that students who ranked their professor after watching a 10-second video gave the same rating as those who attended the professor's entire semester of classes. Educators who made eye contact, smiled, and had open-handed gestures were rated more highly than those who were stiff and fidgety.

▶ Enter with a smile, an outstretched hand, and a ready compliment for those you are about to meet. Be purposeful in providing ways for others to get comfortable in your presence. Researchers at the University of York found that people who communicate in an expressive, animated fashion tend to be liked more readily than the stony-faced variety. Psychologists refer to this as the *expressivity halo*. We feel more at ease with people who are easy to read. It might also explain why you "hated that guy until you got to know him." Help people get to know you. Use your face!

► Be prepared, rather than pretending (or hoping) that snap judgments don't matter. Don't enter a room with your papers askew and your hands filled with bags; they will interfere with the immediacy of making contact with others. Giggling with your friends as you are about to meet new associates sets an immediate tone of exclusion. Finish that funny story outside.

► Pay attention to anticipated assumptions regarding your behavior and attire—and "shock the system" with your flexibility. Are you usually experienced as the stiff banker and are about to meet community leaders? Consider wearing more relaxed clothing. Are you working with colleagues from more conservative backgrounds? Your faith may not require you to cover your legs or shoulders, but theirs does. Wear a shawl and/or long pants.

► Be careful not to assume your rank allows you free entry. Ask for permission to enter a private space and wait for the answer. Pay attention to the action you might be interrupting, and see if you can watch, join, or come back later. If appropriate, figure out a way you can offer help.

► Be curious. If you are the "outsider" coming in, ask open-ended questions to ease any initial awkwardness. Make it your responsibility for conversation to flow.

► Trade in the traditional firm handshake for one that is well matched to the strength and rhythm of the person you are meeting. Don't let chairs, tables, or desks get between you and a gracious hello.

► When you enter as well as when others join the meeting, be the first to make eye contact. Assume they are just as uncomfortable or shy as you are. Predict a good conversation. When you greet people, tell them you are looking forward to talking with them because (insert a heartfelt, truthful reason) and set the stage for a dynamic exchange.

KEEP IN MIND

- "Act happy to see whomever it is you're seeing," says Hillary Clinton. Or as Bill would put it, "Act like whomever it is you're seeing is holding a plate of ribs."

- If meeting people from other cultures, be sensitive to whether handshakes are appropriate. Don't hug. If touching fingertips in a Namaste is the preferred salutation for the culture you are in, do that. Are you working in a society that bows? Bow.

- Once you understand the way in which impressions are made, you can influence others' perceptions of you—and that's a valuable path toward meaningful connection with the people you interact with.

CASE STUDIES

Ask Permission

My mother used to say that hospital staff wake you to see if you need a sleeping pill. Not the most sensitive interaction. By comparison, Wellington Nogueira, founder of Brazil's Doctors of Joy, dons his clown costume and models the importance of asking permission to enter with an exaggerated rap on the door and a tentative placement of his oversized shoe into the patient's room. The patient in the hospital bed laughs, and the doctors watching Wellington learn. Disrespecting the sanctity of someone's space is an assertion of power. Whether it's popping your head over the cubicle and initiating conversation or entering the stock room to review inventory, it's best to ask first.

Join the Action

What do a military man and a medical doctor with a red nose have in common? They both know how to connect with respect. Retired General Jeff Sinclair joined me on a community visit in the Jaipur desert. Our purpose was to gain an appreciation of the local weavers' lives and their relationship with the rug dealer who was committed to the economic development of his suppliers. It was a five-minute walk through the village to get to the carpet company's outpost. The residents were watching us. This wasn't a town that received many guests. Rather than going right to the designated meeting spot, General Sinclair paused to catch a wayward cricket ball and tossed it back to the kids competing on a makeshift pitch. They giggled. I followed his lead and threw a less accurately aimed ball back at the boys, and then we stopped to introduce ourselves. Absent a shared language, the General motioned to the plate miming a request to take a turn at bat. The children squealed with delight.

The exchange took just a few minutes, and we proceeded to the formal meeting where word of our "antics" had already spread. The ice was broken; we were no longer strangers. We started talking about kids, sports, and the challenges of finding good schools. By the time we got to the topic at hand, economic development for the impoverished town, we were treated as interested friends who wanted to learn more about the artisans' relationship with the companies buying and selling their rugs.

17

TELL STORIES

Connect by Hacking Your Colleagues' Right Brains

Stories stimulate oxytocin, the neurochemical that motivates cooperation. Telling stories evokes emotions, enhances empathy, and increases connection. Stories are a primal form of communication dating back to when our "flat screens" were cave walls. Through stories we share passions, hardships, sadness, and joys. Narratives help us find meaning.

Neuroeconomist Paul Zak's research indicates that, biologically, we process stories as if they were real experiences. The listener is feeling and bonding with you. Telling a story in a 1:1 meeting, during a group discussion, or from the stage invites your listener to travel with you back in time or into the future. Sharing a story is a way of saying, "I'm going to trust you with a piece of myself." When you lead with authenticity, others are inclined to follow. The clothes you wear to work is the outline. The stories fill you in as a real person, someone colleagues can relate to, learn from, and befriend.

Stories provide order. Humans seek certainty, and the narrative structure is familiar, predictable, and comforting. Within the context of a story arc we can withstand intense emotions because we know that resolution follows the conflict. We can experience with a safety net. We can listen, absorb, and take in new information without the usual defenses that our logical self asserts.

Work presentations, with their statistics, metrics, and numbers, have traditionally appealed to the left side of the brain. That's changing. As Daniel Pink, author of *Drive*, writes, "Right-brain dominance is the new source of competitive advantage." Rational engagement is based on the stimulation of the mind, whereas emotional engagement is created in the heart. Effective storytelling penetrates our work armor and allows us to establish the personal connection first. Then we can get down to business.

THIS IS FOR YOU IF

- Everyone in this room seems so different. Time to connect as "humans."

- Making a slide deck is your go-to move when asking for resources or just a little help.

- You present as being "all buttoned-up," and people find that boring.

TAKE ACTION

▶ Stop and think, *Why do I care?* Let the audience hear your voice, not "company speak." Don't be afraid to go off script if recent events in your home, office, or the news have touched you and are relevant to the message you want to convey.

▶ Find a short story from your personal life and tell it to a friend first to be sure it hits the right notes before going public.

▶ Practice strategic vulnerability. Remind your coworkers or audience that although you may have designed a beautiful exterior life, your success grew out of mistakes that were the same or worse than theirs. You don't have to turn your speech into a therapy session, but no one believes (or likes) someone who is perfect—so don't project yourself as always having it all together.

▶ Stop and think, *Why should they care?* When asking the management committee to dedicate more funds to product development, don't detail all the reasons why the current system is failing. Instead paint a (true) picture of reduced frustration and more immediate profit from their investment.

▶ Engage the listener's senses by describing what you saw, heard, or even tasted during the experience you are sharing.

KEEP IN MIND

- Remember, your story has to be authentic—and not too long-winded or self-congratulatory.

- Our brains are wired to ignore certain overused words and phrases, so get rid of the clichés to avoid losing your audience.

CASE STUDIES

Tell Them About Being a Gang Member

"Would you hire you?"

Drew was preparing his pitch to human resources executives. He had developed a program to place college dropouts into jobs typically filled by university graduates. Drew was looking for the hook. He was trying hard to appear knowledgeable even though he was new to the world of recruiting. "I think I will begin by asking the audience, 'Would you hire you?'" His rationale was that most employers are setting a higher standard for applicants than they themselves could have met when they started at their jobs. Nah, that wasn't going to do it. Puts them in their heads. OK, how about sharing stats on the number of violent crimes committed by the unemployed? Nope, they'll tune out. What if he started with "Why"?

Drew opened with a personal story. He was a high school athlete, strong and well respected on the street. So . . . he was recruited to sell drugs. He joined a gang. He went to jail, fortunately, for only a short period of time. When he was released a friend of his coach gave him a chance. Without a college education he trained to become a trader on the London Stock Exchange. He made an honest living. Work changed his life, and the lives of his mom and his sisters. Now he's a proud dad, married for more than a decade. Drew stood before the group, polished, accomplished, and articulate, but you wouldn't have known about his journey from athletic star to gang member to trader—unless he told you. The HR directors were captivated. When they heard about how Drew transformed his life, they wanted to *help him* as well as the applicants in his novel program.

Don't Be Afraid to Go Off Book

Getting invited to the startup conference was a real coup for Omera. She had 8 minutes to give her pitch, followed by a 30-minute panel discussion during which she shared the stage with four other female entrepreneurs. There would be prize money. She practiced and practiced. The facts and figures flowed with ease. Omera was proud of her rapidly growing blow-dry business that recruited, trained, and employed women from underprivileged backgrounds. She delivered her pitch with precision. But that's likely not what won the hearts of the audience who voted for Omera to receive the 25,000-euro prize. She anticipated that the moderator would ask about her reason for starting the salons, so she prepared an answer referencing the business school project she had worked on, her love of exercise, and her inability to pay for hair care after her daily workouts.

But then . . . in the moment, Omera went with her heart. Her real motivation was the shame she felt when her single mother couldn't find a job and ultimately swept the floor in a hair salon. For more than a decade it was a clean, safe, and dead-end source of employment that never elevated the family's finances. Omera went to school on a scholarship. She tried to distance herself from her modest roots. On the panel, in the spotlight, she shared what really mattered to her. Telling her story so publicly reconnected Omera to the meaning driving her work and connected her to her audience.

18

DON'T JUST DO SOMETHING, SIT THERE!

Luxuriate in Not Having an Immediate Solution

Taking action is automatic for many of us—in our professional and personal lives. We impose our will rather than let events unfold. To not act, well that's a very difficult choice. I'm not advising passivity or purposeful ignorance. What I am suggesting is to sometimes do nothing, on purpose. Deliberately leave space for others to exercise *their* strengths. Don't rush to find the answer. Trust the system, and allow the group the time to iterate on alternatives.

Living in competitive societies, we learn that success demands drive, commitment, and determination. We must expend a great amount of energy and, if necessary, use force to get what we want. We can, however, consider variations to always muscling through.

When tempers start to flare, when everyone's jumping at the chance to assert their view or grabbing resources, I coach my clients to consider stepping back. Be smart about it; don't abdicate responsibility if there's an urgent situation. But most conditions are not code red. Watch and wait for the right moment. Sometimes all your participation will do is add to the noise. You may have a great idea, but chances are you are not the only smarty-pants, and when the commotion quiets, you may find that the group generated a perfectly reasonable answer. And if they didn't, you can enumerate the reasons why previous solutions didn't work and explain why your concept is worth pursuing.

If you are the more junior member of a team, it's a virtue to demonstrate patience when competition is at a fever pitch. If you are the manager, it's OK to let the group work it out—for a while. As one of my wise clients taught me, "Don't feed the team the instant they are hungry." Demonstrate confidence in their problem-solving ability while maintaining a watchful but not overly involved stance.

If you sit back and let others figure it out and still there's work to be done, coming in to "close" can be the most powerful position of all. Just ask former Yankee pitcher Mariano Rivera whose skill was reserved for the final inning. The "Sandman" would walk across the field (to his own special theme song) to secure the win.

THIS IS FOR YOU IF

- Because you can, you think you always should.

- Responsibility never sleeps. You're like a lighthouse scanning the horizon for boats in distress.

- You have been accused of grabbing power.

- You have ulcers or grind your teeth.

- Not being included makes you nuts.

TAKE ACTION
(OR IN THIS CASE, DON'T TAKE ACTION)

▶ Before inserting yourself, consider whether you are doing this to improve the outcome or to boost your ego.

▶ Treat your energy like a limited resource: appropriate it well.

▶ Resist the temptation to fill the void. Sometimes the system corrects itself.

KEEP IN MIND

- Don't confuse being passive or uninterested with an intentional decision not to act.

- Leaving space for others to act is not the same as delegating; it's an opportunity for others to step up.

Put Away the Cape

Min-jun arrived in my office with every hair in place, his crisp cuff-linked shirt peeking out from his tailored suit. He successfully managed six client meetings in four countries and made it from the airport to my office in time. Mastering the travel puzzle was a source of pride. As Min-jun relaxed into discussion, he also confessed his exhaustion. Min-jun was ready to jump in front of or out of a moving train to get the results he craves. With his Superman cape tucked inside his blazer, Min-jun is always poised for action. He is frustrated (angry) if ever excluded from the epicenter of activity.

After 15 years at a breakneck pace Min-jun's body was beginning to rebel (he was suffering from incapacitating back pain and pounding headaches). Finally, he was able to consider that his relentless control and presence was potentially problematic. Although Min-jun believed he was traveling the globe delivering systemic sunshine to clients and colleagues alike, when we examined the evidence, his inability to let others lead the charge meant he was often the cloud keeping his team in the shadows. We opted to rebrand Min-jun's strength (within the confines of my office) as the magic touch rather than the strongest force. He wasn't going to start shirking responsibility, but he was going to replace jumping to the rescue with standing by, ready to lend a hand, once others had a chance to try theirs. As a result, his team members gained greater exposure and took on more responsibility. They found more meaning in their work.

Being in Meetings Doesn't Always
Equate to Being Valued

Doron, the general counsel for a real estate firm, felt devalued and excluded. When clients were in the office, Doron would watch the CFO, head of sales, and other team members go into the conference room while he sat at his desk. Doron confessed to chatting up assistants to gain access to his colleagues' calendars and then wallowed in self-pity as he tracked all the meetings he wasn't invited to. He made good money, was consistently praised for clarity of thought, and was encouraged to continue to assert his leadership. How could he be considered a leader when he's left out of so many meetings?

We reviewed the facts. No deal ever progressed without Doron's input. He was the go-to man whenever situations became tense. Doron was often consulted on matters of firm culture. He could be counted on to offer the contrarian view when the circumstances demanded a tough decision. And he was listened to! My coaching focused on performing a *mental chiropractic adjustment*. We needed to turn Doron's head around and shift his perspective. What if he wasn't being asked to endure endless preliminary gatherings because he *was* deeply valued? Doron often had an elegant solution to challenging business issues. What if it was important for the company and its constituents to wrestle with various scenarios before calling in the pro? This made sense; it fit the facts. Keeping Doron out of the room was strategically important. Treating him as a limited resource rendered his presence more powerful and made a difference. Doron came to appreciate that in his case, less was more.

19

CHALLENGE NEGATIVE THINKING

Stop Noise Pollution

My mind is like a bad neighborhood;
I try not to go there alone.
—ANNE LAMOTT

"I'm not good enough, not fast enough, not smart enough." That's what I hear from some of the CEOs I coach! On the outside they appear so contained, so in control. On the inside there are days they're a simmering mess. Same goes for the seemingly confident hipster entrepreneur who just opened his third Brooklyn coffee shop. He tells me, "I can't keep up. Everyone's copying my ideas. I'm always one step away from foreclosure." The way people talk to themselves isn't pretty. Often the most destructive dialogues at work are the ones going on in our own heads.

The world outside may seem treacherous, but it's your inner terrain that will trip you up. Sometimes we slip into states of despair so automatically, we don't even realize we are doing it. In order to quiet your inner demon, you have to catch negative thinking. Recognize that you are torturing yourself and fight back. "Be nice to yourself" is fluffy. Let's take a different approach. Be tough with yourself. Don't allow a corrosive inner monologue to dictate your mood. Challenge your thinking. Here's a crash course in cognitive behavior therapy. It's as easy as ABC.

The ABCs of Changing the Way You Think

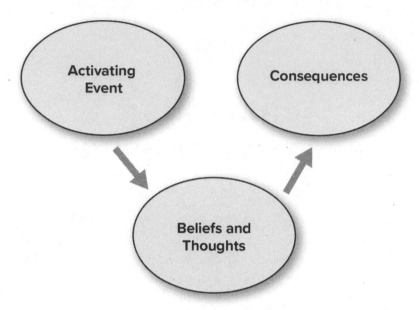

An event happens (A). Let's say you got an email indicating that you have been moved off the Delectable Cake account after working on it for six months. You've been asked to meet with the Mindful Diet team at 3 p.m. tomorrow. Sure, you could just ask your boss what's up, but you need to tame your thoughts before you can have a cogent conversation. You have a choice— yes, a choice—in how you evaluate the event, what you choose to believe (B). You can choose to believe that you were pulled because (1) you are never appreciated for your work, (2) your boss likes *her* better, or (3) this is the first step to being fired, or some combination of the three. The consequence (C) of these beliefs is that you have an awful night, you walk into work the next day grumpy, and you snap at your pal in the next cubicle. You shoot off a terse email to the head of the Delectable Cake account. You opt to check job postings rather than go to the lunchtime guest lecture with your team. If there was any question about how you handle pressure or change, you just communicated that you get rigid and irritable. By the time you have the 3 p.m. meeting, you can barely concentrate.

Now let's try something different. What if we changed B, your appraisal of the situation? I am being transferred from this account because (1) I have trained my replacement and am ready for a more complex assignment; (2) the head of the Mindful Diet team was impressed with my work and requested that I join his group as they could use a boost; or (3) I've developed an expertise in the retail food sector, and I am about to get more responsibilities. The consequence of this more positive appraisal is that you enter work ready for new opportunities, you don't fire off any damning notes, you attend the group lunch and learn something new, and you solidify your reputation as a flexible colleague.

We still don't know why you were moved off the Delectable Cake account, but what we do know is that in the first scenario your negative assessment put you in a bad mood and didn't help your reputation or anyone who encountered you.

The ABC model isn't easy. It takes work, but remember, positive thinking can be learned. Blaming yourself or assuming you won't succeed is a recipe for passivity and depression. Countering destructive thoughts makes us better friends to ourselves and more desirable colleagues to others. Joyful experiences are ignited at work when our inner environment is freed from negative assumptions.

THIS IS FOR YOU IF

- The walls of worry never come down.

- You spend so much time reading between the lines that you forget to read the lines.

- You dread your own company.

- Thinking the worst is your default.

- There's always something "wrong."

TAKE ACTION

▶ Thoughts are just that, ideas in your head—not necessarily facts. Treat them as theories that can be tested, rather than convincing yourself that things are horribly unfair, wrong, or about to implode. Check your hypothesis with friends and colleagues. Reality is an extremely powerful antidote to frustration.

▶ If you can't quiet disparaging thoughts, jot them down rather than perseverating on them. Carry a small notebook. Make a date with yourself to review the list and practice your ABCs.

▶ Don't indulge your inner drama. Write down at least three alternative ways of viewing a situation. Go to work tomorrow and act as if at least one of those alternatives is correct.

▶ Avoid becoming an injustice collector. Have your eyes peeled for a conspiracy of *good* things happening to you.

▶ Listen for the positive internal whisper and try turning up the volume. Sometimes *it is* fun to have voices in your head.

▶ Try some visualization. Open your mental window and let negative thoughts fly out, rather than inviting them to stick around for tea. If you are busy saying, "I'm an idiot, I'm an imposter," try packing "Ima" in an imaginary suitcase and toss her in a dumpster.

KEEP IN MIND

• Sometimes, changing the way you think is not enough. The situation has to be altered.

• You may need to seek professional guidance if you can't alter extreme negative thought patterns.

Drop Perfection and Achieve Respect

A couple about to transition to the United States from London sought my guidance. The American wife was frustrated by her stagnating job. Her Italian husband shared this observation: "She is good at winning, not vacationing; she has to be prepared at all times, which makes her always anxious. She is precise even when cooking. I cook a risotto and talk to my boss. He calls me for advice. The CEO doesn't call my wife; she radiates tension. She's her own worst enemy."

Recognizing that the pursuit of perfection resulted in a force field of nervous energy was not easy for Antoinette. As the regional COO, she had been valued for her ability to anticipate and respond to untoward events, yet, rather than being seen as the safe pair of hands, her fear that she wasn't doing enough was undermining her success. We conducted a series of experiments, tested her thoughts and assumptions versus the actual outcomes, and rewrote the scripts for her internal monologues. As the data emerged, Antoinette's rational self had to admit that she was doing well at her job and that the key challenge was to relate to others from a confident position of authority. As Antoinette relaxed, her voice seemed to drop an octave, she entered the room with more confidence, and she offered her view with greater certainty. The shift in her persona was felt by her colleagues who breathed a collective sigh of relief. Their COO no longer appeared brittle. She was ready to tackle her coworkers' concerns, and as a result more of them sought her counsel.

Creating Mutual Opportunity

Ben generates millions of dollars for his law firm. He's personable, supersmart, and very well connected. Ben has a story and usually a joke for most people he sees. His reviews at the office have been stellar. He has long complained that he doesn't have enough talented people to delegate work to. He's exhausted, and his health and personal life are suffering. Ben contacted me in a mild panic. He had attended a companywide sensitivity training and was asked to stay on for a private session with the facilitator. Ben learned (to his surprise) that a female candidate for a job at his firm had questioned whether she would be happy working with him because he had a reputation of "not including women on deals." There was no formal accusation of wrongdoing, but the comment stung. "I desperately want to staff female attorneys on my deals, but we don't have any at the right level," said Ben. "I would never purposely leave anyone out."

During our discussion it became clear that although Ben never acted to exclude women, he hadn't made an effort to ensure their participation and promotion either. Ben was activated. He would turn this situation (and his reputation) around. Ben asked to join the firm's hiring committee. He sent notes to colleagues requesting referrals of strong female candidates. He made the business case for two lateral hires and insisted that they be female. He personally contacted the recruiters. He started a monthly mentoring session, open to anyone in his department, and wrote personal notes inviting the younger associates to attend. Ben also prepared younger female associates to take the lead in lunches that he organized with clients to ensure that their voices would be heard. Rather than languish in frustration, Ben opted for a positive approach and created opportunities for others.

20

HAVE A POINT OF VIEW

Cultivate an Informed Perspective

I have no special talent. I am only passionately curious.
—Albert Einstein

"What do you see that's out of my field of vision that I need to know to make wise choices?" inquired Jayme Garfinkel, chairman of the board of Brazil's insurance giant, Porto Seguro S.A., after answering an hour's worth of questions from visiting executives. It's a great question to ask and prepare for. Developing and continually refreshing an informed perspective makes you an organizational asset no matter where you sit in the hierarchy. When all you do is repeat what's already known, you run the risk of becoming an expendable corporate commodity—and a dull companion. Dare to differentiate yourself:

- Expand your knowledge about topics that matter to your organization.

- Broaden your company's awareness about topics that should matter to them but aren't on their radar.

- Express an informed view about material that you are responsible for.

Fields Wicker-Miurin, board member of BNP Paribas. thinks of a point of view as a view from a point. If you can articulate your recommendations, people know where you stand, and if they disagree, a healthy debate can ensue. Being open to new ideas or the insights that others provide does not negate the importance of having your own opinion. When working with clients who are eager to advance, I help them shift from being order takers to becoming opinion makers, professionals who can facilitate quality conversation by priming discussions. In earlier chapters we discussed the importance of making the emotional connection. Here's your chance to make the cognitive connection. Rather than showing up at the boss's office and asking, "What do you think? What should I do?" I encourage my clients to arrive with a few novel ways of framing the situation along with some potential solutions. A fear of expressing one's opinion can be experienced as you being too lazy (or unable) to do the work!

It's not uncommon for groups of people, business sector authorities, or experts in a shared field to develop a fixed way of thinking, often with language that reinforces mindsets rather than expanding them. Given all the sophisticated technology for collecting information, presenting only the obvious data can undermine your prestige. And don't just rely on Google for your answers. Try going to conferences outside your immediate field of expertise. Read journals from other disciplines. Talk to people outside of your usual circles. Then bring these pearls of wisdom back to the office.

THIS IS FOR YOU IF

- You are ready to be seen as more senior.

- You want to be a generous developer of people.

- Everyone's using the same sources of information—it's time to shake things up.

- The solutions offered by your team are predicable.

TAKE ACTION

▶ Stay curious. Use travel time to read blogs and listen to podcasts outside your field. Download or carry a book; don't be stuck reading in-flight magazines over and over.

▶ Visualize a time you can interject your new knowledge. Practice beforehand how to make your message simple and relevant to your audience. Be careful not to be boastful about what you know, and others don't.

▶ Make it a point to read material from sources you don't agree with. Add individuals with opposing views to your social media feed.

▶ Subscribe to news aggregators that provide a quick daily or weekly dose of information. Be sure to access reporting outside of your favorite outlets.

▶ Check out books like *Factfulness* by Hans Rosling, which explodes commonly held ideas about the state of the world. Offer up surprisingly counterintuitive information (to help your team be better informed, not to make anyone feel ashamed about their assumptions).

▶ Ask people you respect how they form opinions. What sources do they go to?

▶ Ask, "What don't I know to ask?" Leave enough time to hear the answer. Schedule additional time if needed to fully appreciate what was outside of your field of vision.

▶ Talk directly to the people impacted by strategies and products you may be promoting and bring those insights back to your team.

▶ Participate in defining success. What the (internal or external) client initially asks for is not necessarily what will help them achieve their goal. Arrive with an informed position and the confidence to suggest an alternative approach. Your client may not alter their request, but at least you have added value by contributing to a constructive debate.

▶ Come to work prepared to teach people something new as a way of helping them feel smarter and more informed. Your hobbies or interests outside of work may provide interesting perspectives into problems you're tackling at the office.

KEEP IN MIND

• Timing is important. You don't want to interject new information as a meeting is ending. Don't chase your manager down the hall with a catalog for an exciting new conference as they are leaving for the day.

• Just because you developed an opinion doesn't mean you are right. Test your perspective, and remain open to learning.

CASE STUDIES

Help Define Success

Joan heads marketing for an international consultancy company. She coaches her team not to respond to requests from clients but rather to show up with an informed perspective on what will help them achieve their goals. Her protegee Ava supports the group advising alternative energy companies. The sector leader is quick to suggest the conferences where he should appear, the media coverage he thinks will have impact, and the interviews he wants to conduct with famous names in this space. Historically, Ava would take copious notes during the meeting and return a week later with a plan. "Engage *your* brain first," insisted Joan. "Media splashes may boost egos, but they don't translate into money for our firm." She encouraged Ava to track top influencers in the field, identify what topics were *not* being discussed, see what industry newsletters had the broadest readership, and uncover new alternative energy products that were slated for release in the coming year.

Ava crafted a potential plan in advance of her client meeting. The discussion and the end result were qualitatively different. Not all of Ava's ideas appealed to the client, but she was able to provoke a better conversation, improve her own reputation, and contribute meaningfully to the company's bottom line.

Garner Support by Being Curious

When working with executives at the cusp of being promoted, I encourage them to become thought leaders. Two different investment banks asked me to build a leadership program for their female executives. We focused on increasing each candidate's gravitas, visibility, and value by actively honing their contributions on topics of great organizational relevance. Each woman sharpened her specific recommendations based on uniquely acquired expertise. The executives made time to speak to cross-divisional leaders to learn how they think, what they read, and what fueled their decision-making. Although they feared it would be seen as an intrusion, the women's curiosity flattered their conversational partners. Discussions about emerging trends, current market conditions, and interpretations of key historical moments allowed the women to demonstrate their intellectual vigor. When the women in our program came up for promotion, more of senior management had been exposed to how they process information, in a relaxed and very relational (vs. deal-driven) way. This helped them get the necessary votes to obtain their desired promotions.

21

YOU DON'T ALWAYS HAVE TO BE RIGHT

Trust Me on This, I'm Not Wrong

If you never change your mind, why have one?
—EDWARD DE BONO

Preserve your reputation and help make someone else's by not always being right. A desperate fear of being wrong should signal to you that . . . something *is* very wrong. An overattachment to being infallible is a sign of insecurity. If you want to flex your strength and affirm your position in a group, admit that there are limits to your knowledge and be inquisitive about opposing opinions. Standing resolute, ears closed, arms crossed, and mind shut off from new information signals vulnerability and fear.

People who hold to their ideology so tightly that reasonable dialogue becomes difficult pay a heavy price. They can find themselves isolated. Colleagues work around blowhards or undermine their results.

With a need to be right, you also run the risk of conflating truth with fact. Whose truth? What if two different viewpoints each conform to the truth? Which is more right? Or if I am right, does that make you wrong? Many of us were raised in educational systems that enforced a binary of right and wrong answers. Today's workplace is increasingly specialized. When we are paid to be the expert it's hard to contemplate alternative realities, especially when they are presented by those who are not officially in a position to render an opinion (but may have a very valuable perspective nonetheless). Are you at the top of the hierarchy? It's even harder for staff to challenge you and that much more important to relinquish your grasp on being right.

Are you ambitious and eager for promotion? Sometimes even when you are clearly correct, don't hog the spotlight. You don't always have to get credit for your view. If someone else is promoting ideas that are aligned with yours, and they are gaining traction, show support and let your teammate soak up the admiration. Your generosity will be appreciated and your ability to relax with confidence as the group works its way to a solution you believe in will increase your appeal.

Sometimes you are dead wrong. Experiment with the sweet relief of simply saying, "I made a mistake." The inability to admit an error can cause real damage. It's natural to want the team or boss to be confident in your abilities, so you look for ways to demonstrate all that you know. It's a great plan if all goes well. Which it won't. Mistakes happen. You make the wrong judgment call. Saving money seemed to be a good idea when you awarded the contract to a less experienced vendor. The event planner didn't bring the tables on time. The weather didn't cooperate. The freelancers didn't check their phone messages. Errors spin out of control when you try to hide them. It's best to come clean. The hard work of establishing quality connections can be undermined by a failure to admit a mistake.

THIS IS FOR YOU IF

- You are desperate to be correct. It feels like your job depends on it.

- Being wrong isn't tolerated in your office.

- You live in an echo chamber. Your social media, news feed, and reading material are written by people who share your views.

- You're the boss and believe that staff just need to take instruction.

- You're junior on the team and are eager to show all that you know.

- "They" did it better in the place you used to work.

- When challenged, you talk louder.

- Being asked to explain yourself feels like an insult.

TAKE ACTION

▶ Rather than being argumentative, try being additive. The first rule of improvisational comedy is called "Yes, and. . . ." For example, if you open a sketch with, "Hey, there's a purple orangutan in the bathroom." "No, there's not" is the wrong response. With the denial, the scene goes nowhere. But if the reply is affirmative, "Yes, and I tried to squeeze him into the medicine cabinet, but your pills take up too much room," well, then it gets interesting.

▶ Engage in discussion to reveal other points of view, not demand acceptance of yours. Sometimes someone's perception or counterargument can add complexity or nuance to your position.

▶ Remember that just because you are right, the other person isn't necessarily wrong. Equally, if you are wrong, the other person may still not be right. Enjoy the shared discovery.

▶ Be accountable and apologize for your errors. (There's a later chapter on apologizing, in case you need help.)

▶ Recognize that at a certain point, the discussion is over and the team (and you) must commit even if there's disagreement. Try summarizing the opposing views to demonstrate that they were heard, and then remind the group that a decision was made.

▶ Realize that people who voice a strong opinion may be a little scared inside, or at least more open to a discussion than it initially appears. Ask permission to explore what you think might be right, despite someone else's confidence that you are wrong.

▶ Check if you are creating an environment where mistakes are not tolerated. Even the most junior member of a team can shut down discussion by teasing or gossiping when someone makes an error.

KEEP IN MIND

• Don't let overconfidence in your own opinion prevent you from inviting in or paying attention to alternative views. Sometimes someone's counterargument, even if wrong, can add complexity or nuance to your position/idea etc.

• Don't say, "I told you so." *Resist!*

CASE STUDIES

Your Rule Can Be Right . . .
but Achieve the Wrong Result

Shayna, the manager for a loose association of artisan potters, had it a bit harder. Overseeing the central clearinghouse, she insisted that all products be laced with at least five colors. "It's what sells," Shayna explained. It was true that the export market was responding to cheery motifs, though no exact formula was required. The whole point was to offer unique items.

Shayna was proud to be selected for management training, and she was dead set on managing, even if it meant she had to count the hues on each vessel. The artists were enraged. They were insulted. They understood what the mandate was and most wanted to comply— *their way*. To Shayna, this lack of standardization wasn't acceptable, and her frustration with the "ignorance" of the village women heightened. In her zealous adherence to an arbitrary rule, Shayna disrespected the individuality of the women she represented. The artists expressed their displeasure by crafting ceramics with the requisite number of colors but devoid of any engaging imagery. Only when Shayna was reminded of the ultimate goal did she stop her rigid assessments, and profitable production resumed.

You're Both Right

Jamal and Rajit worked in different regional offices for the same company. Until recently, each office kept their own daily record of profit and loss, but the new senior manager wanted a joint report. "There's no way I can do that and keep my guys motivated," said Jamal, whose shop in the northern region had consistently higher profits than Rajit's. "We are one company, compensated based on our combined year-end earnings," was Rajit's response. "Why wouldn't you show your folks the reality of our organization's bottom line?"

Once the hair on Jamal's neck returned to a resting position, he was able to suggest that they provide a local *and* national report, recognizing exceptional regional contribution where appropriate. It seems easy in retrospect, but it took hours of heated debate before Jamal could accept that Rajit's request was not unreasonable.

PART IV

GROW
LOYALTY

––––––––––––

It's about *them*. Whether the office is a glass skyscraper or your parents' garage, you can't achieve your goals alone. Getting the most out of the people you work with takes more than just money. Tap into what makes your colleagues tick.

When you're plowing through the to-do list it's easy to forget about *them*—your coworkers; the recipients of your latest request who are missing their kids' soccer games, forgoing a date, or skipping sleep, just to help you hit another deadline. The questions coworkers ask you may be about the project at hand, but the questions they ask themselves are: "Do I matter?" "Does my work matter?" At the heart of contagiously positive group cultures are people working because they care and feel cared for. Anticipate what your colleagues need to achieve by connecting first as fellow humans. It's the glue that bonds teams together. Demonstrate mutual commitment by adapting a generous mindset and a readiness to assist others. Reduce stress and enhance success by providing the clarity and context for coworkers to do their jobs.

Don't be intimidated by the concept of *mission-driven work*. There's always a *why* to what we do. Take a few minutes to identify your why, and don't be afraid to share it with your colleagues. Elevate the office mood: secure time to joyfully celebrate each other's success.

This Part Is for You If

- You are ready to make every day matter.

- It's time to deepen team relationships.

- You are surrounded by good people, doing good things, but no one is feeling all that great.

- The long-term goal is far in the distance and interim milestones are needed.

- Noisy, needy team members are grabbing too much attention.

- Work is where fun goes to die.

22

ENSURE ROLE CLARITY

Provide the Context and Permission

All the world's a stage,
and all the men and women merely players.
—SHAKESPEARE

We don our work costumes and act our parts at the office. While I urge people to be their authentic selves rather than assumed characters, bringing out the best in people requires that they know what is expected and the limits of their authority to enact it. I've seen clients who want to do more but fear they will be seen as grabbing power or overstepping their role. Staff on the front line sometimes hold themselves back from generating immediate, creative solutions, concerned they will be rebuked for breaking established practices.

According to Gallup's 2017 State of the American Manager Report, based on a study of 2.5 million teams in 195 countries, role clarity leads to success and stress reduction and is therefore one of the most sought-after ingredients for team effectiveness. Setting specific objectives allows people to manage their time and direct their focus, and it is especially important in small businesses or in mission-driven organizations where staff can take on entirely too much work and risk burning out. The quality of relationships is undercut when there's role confusion. The managers I coach often say, "What do you mean there's 'low role clarity'? They all have their job descriptions!" Job descriptions are a requirement but are insufficient as they are often the document against which staff were recruited rather than a defined role on a team that continually needs to be refined.

Organizational design starts with charts and job titles. Once the positions are populated with real people, their personalities don't easily fit into a box. That's usually when I am called, to do the "psychological clean-up." It's human nature to want to put our personal touch on a role, and many times this imbues work with greater meaning. However, too much modification either by the employee or the manager leads to role slippage. Suddenly, the limits of my job have shifted and it impacts yours, and we both aren't sure who's responsible for what. Tempers can flare: "Who does he think he is?" Paranoid feelings can set in: "Why is my job getting smaller? Are they preparing to fire me?" Whenever possible, be unambiguous about each person's role and the manager's role.

You can't imagine (or maybe you can) how many of my clients aren't sure who their manager is! There's the person who is named as their supervisor, and then there's the guy who acts like their boss—and the directives are not always the same. In a matrixed organization this gets even more mixed up. For example, Sally sells high-end sports cars in Chicago and submits her revenues to the manager in charge of Midwest operations, but she attends the meetings led by the luxury division. The regional manager tells her to push sales this month as it is year-end. Meanwhile, the luxury division head has told Sally not to close deals until the next quarter. He's trying to generate a sense of scarcity. He's planning on hiking up the price. See Sally's head explode. Keep the "Sallys" in your company sane. Be clear about what's expected.

THIS IS FOR YOU IF

- The work product your team presents misses the mark.

- Deadlines slip, and details fall through the cracks.

- "It's not my job" is an excuse not to pitch in.

- Where to start just isn't obvious and "Who do I call?" isn't clear.

TAKE ACTION

- End your team meetings with clear action steps and assign specific people to be responsible. Include a due date.

- When launching a new project, invest the time now to save time in the future. Hold a kickoff meeting at which you review what needs to be done, when, and by whom. If there will be overlapping responsibilities, discuss who will take the lead.

▶ Ensure that the expectations of each role are understood by both the "role-owner" and the other team members. Consider creating cheat sheets of "Who to call if. . . ."

▶ Set up RACI charts: Bring the group together when launching a project, or as a review for ongoing work and fill in the form below. Make sure everyone shares their charts to eliminate ambiguity about who is ultimately accountable for a task, as this is not necessarily the same as the person who is responsible. Colleagues who need to be consulted (e.g., included in communications that require a response) are often confused with those who just need to be kept informed. Reduce email clutter and confusion by agreeing in advance who needs to be included in what correspondence.

Responsible	the person responsible for getting the job done; carries out the task assignment
Accountable	the person who is ultimately accountable for the process or the task being completed
Consulted	people who are consulted but not directly involved with carrying out the task (e.g., a key stakeholder or subject matter expert)
Informed	those who receive output from the process or task, or who have a need to stay informed

▶ Try Ken Blanchard's suggestion in *The New One Minute Manager* to "make sure each goal is written on a separate piece of paper and takes no more than a minute to read" so that staff know exactly what is expected.

▶ If you are one of two supervisors in a matrixed reporting structure, set aside time to meet with the other boss and your direct report so that you can align expectations.

▶ For people transitioning roles within a company, be clear on the time when one role is complete and the new one has begun.

▶ Avoid secret workarounds that ignore official policy or undermine the person assigned to a task. It's tempting to allow your favorites, or high performers, to have a little more responsibility. If circumstances allow for a change in role, be transparent about it rather than creating unnecessary confusion and competition.

KEEP IN MIND

- If you are launching a new initiative and haven't yet defined role expectations, say, "There are no clear guidelines at this time." This gives staff permission to experiment and take ownership of their outcomes.

- Your intentions may be positive, but if you expand an employee's responsibility without communicating this more broadly, you can damage your reputation and the person you are trying to help.

CASE STUDIES

Do I Have the Authority?

I met with Syd, the new COO of a billion-dollar real estate firm. His initial performance reviews were surprisingly poor; he was described as the emergency room doctor reacting to, rather than extinguishing, unhealthy practices. When asked what was getting in the way, he described the lack of clear priorities, the absence of a weekly management committee meeting, and poor adherence to procedures. "But that's your job," I said. Syd agreed that initially he thought it was, but the CEO's actions led him to believe he did not have the authority to establish and enforce the needed disciplines. When informed of the confusion, the CEO readily reinforced the role expectations and gave permission for Syd to "break some glass" if needed, including confronting her when she set a poor example.

Relax, It's Not Your Job

Sometimes people need permission to do less. "Upsell" was the mandate at a restaurant's training session, prompting Natalie to become tongue-tied and awkward in her role as a waitress because she believed she was now expected to entice patrons to order more expensive bottles of wine. Her previously friendly style became stiff as she struggled to talk about bouquets, tannins, and fruitiness. Once told that all she was expected to do was make an engaging introduction to the sommelier, she relaxed, her charm reemerged, and sales (by the wine expert) did in fact go up.

23

CONNECT JOBS TO THE LARGER MISSION

There's Always a Why

*The deepest urge in human nature
is the desire to be important.*
—JOHN DEWEY

Do you bolt out of bed before your alarm rings and skip off to work bursting with enthusiasm? Excellent! Be sure to turn to your neighbor and share your secrets. If you hit the snooze button twice, down two cups of coffee, and are still dragging your feet wondering, *Do I matter? Does what I do make a difference? Does anyone care?*—well, then this chapter is for you (and your boss).

We are not hardwired to pursue money. In "The Human Equation: Building Profits by Putting People First," James Pfeffer reviews studies across dozens of industries and concludes that companies offering challenging and meaningful work made more money than organizations that treated employees as cogs in a production machine. Money can't buy meaning, but work can offer it. Connecting our jobs to a higher purpose makes a *meaningful* difference in recruitment and productivity. McKinsey Co. reported that highly sought-after talent opted to work for companies with an inspiring mission. Bain Consultancy's study of 300 companies worldwide demonstrated it would take 2.25 satisfied employees to generate the same output as one inspired worker.

And here's where it gets tricky. Employees at a mission-driven organization may find that the demands of their daily grind leave them detached from the loftiest of goals while workers performing mundane roles may feel inspired by the impact of their work on their end users. Yes, a factory laborer making the piping that allows people to have reliable indoor sanitation can have more bounce in their step than the social worker approving affordable housing requests.

In *Alive at Work: The Neuroscience of Helping Your People Love What They Do*, Daniel Cable explains that, when stimulated, dopamine (the feel-good chemical released when we have pleasurable experiences) can transform employees into a volunteer army. Since dopamine regulates our perception of time, when we are activated, the minutes fly by. Unfortunately, organizational processes that focus on flawless repeatability often stamp out the flow of invigorating hormones. Remove the monotony by making work real.

Wharton professor Adam Grant reports that radiologists who received a file with the patient's photo wrote 29 percent longer reports and achieved 46 percent greater diagnostic accuracy. Seeing themselves as the first-line protectors of a patient's health connected professionals toiling away in a darkened, often solitary room, to the people they served. Wellington Nogueira, founder of Doctors of Joy, relates a similar experience when hospital kitchen workers received visits from children in a Brazilian pediatric oncology unit. Suddenly, the crew preparing meals were part of the treatment team ensuring the nutritional complements to cancer care. Fewer errors and faster work ensued.

Exposure to the beneficiaries of one's work has been found to be more effective than listening to a leaders' inspirational speech. That's good news. We don't have to wait for the boss to boost our motivational meter, but we do need to look for ways to connect with our clients and customers—to literally go out and meet them.

We also need a break from being automatons to reflect on our accomplishments, to share stories about the times we made an impact. Studies show that meaningfulness is rarely experienced in the moment, but rather in retrospect when people can see their completed work. When given the chance, garbage collectors recognize the significance of their work after they finish cleaning a street and look back at the pristine block. Gardeners stopping by to see the flowers blooming in their customers' backyards and adorning the dinner table feel like artists rather than muddy-booted men and women with their hands in the dirt. Connecting first as people, and then to the mission, is a renewable source of institutional energy.

THIS IS FOR YOU IF

- You feel like a bricklayer, but in fact you are building a cathedral.

- The paycheck doesn't justify the blood, sweat, and tears your team is shedding to make things happen.

- Money is low but passion used to be high, and lately we've all forgotten why we are doing this sometimes dreadful work.

- My friends have sexier jobs. What's wrong with me?

TAKE ACTION

▶ Construct positive identities. When introducing others, contextualize their jobs, illustrating the importance of their efforts in achieving larger objectives. Don't just say, "This is Meg, our night manager." Try "Meet Meg. She's the reason why our hotel has the highest number of bookings from travelers arriving after 9 p.m." Or, "Let me introduce you to Teri who oversees repairs at our taxi depot, making sure your cab gets you to work without injury."

▶ Offer to edit a colleague's bio. Chances are your version will be less modest, and you'll be able to identify your coworker's contribution to the organization's larger mission.

▶ Consider holding a workshop where your team members take turns interviewing each other about their accomplishments and then writing one another's website blurb. Your colleagues are bound to stand just a bit taller each time they read about themselves, for an extra dose of validation.

▶ Reference yourself publicly in a way that sets a positive tone for the entire team. Are you heading business-to-business marketing for movie theater vending machines? Try introducing yourself as an agent of entertainment and your team as the people who make sure the audience has an amusing and yummy night out.

▶ Help the people introducing you. Be sure they have the right facts and emphasis for the occasion. Are you a proud employer of veterans? Do you have three or more women on your public board? This isn't just about your ego. It's a way of reminding your team members who are also in the audience that they are part of a company that's driving change. If the person teeing you up didn't hit the right notes, don't despair. Be ready to add a few lines of your own, "I am delighted to be speaking on behalf of all the physical therapists our department has trained. We literally have your back, and are proud that 50 percent more of our patients this year returned to full functioning within three months of visiting our clinic."

▶ Whenever possible, introduce the people or teams in the room and the role they play in accomplishing your organization's *why*.

▶ Take a field trip. Are you raising money to provide glasses to impoverished communities? If so, set up a time to meet and hear about how the restored ability to see has enabled the women to make money as seamstresses—and buy fresh food for their families. Try to meet the kids and learn about the changes in their lives since their parents' eyesight improved.

▶ Allocate time during your company meetings to share a moment of impact—relieving the tension of a fearful customer, ensuring that emergency medicine was delivered, or catching an error in a product moments before distribution. Be sure to model examples until people get the hang of it.

▶ Hit the brakes, and reflect on what you have built and the good it does for your fellow humans.

KEEP IN MIND

• Research shows that meaningful moments at work are not created by leaders. However, poor management is the top destroyer of meaningfulness.

• Posting a mission statement in your office lobby isn't enough. Help employees make the personal link to why their work is important.

CASE STUDIES

Don't Be Afraid to Say Why

Hopper, a self-deprecating set designer, calls himself the Roto-Rooter man of fashion photography, the one you call in an emergency, not the person you think of first. He prides himself on being the creative problem-solver when artistic aspirations are high, but money and time is limited. Hopper's reputation is strong, yet he struggled with how to price his contracts. Many emerging designers worked in his shop and looked to him as a model. He wanted to give his team the exposure (and the money) to eventually go out on their own. Hopper shifted his narrative from Mr. Fix-It in the background to promotor of creative teams. Once connected to his mission, Hopper was able to negotiate more vigorously for himself and others. After all, his studio was an incubator of fresh talent, and the fees he charged were a means to not only build sets but also to launch the next generation of artists.

Leave a Lasting Impression

I just had to share this note. It was written to my husband.

"I was looking on my Facebook and got a notification that said, 'This day six years ago . . .' and it showed me something I wrote about you after having been employed here about six months: 'I just went to the holiday party at Rockefeller Center and met my boss' boss' boss and you know what he said when we were introduced? He said, 'Oh! *You!* Cayla! [not her real name] Thank you for everything you've done!' and then he turned to another senior-executive-looking-person and said, 'Be friends with her, she takes care of all our money.' *Amazing!*" I was basically star-struck. . . . You set such an incredible example through your leadership as well as through your genuine compassion for the people on your team. It's something I will never forget."

24

OFFER THE GIFT OF TIME

We All Have Too Much to Do

A half-minute of advertising during the Super Bowl costs $5 million. Workers are paid by the hour; lawyers charge by the minute. Time is money. Time is also power.

When you keep me waiting, you communicate that the demands of your day are more important than mine. The person who sets the deadlines or declares when it's time to go home has enormous impact on your professional (and personal) life. Shared calendars allow colleagues to schedule meetings and alter your rhythm for getting work done—without asking. Computers measure your speed at responding to client calls. The factory equipment registers how quickly an order is processed. Vacation days, sick days, they're all counted. Making a living often means surrendering control over your clock.

Many of my clients tell me, "I don't have time to think," yet they are expected to act strategically. Studying the geography of time, Robert Levine found that countries with buoyant economies put a greater value on efficiency. And herein lies the challenge. When we worship at the altar of busy or believe that every second counts, we do so potentially to the detriment of innovation—and sanity.

The feeling of having enough time to do what you want—what's called "time affluence"—is at a record low, according to a 2017 Gallup survey of 2.5 million Americans. In "Time for Happiness," Ashley Whillans observes, "Time poverty exists across all economic strata, and its effects are profound. Time-poor people experience higher levels of anxiety, depression, and stress. They laugh less and are less healthy. Their productivity is diminished."

Giving the gift of time benefits the individual and their institution and comes in many forms: months to explore a passion, a few days off, or even the return of a few precious minutes. Professors have long enjoyed sabbaticals, a semester off after seven years of service. It's a chance to dive into research, write a career-defining book, or just recover. The idea is catching on in business. A quarter of the organizations on *Fortune*'s 100 Best Companies to Work For list offer employees extended leave to explore their passions—and get paid for it. Rather than months off, some establishments allocate space each week for employees to experiment. 3M led the way with its "15 percent time." In 1974, 3M scientist Art Fry used this opportunity to apply an adhesive to the back of a piece of paper to create the perfect bookmark. Voila! The very profitable (and convenient) Post-it notes were born. Other enterprises have followed suit, resulting in equally monetizable ideas. Gmail and Google News were invented during Google employees' 20 percent time.

You may be thinking, "Sure, sure, a large company can offer unstructured time to employees, but what about my little organization?" Don't turn the page. Try getting creative instead. I've been called Melanie-the-maniacal-minute-manager because I arrive at meetings with a clear agenda, track our progress throughout a session, and ensure that we always end on time, if not early. It's a sign of respect. Try reviewing your meeting structure to see if you can excavate some extra minutes. If you're a middle manager, it's likely you are spending about 35 percent of your time in conference rooms, and if you're in upper management the figure swells to at least 50 percent. Americans waste more than $37 billion annually in unproductive meetings. Do you really need all those get-togethers? Do they have to be so long? Can you end before the allotted time if you complete your agenda?

Returning the unused meeting minutes to your coworkers rewards them for their focus, allowing them to get other stuff done, socialize with each other informally, or simply get out of work earlier. Want to make your office a happy place? Give back time.

THIS IS FOR YOU IF

- Meetings start late because all conferences are scheduled to begin and end on the hour with no time to get between sessions.
- You want to do your part to insert some breathing room into the day.

TAKE ACTION

▶ Hold 45-minute meetings rather than an hour. It gives people a break or chance to transition between gatherings held on the hour. Initiate the trend.

Take the first step by sending calendar invites with the subject "45-minute meeting to discuss . . ." and then be sure to keep it to 45 minutes or less.

▶ Experiment with standing meetings. And by standing I don't mean *regular*, I mean *chairless*. They are shorter and more focused. It's very hard to multitask when you are vertical and in such proximity to your coworkers.

▶ Start meetings on time and let the stragglers catch up. Don't start from the top each time a new person enters. Latecomers will get the message that you won't wait for them, and those arriving on time will be respected for making the effort to be prompt.

▶ Encourage people to put away phones and personal electronics during meetings so that they can focus efficiently on the shared task—and potentially end early. When possible, use video meeting technology instead of conference calling. It's harder to multitask when colleagues can see you.

▶ Use whiteboards or paper calendars in order to *see time*. It's hard to appreciate the rhythm of a month on a phone or computer.

▶ Initiate meeting-free days. For example, block out Wednesdays for uninterrupted time to focus, for everyone.

▶ Consider rewarding employees who just completed major projects with time off rather than expensive company dinners.

▶ Be sure your colleagues take the vacation time that is coming to them. Use it or lose it policies aren't enough for overly motivated team members who may work themselves to the point of collapse. Be sure to remind and give permission for hard workers to take breaks.

▶ Volunteer to help keep a meeting on time. You don't have to be the boss to offer to manage the minutes. You can politely insert a "progress check" and let the assembled know how much time is left and give them a chance to make any necessary modifications to the remaining agenda.

▶ Practice offering spaciousness. Don't book conference or seminar sessions back-to-back. Recognize that participants want a few moments to themselves or a chance to catch up with colleagues.

KEEP IN MIND

• Everyone, at all levels, enjoys the gift of time. Surprise the receptionist with a chance to leave at noon on a slow Friday. Ask your manager what you can do to help them end the day early.

- Remote workers don't have the visual cues indicating that the folks in the cubicles are taking a break. Provide the verbal prompt to "take a breather" to your colleagues living "in your computer."

CASE STUDIES

You Deserve a Minute

At the fifty-ninth minute of every hour, wonderful chimes tinkle through the office air. The place falls silent. Those on calls with clients stop talking. Christina Carvalho Pinto, president of Full Jazz Communications in São Paulo, Brazil, says, "My team devotes so much of their day to our work; I can give them back a minute of every hour." It's effective. And contagious. The minute changes shape. Initially, it feels like an interruption, and then it becomes luxuriously indulgent. At the 45-second mark it feels uncomfortably long, and by seconds 58 and 59 one emerges refreshed and ready to resume discussions with greater clarity. At first, it's disorienting, but then clients on the other end of the phone report delight at having that peaceful moment for themselves.

Take the Time!

Sometimes we all need encouragement to *take time* (even the phase sounds like we are stealing something). Michelle is a project manager for a construction company. She noticed that her team members seldom used their personal days. She made it a point to inquire about anniversaries and school plays and in the week or so prior would prompt her direct reports to request the day off. Michelle proudly relates how she has given "magnificence to life's special moments" by the simple act of encouraging her staff to take time off to enjoy them. Hard-driving Michelle relishes the thank-you texts and photos from first birthday parties and state finals from the men and women on her team. By securing the time for her team to partake in life's joyful moments, Michelle also experiences happiness.

25

KNOW WHEN YOU ARE DONE

Clear Goals Enable You to Declare "Finished!"

Done is better than perfect.
—Facebook mantra

But when are we done? When has the subcommittee completed its work? When has your special task force ceased to be special? How can you tell when the formal portion of the program is done and hanging around to socialize is optional? Recognizing when the mission has been accomplished is harder than it sounds for organizations as well as individuals.

In a perfect world, projects have clear kickoff and due dates. Team members manage their time toward these goals and take satisfaction when completing their tasks. In the real world, there are many instances in which "the end" isn't as clearly defined as it should be, leading to wasted resources and frayed nerves. This may be due to an ever-expanding set of deliverables (scope creep) or the inability to articulate what done might look like as the project itself is an exploration.

Put a bookmark in this chapter and pass it around to your colleagues. Protect against the two dirtiest words in project management: scope creep. Scope creep occurs when contractors or team members want to exceed expectations and deliver "more value," unexpected events impact when or how a product can be delivered, or little requests add up to time-consuming (and potentially expensive) labor. Before you know it, the extent of what will be produced and what it will take to finish has swelled. Failure to point out "this wasn't in the original remit" leads to frustration and potentially unpaid time. We sometimes avoid anticipated conflict and figure it will all work out in the end. But it doesn't.

Another reason why we don't declare "Done!" is that the familiar gets comfortable. Mastering a problem feels good; becoming the expert is fun. Why stop now? You've gotten into a rhythm with the other people on the project, you've found your favorite lunch place to hold meetings, and you've developed a group shorthand. Shifting attention from what you know to delve into the unknown takes energy, and it requires disbanding your gang. No one dares to declare "finished," so you keep on perfecting—and spending time together. Keep those great connections going. Look for ways to nurture the new relationships you formed (plan a reunion of your work group), and give yourself permission to enjoy each other, separate and apart from the task.

Depending on how you are wired, a terrific evening may constitute observing germs through the microscope, wordsmithing the perfect opening sentence, debating the appropriate prompt to facilitate a discussion, or contemplating which image should open an art installation.

There's banter and camaraderie. Some of your colleagues flew in from out of town and have no evening plans. Or your company pays for dinner and/or your transport home if you work past a certain hour. The conversation continues. Half of your group has relaxed into the activity, while others have to relieve the nanny, go to rugby practice, or buy groceries. Who's going to say, "Thanks for your input. Anyone who wants to stick around, please do. Anyone who has to leave, see you tomorrow."

Sometimes the devil preventing "Done!" *is* perfection. Psychologist Barry Schwartz found that people who do good enough work, "satisfiers," are consistently happier on the job than "maximizers." Although maximizers seek the optimal choice, their ultimate decisions are not necessarily better. So what's good enough? Clear communication of what is expected takes you part of the way toward proclaiming, "Completed!" The other necessary ingredient is the courage to say, "We're done." If you want to foster respect and loyalty among your colleagues, learn to open and close a meeting, project, or initiative with grace.

THIS IS FOR YOU IF

- Your team enjoys their work and each other.

- It's hard to get on your calendar. You're always in a meeting.

- There's always something more to do.

TAKE ACTION

▶ State goals clearly, and continually refer back to them. When expectations expand, complete the initially stated task and then agree to the new objectives. Everyone involved should be able to state what the overall goal is and their contribution to it. As work unfolds, remind your team of project plans and deadlines.

▶ Avoid the trap of working on the familiar at the expense of starting a new, more challenging project. When kicking off a special committee, assign a date for it to disband. Don't allow continuing ad infinitum to be the default.

▶ Set a clear agenda for meetings and dismiss the assembled if you have achieved your goal before the allotted time is up. Left unchecked, meetings will fill all available minutes. Pay close attention to how time is used. If participants spend 15 to 20 minutes at the beginning or end of a routine meeting discussing a coworker's golf game, try to schedule less time for the session in the future.

▶ If you have gathered colleagues together for coffee or a cocktail to plan or debrief a piece of work, be sure to note when the formal portion of the discussion is over. Let the people who want to socialize stay on and give permission for others to depart.

KEEP IN MIND

- You can declare one project done and then agree on terms for a new initiative. Recognizing the end can kindle new beginnings.

- Read the room and check the goals. Just because you're getting antsy doesn't necessarily mean the meeting is done.

CASE STUDIES

Contain the Creep

Jules has saved her money for years, waiting for the moment when she can convert her very tired kitchen into an Italian oasis in the middle of Sussex. Her files overflowed with design magazine clippings. She lugged tiles back from her summer trips abroad, blue for the backsplash, Moroccan hues for the counter. Now that she's retired, Jules has time to devote to the project and a chance to cook for and entertain all the people she loves. She interviewed five architects and hired Wyatt. He had just started his own shop, could work within her budget, and understood that this was more than just a renovation for his very engaging client.

Jules liked this design. And that one. She cherished the time she spent with Wyatt. She asked for a change here, another alternation there. Wyatt couldn't say no. Jules reminded him of his mom; she always brought him a treat and lit up in his company. The junior architects in his office didn't share the same delight. They were getting exhausted, resentful, and sloppy. "Does this project have any end?" they moaned. Jules reinforced the very reason Wyatt became an architect, to build people's dreams. But to maintain a viable business, he had to temper that with realistic boundaries. He explained his devotion to Jules and her project and the necessity of setting some limits. She was embarrassed at having overburdened him, reined in her imagination, and made choices she stuck with. The kitchen got built, and Jules hosted a party for Wyatt, his team, and a few of their prospective customers.

Release Your Audience

Professor Lee is a lovely guy. He's also quite shy. Some call him socially awkward. His science is top-notch. Dr. Lee has funded fellowships for budding professors from around the world. He's a natural when presenting at academic conferences but becomes quite anxious when speaking at industry events. He likes to get input on his slides before he gives a talk, so he often sponsors a dinner in a lovely hotel suite. It's a privilege for junior faculty to be invited. Well, at least that's how it feels for the first hour. Then it gets long. Dr. Lee iterates, questions, and ponders alternatives. Some of the invitees love to watch his thoughts unfold. Others want to join the networking sessions in the lobby. Although the professor can sense the crowd's impatience, he often attributes it to displeasure with his ideas, which results in even more requests for feedback (and the feeling for some that they are being held hostage).

One night a caring colleague came to the rescue. Dr. Jones offered to introduce the evening, laid out the timing for discussion, and was specific that the formal portion of the dinner would last 90 minutes, after which time guests were free to go. True to his word, when an hour and a half passed, Dr. Jones gave permission for people to leave. Everyone had a better time, especially Dr. Lee!

26

THERE'S PLENTY FOR EVERYONE!

Assume an Abundance— Not Scarcity—Mentality

*If you look at what you have in life,
you will always have more. If you look at what you
don't have in life, you will never have enough.*
—OPRAH WINFREY

During a multidenominational Thanksgiving service, my husband and I were struck by the simplicity and applicability of a preacher's teaching: "See the world from abundance, not scarcity." Raised by a mother who firmly believed we had nothing to eat if we didn't have three options in each food group, I wondered what would happen if I flipped my default to there being *more* rather than *less*? In *The 7 Habits of Highly Effective People*, Stephen Covey observes: "Most people are deeply scripted in the *Scarcity Mentality*, they see life as though there were only one pie out there: if someone gets a big piece of the pie, it means less for everybody else." People with a *scarcity mentality* have a very difficult time sharing recognition and credit, power, or profit. Their difficulty being genuinely happy when other people succeed prevents them from connecting meaningful with others.

The *abundance mentality* assumes there is enough for everybody. Another person getting a raise is not a source of jealousy or internal pain because you know that person's achievement doesn't take anything away from you. Leaders who adopt a not-enough attitude and complain about the shortage of time, money, or resources typically frame their challenges through what they lack. The focus becomes preservation rather than growth. In contrast, leaders with an abundance-based mindset are prepared to search for and often develop people and new ideas. Meaning and joy more readily emerge at work when the richness of opportunity is celebrated.

THIS IS FOR YOU IF

- Giving warms your soul.

- More for you means less for me.

- Restrictive budgets and reduced resources are your focus.

- "If only" enters your conversation monthly.

- Sharing makes you feel vulnerable.

TAKE ACTION

▶ Be generous. Immerse yourself in the fullness of all you have to offer and share intangible assets such as your knowledge, your network, and your compassion. "Giving away" what is so scarce in organizational life—appreciation, information—replenishes the supply.

▶ Experience time affluence by spending time on others. Research shows that hoarding time slows down the clock.

▶ When performance pressure is soaring just before a big presentation or company event, rather than worrying about whether you have what it takes to succeed, try asking your teammates, "What can I do to help you shine?" Recognizing that you can help others often quiets the internal doubts about what we may be lacking.

▶ Create your own environment of abundance: spend time with people who see possibility. Challenge colleagues who are quick to note what's missing and forget to celebrate what's working.

▶ Become aware of the thoughts in your head and make a conscious effort to focus on all that you have. Sometimes it helps to make a chart. Go for it. On one side of the page, write down all the curmudgeonly, miserly thoughts that are almost too embarrassing to share. Then in the other column, write down the expansive, positive interpretation. Don't worry if you can't quite believe the abundant view (yet). It takes practice.

▶ What you tell yourself and others shapes your reality. When you address your team, share work news with friends, or update your family, are you telling stories of scarcity or stories of abundance? Do an experiment. For the next week, only share stories about excess. See how you feel. No, don't tell tales about excessive work (nice try, but I heard what you were thinking). Focus on times this week when you were the recipient of goodwill. Did someone let you take their parking spot, offer you a phone charger? How about the colleague who spent an hour helping you with your computer? That counts. So does the fact that the guy you call your underminer just whispered in your ear (not in front of the group) that you had added the numbers wrong in your audience engagement report.

▶ Keep a gratitude journal. Write down what you are grateful for every day. Aim to record at least 10 items. Remember to list the simple things that often get overlooked, such as having an interesting coworker to share coffee with (and the money to pay for it).

▶ The enemy of abundance is a contracted awareness. Widen your peripheral vision and see all that is around you. Look up from your desk.

▶ Practice purposeful wonderment. An abundance mentality craves learning and growth. Seek out novel experiences and soak up the rich enthusiasm and energy that is released when you jump into the unknown.

KEEP IN MIND

• Avoid feeling like a victim. Don't tally instances in which you were *cheated*.

• Small pockets of joy and generosity add up to happier days at work and beyond.

CASE STUDIES

Therapy in the Stairwells

Bellevue Hospital, founded in 1736, is the oldest public hospital in the United States. When I started my internship there, the furniture and carpets looked like they had never been replaced. There was a shortage of everything. Ambulances roared in, medics ran, patients and doctors crowded into the too few elevators. You couldn't find a pen to fill in a chart note. Reception areas were standing room only. Snagging a chair was a competitive sport. Since there weren't enough offices, more than once I conducted therapy in a stairwell. Landing an internship at Bellevue was hard, but figuring out the system was virtually impossible. How do you get things done? There was no manual for patient care or a centralized repository of desperately needed referral sources.

And yet I look back on those times with great fondness. As my fellow psychology interns at Bellevue quickly learned, we may have battled to win our positions, but we would only thrive in this crazy place if we had each other's backs. We vowed (out loud) to share what we learned, to tell each other if we heard anything about someone's performance, and to speak positively when asked about each other. For the duration of our internship, we agreed to meet for drinks every Thursday night at the same place across the street. The challenges we faced were fodder for Thursday night stories. We laughed away the absurdity of some of the situations we endured. More than three decades later, many of us are still in touch. We marvel at the effectiveness of our mutual experiment. Among us we found what we needed. The underfunded, overcrowded hospital was overflowing with passionate professionals who took pride in relieving (at least some) patients' pain.

Focusing on the Mission Increases Resources

You would think that someone whose job title was "Head of Corporate Social Responsibility" (CSR) would be naturally inclined toward generosity, or at least to seeing possibility. But that wasn't the case with Beca. Around every corner she saw rivals. She felt that the marketing team and client relations team were encroaching on her territory. Beca complained she didn't have enough staff or budget to have the impact she desired. Her coaching sessions helped clarify her purpose. She initially went into law because she believed in equal access to justice. By her own admission, she wasn't a stellar legal advisor and had transitioned into the CSR role because she was very good at building bridges between people and organizations (when she wasn't feeling threatened). Using access to justice as the organizing principle, Beca rewrote her business plan. She presented it to the marketing team, who enthusiastically supported this focus (previously Beca's group was doing projects on education, sanitation, and nutrition). Motivated by her mission, members of the client relations team asked Beca to join them when they went to sales meetings. Beca's sphere of influence grew, and her initiatives were better resourced.

27

BANK SOCIAL COLLATERAL

Give Now to Succeed in the Future

I encourage my clients to build *social collateral*. You don't want to be over-drawn at the moment you need help. Build up a positive balance. I'm not suggesting tit for tat, or a transactional approach to relationships. I am asking you to think more about what you can do for others than what you can get in return. It feels good and it's good for you. In the previous chapter we discussed the importance of an abundance mindset and the advantage of making gener-osity your default. This chapter goes deeper into that discussion.

"As a leader of a growing team or company, the single most important thing you can do to ensure your success is to invest in building a culture of givers," says Adam Grant, author of *Give and Take*. Nice guys *don't* finish last. "It's good to help others. That's news?" asked a friend of mine, after attend-ing a community talk given by Dr. Grant. Sadly, yes. Advancing one's own agenda frequently trumps assisting others. Time poverty is the usual excuse, and yet many acts of great import to your peers take just a few moments. Mak-ing a well-placed introduction, pointing a colleague to pertinent research, or sharing an invitation to a relevant, but lesser known professional conference all take about five minutes. When working in highly competitive environ-ments, it's tempting to assert your status by gobbling up or guarding limited resources. Resist.

People don't care how much you know until they know how much you care. That's a key reason to connect first. To gain an audience for your ideas, first capture your coworkers' hearts. The importance of anticipating a colleague's needs—intuiting what he or she needs even before that person may know—underpins the ancient Chinese concept of *guanxi*. You can't simply ask, "How can I help?" You have to watch carefully to determine proactively what might be useful. *Guanxi* translates into "establishing human relations to open doors for opportunities." It's a long-term investment in your reputation that extends beyond any job.

THIS IS FOR YOU IF

- You want to sleep well at night and feel even better during the day.

- It's time to invest in your future.

- Things are going well for you.

- You think greed is good.

TAKE ACTION

▶ Build a network of goodwill by paying it forward. Do a five-minute favor for anyone who asks. Yes, anyone.

▶ Try being generously attentive to those with whom you are in conflict. It may seem counterintuitive—it's hard and destabilizing but very effective. Our opponents are often the ones we watch most closely, so you are likely an expert in what they need. Rather than compete, reverse tactics: offer to help.

▶ Don't sit passively during company meetings. Did your colleague, boss, or junior team member just present an important idea? Identify at least one thing that's easy for you to do to help that person achieve their vision. Don't wait to be asked. Tell them what you have in mind.

▶ Do not assume a coworker has it all under control. Offer to help. Allow the recipient of your offer the privilege of saying no.

▶ Sign up for Givitas (cocreated by Adam Grant, Wayne Baker, and Cheryl Baker) at https://go.giveandtakeinc.com/granted. It's a software platform on which employees can ask for help *and* offer to solve real problems.

KEEP IN MIND

- Self-interest and ambition can coincide with generosity.

- If you are keeping a mental scorecard, you aren't *really* relaxing into the power of generosity.

CASE STUDIES

Don't Get Mad, Get Dinner

During a coaching session, Frank related that he wanted to throttle Carmine, the sales rep who bypassed Frank's authority and went directly to his team for information. "Who does he think he is? Our group is already working long hours. Carmine can't just push his way in and demand to get a response. He's a notorious bully." When I probed, a more compassionate response emerged. Frank realized that his department was underserving the needs of those in the field. Rather than pick up the phone to register his fury as he initially intended, Frank asked his colleague to meet for a drink, and together, they brainstormed better ways to partner. This allowed Frank to anticipate Carmine's needs and offer solutions.

Once Frank expressed interest, Carmine's shoulders dropped from around his ears and his tone softened. Carmine explained that the traveling reps who reported to him were frequently on the road and felt cut off from the home office. Even when they were in town, they didn't have easy access to the people who supported them. Frank agreed to organize meals when the sales reps were in town, and surprised Carmine's group with invitations to impromptu office activities. What could have been a companywide conflict became the basis of an enduring friendship, and Frank's reputation was sealed with those in the field as the guy who cared, rather than the one who failed to deliver the data when needed.

A Swedish Secret

Making expectation-free deposits into the social repository is more than doing a series of favors, it's a mindset, a way of life. A longstanding client of mine, Karin Forseke, sets a wonderful example. I first met Karin when she was the COO of the London International Financial Futures Exchange (LIFFE). Karin went on to become the CEO of Carnegie Bank and the chair of Alliance Trust. She has held multiple board positions, and was the deputy chair of the Financial and Securities Authority (FSA) in London. The list goes on. Impressed? I certainly have always been. Upon meeting Karin, you readily appreciate her formidable focus on fairness *and* profit. She's smart, connected, and informed. It's easy to be daunted by her accomplishments, yet Karin consistently does more for you than you could ever have considered asking. As one of the most senior women in banking, Karin has been thrust many times into the often-critical public eye. She once asked for directions to the grocery and that made news in Sweden. How could Ms. Forseke advise the finance minister if she doesn't know where to buy milk?

Despite efforts to discredit her, Karin's spirit has not been submerged. Her method for survival? Karin has a clear mission and an unswervingly generous approach to the world. She's constantly on the lookout to praise, promote, and do for others. As a result, Karin has amassed many loyal supporters who continually bear witness to her best intentions—true believers who are ready to counter any bad press. For Karin's birthday, Swedish musician Fredrik Swahn wrote a song entitled "In Totality" that captured Karin's ethos. "You can't separate who you are from what you do and who you do it with, so it's best to celebrate the whole of you and the totality of us." Who can argue with that?

28

STROKE THEIR NARCISSISM

All Egos Need a Little Love

People never get tired of talking about themselves.
—My Aunt Roz

Let's be honest. We all want to be appreciated for our greatness. You're not seeking praise (we have a chapter on that) or a task-based thank you (there's a chapter about that as well). What we are talking about here is *acknowledgment* of what you have contributed over time, the history you have with the company, the pioneering research you have done, the importance of your role or your experience in the sector.

This desire for recognition may be close to the surface, or it may be your guilty secret. Although you "should" be above the drive for appreciation, you're not immune to a touch of *normal narcissism* and neither is the person next to you. Belief in oneself is a sign of mental health. Sustaining a healthy ego requires periodic nourishment, but here's the secret—feed your colleagues' egos first and you won't go hungry. Even the most self-assured colleagues who carry themselves as if they are above it all will find well-placed ego strokes irresistible.

When you aren't recognized for your position or contribution, at first you may feel badly about yourself, but soon that simmering discomfort bubbles into feeling even worse about your colleagues. That's when trouble sets in. "Why aren't they seeking out my opinion?" "Why am I suddenly so disrespected?" Their perspective: You've created the conditions for others to succeed and are likely moving on to new endeavors. After all, you are a pro. Your perspective: Don't they realize all I have done?

What do your successors want? Your approval! What are you not willing to give them now? Any recognition! The result? A narcissistic desert devoid of ego gratification for everyone. In the war for appreciation, stroke first.

Drew's shirt is always crisply ironed. He wears cufflinks and a big gold watch. He walks with a swagger, he drives a convertible, and he's boiling inside. He's made the money; he's on the management committee. He recruited the new Chief Investment Officer. All he wants is a nod to his influence, a stroke of his natural narcissism. "Can't they see that I've launched this new field? I was investing in bitcoin before there was even a name for cryptocurrencies, and now no one is putting me on the agenda to address the latest developments. Sure, we've hired an alternative investment specialist to lead our firm's effort, but don't these guys know that I convinced management to take the initial risk that brought us millions?" Drew's ire could have been avoided had his colleagues kicked off the meeting saying, "We wouldn't be here today if not for Drew's creativity and foresight." Or, perhaps, they could have asked him to comment at the end. Instead, Drew, an infuriated and highly influential senior executive, set out to undermine the credibility of his new associates.

On the spectrum of ego needs, Drew is more like most of us, exhibiting a normal narcissism. Further on the continuum are folks whose hunger for acknowledgment can feel insatiable. These are *extreme narcissists*. They are plugged in, dynamic, and inspirational. They're winners and you want to be part of their plan. Are they magnets, you ask? Good question. These charismatic folks may be magnetic at the onset, but they lose their luster once you realize it's all about them. Initially, you want to work for their campaign, join their startup, or take a pay cut to chase the vision they made you believe was possible. We're in this together (you think) and it's invigorating. And then . . . you start to feel depleted; motivation wanes as you have a rising sense that you have been robbed—of your achievements. If your ego got kicked to the back seat as you aimed to please the now irascible (previously irresistible) boss or coworker who relentlessly pursues affirmation, you may be working with an extreme narcissist.

Although data indicates that the true ingredients for success are competence rather than confidence, altruism rather than egotism, and integrity rather than charisma, many extreme narcissists make it to the top. Innovation, pioneering policy, and perseverance in the face of adversity are fueled by a majestic sense of self. As a result, it's likely that over the course of your career you will find yourself working for (or with) someone who has an extremely hungry ego, limited empathy, and an inflated sense of self-importance.

Don't be fooled. Confidence can coexist with a desperate desire to prove one's worth. To protect themselves from feelings of inadequacy, they can put on a cloak of arrogance and self-aggrandizement. There's often an inverse correlation between an overt pursuit of praise and strong self-esteem. Those peacocks strutting their stuff at work (no matter their place in the hierarchy)— the ones you are least motivated to applaud—are often the very people who could use a little love. When in doubt, stroke their narcissism. Really. It helps them relax.

Here's a common dynamic: The narcissist makes you feel like what you do doesn't matter. They don't give you credit for work you did, and they flaunt their accomplishments and grab the spotlight. It's not fair. It's disrespectful. This flagrant disregard for your contributions makes you want to ignore or downplay their successes. You don't want to laud them; you want to punish them. Resist the urge to strike back. Rather than assert your value, demonstrate a deference to theirs.

You are probably wondering why I am encouraging bad behavior. Shouldn't we recoil from the enveloping egoist and make them suffer the consequences of their exasperating behavior? I hear you, but surviving the extreme narcissist requires counterintuitive action.

Narcissists have super-sensors for rejection. You can get attacked for anything the narcissist sniffs as criticism. That's the bad news. The good news is that although narcissists are notorious for ruthlessly manipulating others, they're exceptionally vulnerable to being duped themselves because their super-sized egos require continual affirmation from others to remain securely (though artificially) inflated. Don't throw water on a narcissist's electrical storm. Tame the beast by acknowledging their awesomeness. It's OK to make it about them. Try these helpful phrases: "You are the only one who can help me." "How can I help you?" Chances are, when your insecure colleague sees you as a nonthreatening extension of themselves, they'll be the first to sing your praises.

THIS IS FOR YOU IF

- You forget to consider who needs to be complimented, consulted, or recognized publicly.

- Established professionals in your field are giving you the cold shoulder.

- Your colleague has an insatiable desire for admiration.

- You dream of strangling coworkers who can't seem to acknowledge your accomplishments.

- You want to gain support for your ideas.

TAKE ACTION

▶ When you are surrounded by lots of egotists, you run the risk of feeling badly about yourself. Fight the urge to assert your own worth to recoup your self-esteem. Instead, give praise and relax into your social power. Those who are devaluing others are signaling their desperate desire for admiration. Look for a legitimate way to levy praise. There's usually something you can compliment. Consider commenting on effort, even if the outcome wasn't so impressive.

▶ When there is tension between you and another person, you may be least likely to find something positive to affirm in their behavior. Push yourself. Elevating another person's self-worth is a very powerful way of defusing conflict.

▶ As a means of forging a deeper relationship, try reflecting back to a person what they most personally value. For example, when entering Emma's postage stamp–sized bookshop, be sure to comment on her courage to enact her dream. Note how the store is designed, and definitely underscore Emma's ability to arrive in a new city and establish herself so quickly with the glitterati (yes, yes, you get a little nauseous with what you experience as social climbing, but to Emma it's about assimilation and sponsorship, so go with that).

▶ Replace *but* with *and* to avoid going head-to-head with an overly cocky counterpart. Try building on that person's idea to advance your own.

KEEP IN MIND

- Respond, don't react. The management of the narcissist's ego is a sport, not a personal affront to you. Ultimately, you have to take care of yourself. If you have tried everything you can think of during at least a year's time and the situation is still too debilitating, you may have to explore alternative employment.

- Watch your timing! Don't overcompliment your boss before a promotion or review. That can be seen as overtly manipulative.

CASE STUDIES

Seeking a Colleague's Endorsement Demonstrates Respect for Their Position

Cathy thought she was protecting her former boss, Dick. But Dick felt deeply disrespected. What happened? Dick was an avid supporter of his star employee for years, always looking for ways to advance Cathy's career. Just before Cathy came up for promotion, Dick was transferred to a different division. Dick offered to coach the new manager through the process to ensure that Cathy's role was elevated, yet no one sought his expertise. Cathy heard that Dick was having health issues and that combined with his increased seniority resulted in a decision not to bother her old boss. The radio silence enraged Dick, who felt extremely devalued. He wondered if Cathy "respected him enough to ask for advice and possibly an endorsement." Not recognizing her mentor's superpowers within the system cost Cathy her long-awaited seat at the table. Spurned, Dick opted not to speak on his protégée's behalf. She missed her chance to advance by one vote. Dick was just a *normal narcissist* whose feathers got ruffled, but Cathy's promotion stalled because of it.

It was a surprise to many that Cathy didn't make the cut, and I was engaged as her coach to prepare her for the next vote. I interviewed many executives on her behalf, including Dick. He sounded exasperated with her in a way that no one else had expressed. I sensed his anger. When I dug in, his disappointment and hurt were revealed. I asked him if had shared this with Cathy. Not surprisingly, he had not (this is the behavior that keeps coaches in business). Dick gave me permission to tell Cathy, who was stunned. She immediately called him, cleared the air, and affirmed just how important to her his guidance has always been. Dick was flattered and relieved and resumed his mentorship. Cathy was promoted.

Give Them What They Crave—Confidence

At 65, Vicky was ready to work four days a week. As a beloved property manager reporting to the newly appointed CEO of a family business, she knew that her boss, John, really relied on her. Reducing her availability would surely upset him. Vicky believed that John could succeed without full-time access to her input. However, he was more comfortable knowing she was there. John's insecurity was not a good enough reason to resist change. Vicky's strategy? Rather than make it about herself (and why, after 35 years of employment at the firm, she deserved a modified schedule), Vicky focused her attentions on what John really craved, confidence. Most people experienced John as the Ivy League–educated heir of a successful family business. He came across as the man who needed no one. Vicky saw beneath the bravado and appreciated that her presence bolstered John's self-assurance. As a result, she identified moments to privately and publicly acknowledge John's leadership acumen while working to reduce his reliance on her (no matter how flattering it was).

John would seek Vicky's advice about the latest round of vendor bids with urgency and offer to send a car (or, if needed, his private helicopter) to bring her back from her holiday to bask in her expertise. As glamorous as the sky-high ride may seem, Vicky responded with, "John, at this point, no one is as good as you in assessing the numbers." Subsequently, when investors gathered to determine the next steps following a hurricane, and John turned to Vicky to describe the damage to their company's properties, Vicky told the group, "That John, he's so modest. He's the one who toured every asset as soon as the storm hit. He knows the condition of the real estate better than me."

When Vicky ultimately approached John about a shorter workweek, she reflected on the quality of his leadership and how much he had grown. Vicky positioned her request for reduced hours as a way of clearing the way for others to transition (with John) into the next generation of leadership. John's answer? Of course!

Fight Back . . . with Praise

"Arun, we already know you are the most important one in the room." That comment was the tell. Arun's move to this well-known fashion company was reported in the news. He was going to shake things up! "The world was watching." But so far, his first 90 days were not so successful. At every turn, Arun was being blocked by Keenan, a very talented designer. Arun's appointment was effectively a demotion for Keenan, who no longer reported directly to the team leader. Arun tried being nice. That didn't work. Arun expressed frustration with Keenan. That didn't sit well with Keenan's loyal and longtime colleagues. Arun knew Keenan was angry and humiliated by the change in management, yet Arun was reluctant to pump up Keenan's ego. Keenan reported to him! Meanwhile, Keenan was fairly adept at undermining Arun and distracting the rest of the design team with constant examples of Arun's incompetence.

Arun and I agreed that he would go to Keenan and articulate the many ways in which Keenan's talents remained not only valuable but critical to the company's expansion. Arun asked Keenan to indicate what success would look like for him, given the new structure. If Keenan cared most about seeing his designs worn by Emmy Award winners, how could Arun help make that happen? More press coverage for the creative team? Arun would investigate that. Complimenting Keenan, Arun offered to use his position to support these goals.

Publicly, Arun made a point of calling out Keenan's contributions. By recognizing the ego blow his arrival meant for Keenan, Arun was able to shift his focus to enabling, not fighting, his new direct report. Keenan responded as hoped. He started telling the team how lucky they were to have new blood and an experienced manager!

29

CREATE RITUALS

Celebrate Success and
Grow from Mistakes

Most organizations have rituals—from the everyday routines (coffee breaks, tea time, etc.) to major events such as annual meetings and retirement parties. Successful companies recognize the importance of tradition and are intentional in creating recurring experiences that give staff something to look forward to, aspire to, and reminisce about. They don't have to be costly and can be created by employees at all levels of the organization. Bestowing a humorous prize for greatest recovery after an indelicate error normalizes mistakes and supports growth. Booming classic rock tunes for two minutes when a big deal is closed boosts morale. Gathering as a group and doing a cheer before making the sales pitch communicates that this is a special moment, we are in it together, and we are ready.

Recognizing significant milestones creates a sense of shared history and team cohesiveness. Noting the comings and goings of team members provides the personal touch that expresses an appreciation for the individual beyond the service they provide to the organization.

Daily ritualized actions between just two people can give the day form and reassert the personal connection (especially when working remotely). For example, Gerry Sanseviero, the administrative director of Katzman Consulting, always starts the day by sending me a Good Morning message that reviews immediate goals and wishes me well. I do the same for her. Our days always end with a signoff email, a quick appreciation for what was accomplished and the hope that the night will be fun, restful, or both. Sometimes Gerry includes a picture or cartoon to make me smile. She's very good at that.

Big companies have Human Resources departments that design firmwide initiatives, but sometimes the best rituals are organically grown and local to your team. Effective rituals fire up our emotions and prepare us for action. The New Zealand rugby team, the All Blacks, has been performing the legendary Haka, a Maori war dance with vigorous feet stamping and rhythmic shouts, before its matches since 1905. In addition to being really cool to watch, neuroscientific research shows that acts like the Haka trigger feelings of connectivity, which stimulate mental flow states. These in turn reduce anxiety and increase energy and focus.

THIS IS FOR YOU IF

- The end point of your project is far off into the future.

- Your team works together but doesn't actually take time to be together.

- An infusion of pride and joy isn't such a bad idea.

- You want to help shape your team's culture.

TAKE ACTION

► Honor significant years at the company (e.g., 1-, 5-, and 10-year anniversaries). Get a large card and have everyone sign it, or collect notes and put them in a nice box. If you work virtually, set up a private electronic page where colleagues can share positive affirmations for the employee you want to recognize. HR may have the records, but it's easier if there is an appointed person who keeps the master calendar of your immediate team members' start dates. Why not volunteer for the job? It's an easy way to spread joy and respect.

► Celebrate all of the employees who are having a birthday in a given month with one cake and quick toasts for each person.

► Recognize the rhythms of work. Acknowledge project milestones, especially if the final goal is far off. Host a "we are halfway there" gathering. It's a good chance for staff who have been on the project from the start to share stories of how far you have come. Restate the dream. Why are we doing this? What's the goal? Ask community members or customers who are going to benefit from your work once it's done to join you at this celebration of progress.

▶ Have a monthly award for fabulous mistakes. You can only nominate yourself (the aim is not to shame others). You can do this even if you work virtually. The first Tuesday of each month may be when the team hops on a call to tease (and learn from) the person who wins for biggest blunder. Ask everyone to share one regrettable moment. "Presentations" should be no more than three minutes. This is meant to be fast and light. The goal is to clear the air, offer support, and have a chance to say, "What could we do differently in the future?"

▶ Consider rituals to contain negativity. For example, declare Thursdays "Complaining Day" and self-police the rest of the week to maintain a positive attitude.

▶ Book the "we did it" celebration *before* the final push toward completion. You can then just show up and party once you have hit your target, rather than risk your team being so exhausted from delivering, they won't have the energy to plan.

▶ To maintain rituals, you can't always wait for everyone to be free, especially during busy times. The more consistent you are, the more likely staff will make an effort to attend. Be sure you are clear on who is responsible for coordinating activities. If any of the ideas you just read appeal to you, present them at your next team meeting and ask for volunteers. Put the date and person in charge into your calendars.

KEEP IN MIND

● Don't let a poorly performing ritual become another bad habit ingrained in your company's culture. If it doesn't work, drop it. Keep on experimenting.

● If you work in a family business, be sure your personal celebrations aren't hijacked by business tensions and demands. Agree to have a moratorium on office discussions at key events.

CASE STUDIES

Institutionalize the Unexpected

During one of our early *Women@Work* radio broadcasts, our experienced guest Sallie Krawcheck registered my anxiety and that of my co-host, Laura Zarrow. The producer was counting down, "three . . . two . . ." —and Sallie said, "Don't f--k up"—and "one" . . . we were live! It was a destabilizing comment in the moment. As Laura observed, "Once we vanquished the two demons, judgment and fear of failure, we were able to see how funny Sallie's coaching was." During the shows that followed, Laura and I routinely told each other at the 30-second mark "Don't f--k up," It was our way of kicking self-doubt out of the room so we could freely enjoy being with each other. The routine also had the reliable effect of making the guests in our studio laugh (and relax) at the unexpected off-color comment. We would then quickly explain the derivation, normalize the inevitable shared nervousness at the start of the show and . . . we were on the air!

Yesterday's High Point and a Chance to Make Today an Even Better Day

Ricky runs a food truck that pops up at different points in the city. His staff is an ever-changing team of hourly workers. Just before they open the hatch, Ricky asks each person to think back to their last time in the truck and to share one high point and a suggestion for how to replicate or improve upon that moment. The result is a chance to share a laugh and celebrate some energizing experiences. This ritual also allows the staff to identify the role they played in creating these memorable interactions. Sometimes it's as simple as starting a conversation with a customer that leads to an enjoyable exchange rather than being overly focused on prepping the food and sending them on their way.

30

GENERATE JOY AND LAUGHTER

Energize Your Workplace

Do you want a bigger bonus, a boost in creative thinking, increased credibility, and greater opportunity? Start laughing. Humor at work is a serious business advantage. Check this out:

- Eighty-two percent of employees at Fortune 100 companies that were recognized as "great" places to work agree with the statement "I work in a fun organization."

- All things being equal, 89 percent of CEOs believe they'd rather hire someone with a good sense of humor.

- Managers displaying a good sense of humor are given more opportunities in organizations than those who take themselves too seriously.

- People who can inject some lightheartedness, particularly in stressful positions, are viewed as being on top of things and in control, whether or not they actually are.

- The "funnier" an executive is, the higher the bonus.

- Supervisor use of humor is associated with enhanced subordinate work performance and workgroup cohesion.

Don't panic. You don't have to put this book down and run to a standup comedy class. Instilling joy and laughter at the office doesn't require a pocket full of jokes or a stream of one-liners. It's about relinquishing the relentless sense of urgency. Everything you do doesn't have to be approached with grave importance, and you don't have to always take yourself so seriously! Like the team at Nickelodeon used to say, "We are selling SpongeBob, not curing cancer. Why is everyone so tense?"

Upbeat atmospheres are associated with increased productivity and creativity. The more playful your culture, the easier it is to brainstorm ideas without the fear of being shot down.

Daniel Goleman wrote, "Laughter may be the shortest distance between two brains." It builds cooperative bonds. Negotiations that begin with shared laughter more often result in mutually beneficial outcomes. Laughter is also a potent stress buster. If you are laughing or enjoying yourself, you can't be feeling pressured or stressed. It's like a mini-vacation.

Wharton professor Sigal Barsade has done extensive research revealing that employees are not *emotionnal islands*. We continuously spread our moods, receiving and being influenced by the affective states around us. The giggles of your colleague in the next cubicle can brighten your day. Neuroscientists have demonstrated that when we hear others laugh, mirror neurons are stimulated in our brains. We experience amusement as if we ourselves are laughing. Those who counsel that "work is no laughing matter" have it all wrong. Your mood affects my mood; my mood affects your mood. We all have a responsibility to insert a bit of levity. A lightness of being is contagious, and a key ingredient for success.

THIS IS FOR YOU IF

- It's time to replace the *b* in *job* with a *y* (*job* → *joy*).

- You are very important.

- Brains are shut down and creativity is lacking.

- Everyone's afraid. It's tense. It's no fun here.

TAKE ACTION

▶ Most emotional communication occurs through body language, facial expression, and tone. Change your facial expression to the one you would have if you were happy, even if you don't feel it in the moment. It will improve your mood.

► Greater self-awareness is associated with occupational success. Be the first to joke about your idiosyncrasies. Be the source of levity, rather than the font of office tension.

► If appropriate, consider introducing laughing yoga at work (https://laughter yoga.org/).

► Have a board by the coffee machine and invite colleagues to post industry-related comics. No one laughs louder at a lawyer joke than a lawyer. Get the ball rolling. Post a few cartoons of your own.

► You can't mandate humor, but you can model it. Start small. Share a joke or a funny passage, make a play on words, or create an unexpected acronym for the latest project. If you get a smile from one person today, that's success.

► What if you're just not funny? Or don't find other people funny? That's OK. Don't force it. But don't be a spoilsport by frowning at your chuckling team-mates. Laugh with them or simply soak up their positive vibes.

KEEP IN MIND

• Resist making inside jokes or laughing at another person's expense.

• Building an inclusive community requires that everyone get the chance to be the subject of (appropriate) humor.

• Don't overly rely on humor to deal with conflict or tension. Sometimes a serious intervention is necessary.

• Adding a smiley emoji after a terse comment does not make it funny.

• Not every form of humor is appropriate. Work is no place for locker room and bathroom humor or political, sexist, malicious, religious, homophobic, and xenophobic jokes.

Pack Your Rubber Chicken

The Institute for the Future chose Wellington Nogueira, a clown, as an advisor on the future of health care. Makes sense. Clowning is one of the oldest disruptive technologies. In 1991, Wellington founded *Doutores da Alegria* (Doctors of Joy) in Brazil to promote the importance of joy in the healing professions (and beyond). "Don't underestimate the importance of the fool," says Wellington. It's an ancient profession. Most great regimes have relied on court jesters to keep the ruler in check, break the tension, bring attention to inappropriate behaviors everyone is trying to ignore, and offer an alternative way of seeing what is right in front of you.

Wellington traveled with me to rural China looking for jesters. Adventuring with a clown is a great recipe for making friends. Wellington was invited to the home of a Communist Party leader. In appreciation, Wellington left a special gift—a rubber chicken. His new host promptly placed it on a bookshelf along with his souvenirs of political service. We all cracked up. Now that's diplomacy.

Let Loose and Do a Goofy Dance

When Peri's pals asked her, "Do your new coworkers like your fake falls and goofy dance?" she exclaimed, "OMG, I've been at this job six months and never really let loose!" No wonder she went home exhausted, and was having a hard time adjusting to her position.

The next day she found an opportunity to take a risk. She "melted" on purpose just before a meeting with subordinates. Everyone giggled. "How else will you surprise us?" they asked. They were used to seeing Peri as a buttoned-up, slightly miserable person. "Well, I have a few dance steps," she admitted. Laughter spilled out as the air cleared. Peri had given permission to herself—and others—to take an energizing moment for silliness. Then they got back to work.

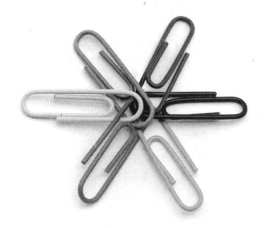

PART V

RESOLVE
CONFLICT

When trouble happens, your heart hurts, your body rebels, and even your best friends tire of your complaints. You can't get work out of your head. It's time to clear the conflicts.

Odds are things won't go as planned. Even the most mission-driven organization has a simmering stew of misunderstandings. The more you care, the more heated things can seem. Sure, you're aggravated. You're likely not alone.

A foundation of respect, trust, and generosity prompts everyone to assume best intentions. In reality that's often not enough. When emotions are high, things get complicated. This part helps you contribute to the solution by remaining curious and bravely labeling your own errors or limitations. Responsibly sharing your feelings reveals commonalities among colleagues and helps dispel destructive assumptions—bringing people to your side rather than prematurely gearing up for confrontation.

Deep connections are forged from, not in spite, of conflict. Your ability to work through differences allows you to engage a wider set of collaborators and learn more by experimenting with new ideas. Expanding your knowledge and network of relationships gives work meaning and sets you up for success.

This Part Is for You If

- You crave honesty and the calm that comes with it.

- You are starting a new initiative within an established organization.

- It's time to ask for a raise or new opportunity.

- You've been told that you are the problem.

- The processes and procedures you put into place aren't working.

- There are too many meetings and memos.

- Emotions are at a fever pitch.

- People are afraid to say what they really think.

- Cliques are forming; gossip is increasing.

31

STAND IN SOMEONE ELSE'S SHOES

Experience Their Point of View

No matter how flat you make a pancake,
it's still got two sides.
—Dr. Phil

In order to move people, I've learned that sometimes I have to . . . move people. Literally. Get them out of their seats and into the streets, into each other's neighborhoods and offices, homes, and gardens. Some call this kind of education experiential; others call it action learning. One thing I know for sure is that *doing, sharing, and being* together beats reading any theory. We each look at the world from our own subjective perspective, a bias that is more pronounced when the stakes are high.

The resolution of any conflict comes down to the question: What really matters? The answer is seldom one you can ascertain alone. What was once crystal-clear blurs out of focus when you stand in someone else's shoes and see the view from that person's point. You can't always reason out a conclusion at your desk. Sometimes you have to travel on the elevator or cross-town bus or maybe take an airplane (if you can afford to). Remember to take your *Connect First* tool kit. The basics will help set the stage; the tips in earlier chapters will kindle quality conversation and the act of physically going to another person's place will deepen your relationship. Standing in someone else's shoes helps you solve their problems, offers a new perspective on your challenges, and generates lasting goodwill.

THIS IS FOR YOU IF

- You want to have an expansive positive impact.

- The unintended consequences of your actions can be costly, and you want to widen your aperture.

- It's an interconnected world, and you want to learn more about your place in it.

TAKE ACTION

▶ Start your conference call by asking what everyone is seeing out their windows. This anchors you in their reality. Restrict the response to one sentence. It won't take long, and it literally "places" your remote team. The quick opening question humanizes the conversation that follows.

▶ Skype, Google Hangouts, Zoom, FaceTime—video technology doesn't replace the experience of visiting other offices. If you can afford the trip, see the engineering team in Bosnia. How are they recording the instructions from the head office? What? They don't post project plans, yet you always reference the flowchart as if your respective walls share the same visual images. Agree on a mutual way to communicate and capture progress now that you know better.

▶ Sometimes the engineers coding your latest product are working across town. They are frustratingly slow, and they miss deadlines. Go to their office (even if it's in a garage). Is it noisy? Cold? Does the sensory environment impact your ability to think? Do your colleagues share the same experience? Did they know they could ask for noise-canceling headsets? What changes can you make right away to help?

▶ Visit the recipients of your work. Do you manufacture safety glasses? Visit the factories that use them. Connecting to the end user provides a sense of purpose. Look around. Taking in the environment may also inform innovation. You hadn't realized that the factory workers were repurposing your packaging material as stuffing for children's toys. Can you help market those teddy bears? Can you offer to buy some for your team? Do a joint project.

► Do you know how the environment will be impacted by your latest building plans? Government officials blithely said they can "move the water." What does that mean? Will homes be affected? Trees? Transport routes? It can sound easy until you arrive on-site. Once you visit the community, the neighborhood complaints become clear.

► Did you just have the second tense phone call after five increasingly hostile email exchanges? Don't just sit there, do something. Ask the person you are sparring with if you can meet at a place that matters to them. It may be their office, the building site that's raising blood pressures, or the music shop that brings that person joy. No matter the choice, you will learn a great deal and connect more.

► When meeting someone on their turf, come prepared to talk in terms of their interests. Do research in advance so you can ask informed questions. Check the local newspaper or blog to tap into timely concerns.

► Ask open-ended questions and be prepared for answers you didn't expect. Don't be afraid to ask for explanations of jargon, abbreviations, or words you don't understand.

► Engage in active wonder. Relinquish the urge to judge; instead, allow yourself to feel the moment. Listen to understand. Don't be pressured to match their story with one of yours.

► You've invested the time and resources to meet community members, collaborators, and colleagues where they are. Now what? Take the time to reflect. If you are organizing the trip, agree on a place for everyone to gather after an interaction to ask: "So what? What does this mean for me, for my company, for the wider world?"

KEEP IN MIND

• The excitement of entering someone's space and all of its novelty may feel like an Instagram moment for you. Don't take pictures right away. Have your meeting. Bond. Then ask if you can take a photo. The camera will capture the connection (if you made one), and it will be a much more valuable image than a tourist shot grabbed without permission.

• Pack your flexibility and sense of adventure. It's what you don't expect that can teach (and delight you) the most.

CASE STUDIES

Your Germs Are My Germs!

Lindsay Levin founded Leaders' Quest in 2001 to create immersive experiences (quests) that allowed people from all walks of life to visit the lives of individuals they might not otherwise meet. A poignant moment is captured in Lindsay's book, *Invisible Giants*. An international group of business, community, and cultural leaders visited a crowded men's shelter off one of Delhi's main roads. When asked, "Do you have a job?" the residents replied, "We work in catering, serving food." "What do you do for sanitation?" "We manage." "Toilets?" "There aren't any."

During the course of our week in India, many of the travelers had suffered from Delhi belly (violent diarrhea). Suddenly, the conditions contributing to their extreme discomfort came into full focus. "These people are our cooks, but they don't have a place to wash." In that moment the relationship between farmer, kitchen, food server, and dinner table took on a whole new meaning. We share the same water, air, and contaminants. whether we like it or not.

Our group returned home eager to learn if their employees could access proper sanitation after work. Had they unfairly assumed that everyone in their supply chain had running water? Others asked, "Does my organization depend on laborers who don't receive social services?" Seeing, smelling, and talking on site prompted a deep reflection on our individual and corporate responsibilities in an interconnected world.

Calculations Tabulated at Your Desk Won't Cut It

To understand another person's perspective, you don't have to go half-way around the world. Sometimes you just have to walk the halls of your office. Kara, a newly appointed actuary in an insurance company undergoing a major transformation, kept long hours to develop revised projections, which she presented with pride. In the audience was Evan, the organization's most profitable salesman. The renowned "superstar" was furious to learn that Kara (whom he had never taken the time to meet) had recalculated his business unit's risk profile, which meant that Evan's previously top-ranking team would now miss their targets. There would be no bonuses; compensation would decrease. Evan, who had deleted the email announcing Kara's arrival six months prior, now jumped into action, firing off questions and offering alternative calculations. The CEO experienced Evan's attack as undermining the new regime. "Change your behavior or start looking for a new job."

Evan went on a listening tour (to all five floors of his office), patiently getting specific illustrations of how his team could support the new processes. He spent the most time with Kara, honoring her skill set by asking to learn from and with her. Evan apologized. Ultimately, Kara and Evan coauthored a companywide report that delineated why the new actuarial models were needed for long-term success.

32

DECODE YOUR COLLEAGUES' EMOTIONAL CLUES

They're the Key to Connection and Success

Group dynamics run on two roadways. The hallways connecting offices are akin to the local thoroughfare—lots of stop signs, distractions, and potential delays. Let's call this the cognitive passage. It's the path you are likely most familiar with. You can orient yourself with recognizable signposts—there are memos and meetings, formal presentations, and snack room chatter. There's an alternative route, faster but daunting to enter. You have to go deep through confusing muck, shift gears, and invest in the journey, but once you access it, there's plenty of fuel for new projects, traffic clears, and suddenly there are multiple connecting routes to reach your destination. This is the emotional speedway.

Here's what I've learned during the past 30 years: Sticking with what you can readily see and label is comfortable but often inefficient. Taking a break from words to pay attention to mood (yours and theirs) marks the difference between average and superior performers. Pause to experience and respond to the tension in the room, the worried looks, the giddy anticipation, or the detached gaze of your peers. These are vital data points. Many professionals sense what's going on beneath the surface, and to their detriment, choose to ignore it. In most offices, employees are reticent to articulate what's motivating them, complicating their production, or scaring them silly. Your ability to decode (and respond to) your colleagues' (not so hidden) emotional clues is your competitive advantage.

To enhance your interpersonal savvy, try this psychological hack—it's the foolproof secret. It requires you to use your own psyche as an investigative instrument. I call it *checking the emotional mirror*. Begin with the hypothesis that *if you feel it, likely they feel it, too*. When confronted with a new opportunity, an intractable conflict, or an unfamiliar collaborator:

1. Take a minute, maybe even 180 seconds; breathe deeply and tap into how you are feeling. Are you uncomfortable (or excited)? What negative outcomes do you fear? Why is success so important to you in this instance? Keep going. Are there core beliefs that are being challenged by the circumstances? Is a raw nerve or insecurity being tapped? Is there something "wrong"? Does the air "smell bad" in the office? Go down another level. See if you can venture below your work veneer and find some words to express what's bubbling up. Remember, our gut is filled with neuroreceptors. At times our brain fails us, but our body doesn't lie. How does your stomach feel? Are your teeth clenched? Is your back aching? Try to name the experience.

2. Scan your environment. Who else might be sharing the same feeling (positive or negative)?

3. Practice strategic vulnerability: Start a conversation with your coworkers, not about *what* has to get done but *how* the work is impacting you. Label your concerns or excitement. Leave lots of room for them to respond and share their experience. How is the work affecting them? If they ask why you are inquiring now, tell the truth. Your emotional radar was activated, and you thought it might be signaling some discomfort (or happy anticipation) on their part. By connecting in this way, as fellow humans, you are giving permission for a peer, direct report, or partner to transition with you to the superhighway.

WHEN THERE'S TENSION BETWEEN YOU AND SOMEONE ELSE

If you feel angry, perhaps your colleague is also seeing red. He appears calm, but then again, he's reticent to give you the information you need in a timely manner. I know, I know, you can't imagine why this cocky creature would be unhappy. After all, he has access to all the information and his slow response time is provoking *you*. But if you want to continue this necessary partnership, rather than approaching your coworker with a litany of missed deadlines and a demand that he shape up, ask about his experience. The conversation may release pain on both sides and produce a new level of understanding. Chances are, the speed of your collaboration will escalate as well.

If you feel undermined by your direct reports, drop your defensiveness and see if you can uncover ways that you may be making people feel small. Feeling disrespected? Are you sure others feel respected by you? Ask them.

WHEN YOU NEED TO MOTIVATE GROUPS

Rather than kicking off a new project with spreadsheets and deadlines, try sharing your definition of success and why it's important to you. Then ask others to do the same. For example, the leader of a Pan-African bank started her management offsite saying that as a white South African she was committed to training black managers to become company leaders as a means of making amends for the shame she felt post-apartheid. Group participants followed her lead. One man related that he was the first in his family to graduate from college, and all eyes were on him to do well in this job. Another manager shared that his mom, who grew up shunned by the system, saved money by sewing it into the hem of her skirt. He wanted her to be unafraid of opening a bank account. The gathering was ostensibly to refine sales strategies for the next generation of banking needs, but what resulted was a shared sense of purpose fueled by personal determination and fear of failing.

My daughter gave me a motivational calendar. One of the entries says: "You're unique, just like everyone else." We are all so different. We individualize our coffee orders; gluten-free, dairy-free meals; tattoos; and religious customs. Yet peel back a layer, and we are astoundingly alike. Stopping to consider *if I feel it, do they feel it* is a great way to recognize our shared humanity, to clear obstacles, get the job done, and overcome that lonely feeling at work (and beyond).

THIS IS FOR YOU IF

- The conversation in your head about and with colleagues is taking more time than any real discussion you may have had with a coworker.

- You have no clue what he or she must be thinking, and you are close to no longer caring.

- The tension is thick, and you're ready to try a new tactic.

- There have been *so* many changes in your group and nobody has taken a breath or stopped to ask, "How are you doing?"

TAKE ACTION

▶ Do an emotional body scan. What's giving you the zip in your step? Why is this project such a drag? Why are you suddenly dreading going into the office? See if you can articulate the experience and share it with the colleague in the cubicle next to you. Feeling "off" before a big event? Don't be afraid to open the meeting expressing your internal turmoil. Ask the assembled if anyone else has similar sensations. Demonstrating your "personhood" makes even the most intimidating manager that much more approachable. The more you seem like "one of us," the less frightening it is for employees to share less than perfect updates—which is how you get the information you need!

▶ Before you build your case against a colleague, consider your impact on them. Slow down long enough to recognize how you and your current antagonist may be experiencing the same thing. Take a deep breath and ask if your "opponent" feels what you feel.

▶ During performance reviews and project kickoffs, ask your colleagues what feelings you evoke in them (and why)—especially when you are at your best. Use this precious data to further your development.

▶ Begin meetings with a check-in. Asking how participants are feeling in a workshop or strategy session may seem counter to many corporate cultures and yet it truly warms the room. If you are leading the meeting, it's a chance to model the importance of emotional centering. Share a story, or simply reference what's in your heart or gut (before launching into what's on your mind). Bringing together diverse perspectives is often the goal, but start-ing from a place of difference often stalls discussions. Go under the skin to leave roles and rank behind.

▶ Ask, "How is what I experience of this person true about me?" This process of identification removes judgment, builds empathy, and is a great way of forming authentic bonds—especially when working with people of differ-ent backgrounds. The next time you want to accelerate relationships among new collaborators, invite team members to speak in pairs. Take turns. In-struct one person to share a story about a career-defining moment. Have the listener comment on the personal qualities the narrative revealed. Compliment your conversational partner by noting why these character-istics were admirable. Then have the listener reflect on how they, too, may share these same qualities. Reverse roles. Try it. It's powerful.

KEEP IN MIND

• As tempting as it might be, don't always assume your reactions are the same as someone else's. You have to test your hypothesis!

• Have an inclusive set of eyes. When evaluating who around you may be sharing the same emotions, be sure to consider people at all levels of the enterprise.

• While the goal is to be more transparent with your feelings, this does not mean you disable all censors. Don't release emotional weapons.

• Read your audience. Don't force someone to have an impassioned dis-cussion when they are racing out the door. Set a date that's mutually con-venient.

CASE STUDIES

Managers Feel Unappreciated, Too

"She doesn't see all that I do for the company. She doesn't care about me. I have been so devoted to her," exclaimed Nica, a human resources director working in Japan. Two months earlier, Nica had applied for relocation after successfully hiring and training her successor. The process was in motion when Nica received a note from her boss, Ruth, asking, "How committed are you to the new role?" The question infuriated Nica, setting off a tornado of insecure thoughts: *How in the world could Ruth see me as anything less than 100 percent committed? Is my company building a case to push me out?* As our conversation continued, Nica related that, in her fury, she had not responded to Ruth's request. Nica was asked to write the business case for the transfer, including an affirmation of her commitment to the firm and intentions to live in Asia for the next three years. Ruth needed this information to lobby on Nica's behalf.

On the other side of the globe, Ruth sat in the company's headquarters and wondered to herself, *I've done so much for Nica. Doesn't she care about me? Why isn't Nica providing the information I asked for?* Ruth feels disrespected by Nica. *Doesn't she see how committed I am to her?*

I challenged Nica to consider whether Ruth's questions about her commitment were coming from a positive place—an effort to help, not question her. Nica's attitude shifted from suspicion to compassion as she recognized that Ruth might herself be feeling devalued as Nica never seemed to notice all that her manager had done to support her growth. Nica called Ruth to express her appreciation for her extraordinary support and to affirm her desire to do what it takes to contribute to the company goals. Ruth was appreciative that Nica recognized her efforts and relieved to obtain the necessary assurance. The tension broke, and the transition plan progressed smoothly.

Building Bridges from the Inside Out

Vihaan managed a newspaper in India that often ran exposés on the lives of underprivileged workers, yet he seldom spoke directly to the very people whose lives differed from his own. Connecting people from different walks of life to foster an appreciation of common social issues was the goal of the program I was facilitating. Vihaan was quite nervous about meeting a domestic maid who traveled two hours each way to work, and was living with her daughter in the rented corner of a room above a brothel in the Khetwadi district, outside of Mumbai. He said, "I am so curious and also ashamed of what I don't know about her situation." Days before, as we prepared for the visit, our hostess, Aadhya, had expressed almost the exact same sentiment: "What will I say to these businesspeople? I am so embarrassed by my situation."

To build a bridge between their worlds, I encouraged Vihaan to begin by sharing his shame, which relaxed Aadhya, who shared her discomfort. This, in turn, reduced Vihaan's anxiety. They bonded based on how they felt rather than focusing on the different positions they held in society. This allowed the exchange to move naturally to a deeper level, a discussion about parenting. Aadhya expressed fears that her daughter might be tempted by bad influences; the media mogul worried about the same thing. That we were sitting above a whorehouse wasn't relevant; their conversation flowed and ended with Vihaan having a sincere respect for a woman working so hard to ensure a better life for her child.

33

APOLOGIZE

Don't Justify or Explain Why

Holding on to anger is like drinking poison and expecting the other person to die.
—BUDDHA

Have you apologized recently? No? There's something wrong. Quick, take your pulse! Surely, there must have been something you cared enough about that you drove your perspective a little too hard, took a shortcut that backfired, or pissed off your colleagues. If you aren't periodically pushing the boundaries, you risk boredom, block innovation, and can become profoundly dull. If you blithely do as you please because you are the boss, the funder, or today's beloved employee, you may *think* you are getting away with organizational murder, but the court of public opinion will eventually deliver your punishment (potentially at an inopportune moment). Making errors isn't the problem. Failing to apologize when your actions negatively impact others—that's when the trouble sets in. Sometimes we inadvertently hurt or undermine others. It's embarrassing when we find out, and, in the moment, gulping disappearing potion has huge appeal. If no one notices or mentions your bad conduct, maybe we can all pretend it didn't happen. Wrong. What if I had a good reason for acting inappropriately? Nope, that doesn't get you out of apologizing either.

People get angry at work. That can't be avoided. I consider anger the basecoat of emotions. It lies beneath many of the other occupational feeling states. Shame, betrayal, exclusion (and affection) all beget anger. Without the fire in our belly, action attenuates. A study using fMRI technology allows us to see emotions by mapping elevated physiological sensations based on the activation of facial muscles, skin temperature, and limb activity. Happiness, love, and anger all produce a similar glow. These are called "emotions of approach"; we move toward someone or something when we love them, if they make us happy . . . or if we are out to get them because we are mad. Physiologically, anger is akin to positive emotions. If you don't care, then you don't engage, you don't light up. If we want people to be passionate about their work, expect to find its red-hot twin, fury. Anger gets a bad rap and should if it leads to abuse or relentless negativity, but let's give it some respect. Don't pretend everything is alright when we have provoked our colleagues or slimed them with our frustration.

Given the frequency of human error, you would think we would be better at asking for forgiveness and enabling others to admit their mistakes. If only it were that easy to be accountable when we screw up. Although it's possible that drawing attention to our missteps may tarnish our reputations in the immediate, in the long term, team trust and performance are often enhanced. Stanford management professor Robert Sutton, author of *Good Boss, Bad Boss*, says the first thing to do is not to sugarcoat your error, but to take the blame fully. Affirming your responsibility is a form of taking control. The conversations stimulated by your apology often lead to strengthened relationships.

Openness about your mistakes sets the stage for others to share their errors. Employees who fear fessing up hide issues that could have been solved had they been aired. If you are honest about your failings, you have a greater chance that important truths make their way to your ears.

The gurus of regret concur on the recipe for an effective apology. It should demonstrate humility and when possible be delivered face-to-face. While email can be a tempting alternative, if you can't look a person in the eye, at least pick up the phone. It's important to say the words "I'm sorry" or "I apologize" and to provide a clear, succinct indication of exactly what you're apologizing for. Endure the awkwardness. Incomplete or insincere efforts can backfire. Offer suggestions on how you will work to avoid the mistake in the future, propose ways to make amends, and then sit back and let the other person vent if needed. Don't make excuses for yourself. Don't interrupt, argue, refute, or correct. Resist bringing up your own criticisms and complaints. Even when the offended party is largely at fault, apologize for your part in the incident, however small it may be. In some instances, your vulnerability may set the stage for others to explore ways in which they may have contributed to the problem—but don't count on it. Be prepared to learn something unexpected by listening deeply. For example, you may find out that another error you made was even greater than the one for which you apologized!

THIS IS FOR YOU IF

- You are human. Even if you are a robot, you should learn to say, "I'm sorry."

- The air is thick, there's no place to hide, and yet you want to pretend that everything is OK.

- You find yourself taking the long route to your desk to avoid *them*.

- Maybe, just maybe, you did something wrong.

TAKE ACTION

- Extend an invitation for an in-person meeting to the colleague you slighted. Avoid the excuse "this person works for me."

- Find the fun in admitting your error. Mock yourself before others do.

- Say what is necessary. Keep from over-apologizing. The best apologies are short and don't include explanations that can undo them.

- Leave room for the other person to respond, and remember to listen.

- Once you've expressed your regret, put it behind you and move on. We are all fallible—no need to beat yourself up.

- Don't offer "I'm sorry" gifts like flowers, which can be misinterpreted or seen as too personal a gesture. The best investment is a heartfelt expression of regret and ownership of your error.

- Concentrate on what you have done and how others have been impacted by your actions. Avoid saying, "I'm sorry that you feel. . . ." Blaming other people for their reactions puts the onus of the problem on them and turns "I'm sorry" into "I'm not really sorry at all."

- It's never too late to say you're sorry. However, it's better to admit your error quickly and emphatically.

KEEP IN MIND

- Anger at oneself and frustration at another person are frequent bedfellows. We inflict internal pain when we judge ourselves by unrealistic standards: "I should have seen that coming." "I never should have trusted her." Check the source of your fury. Calming your inner demon is protection against attacking the innocent guy at the desk next to yours.

- While it's hard to admit mistakes, it's sometimes even harder to accept an apology. When the tables are turned, allow the person to express their remorse, listen carefully, and show appreciation for their efforts in making amends.

CASE STUDIES

All He Wanted Was an Apology

Close friends and coheads of a regional office, Chu and Andre were passed over for promotion by their law firm. Management said they wanted to make them partners at the same time and, economically, it was prudent to wait another year. Chu argued that he was responsible for more of the office income, threatened to quit, and was subsequently offered the promotion. Andre, by his own description, "went insane." Witnessing Andre's outrage, Chu changed his tune and told his boss that he would wait the year. Going forward, Andre refused to work with Chu. The success of the office required that Chu and Andre recover from this relational rupture as it wasn't realistic to have two warring managers polarize their subordinates.

Both men believed it would show weakness to take responsibility for the conflict and waited for the other to say, "I am sorry." The standoff ended when Andre acknowledged that, although he felt betrayed by Chu, his own behavior was inexcusable. The tension was exhausting, Andre missed Chu and took the first steps toward reconciliation. Andre's apology released the pressure. It was the start, not the end, of much needed conversations between the two men.

Take the First Step

Gyeong oversees talent recruitment at a major real estate company. Adele heads a prominent search firm and frequently finds candidates for Gyeong's company. From very different backgrounds, the two colleagues get a real kick out of each other's no-nonsense approach, and they have shared ideas, resources, and many lunches for years. And then Gyeong hired a new head of construction and refused to pay a commission to Adele. Adele was enraged. After all, years back, she was the one who introduced the candidate to Gyeong. From Gyeong's perspective, that connection was made a long time ago. There was no contract. In recent months the candidate approached her directly. Adele voiced her displeasure loudly, in front of others, and was steadfast in her assessment—she had been robbed of her fees. Gyeong said she would never work with Adele again.

Six months later Adele heard that Gyeong was going through some hard times and called to say, "I'm sorry. I don't want us to be estranged. I shouldn't have been so harsh or public in my reaction. I'm disappointed that we couldn't agree on payment, but our relationship matters too much to me. Here are some ideas about how I can help you." Gyeong readily accepted Adele's apology and added one of her own, "I was under pressure to show that I was reducing costs. I should have paid you a portion of your fee." They went out to lunch and laughed at how tough they both were (and what softies they were inside). Gyeong and Adele have subsequently told their story with pride to both of their teams. The moral? Push hard, and then know when to say enough and make amends.

34

ACCEPT THAT YOU WON'T BE UNDERSTOOD

Sometimes the System Isn't Ready for Your Ideas

Every society honors its live conformists
and its dead troublemakers.
—MIGNON McLAUGHLIN

Today's startups and multinationals alike are seeking to disrupt and innovate within their industries, but most are not terribly good at it. Data suggests that the most successful industry solutions come from people with outsider perspectives. Why? Because insiders are prone to *déformation professionnelle*, the tendency to assess information through the lens of one's specialty. What happens when you are hired to be "inside" because you have astute knowledge from outside the sector? After popping the bubbly, sober up. Research reveals that intrapreneurship efforts fail 70–90 percent of the time, most often because these efforts are treated as add-ons to required activities rather than critical innovations for the future of the organization. The corporate immune system works hard to reject challenges to the status quo. Appropriate levels of staffing, time, and funding are often denied. Even successful intrapreneurs struggle to find a place in the corporate structure and have to chase management for decisions that are delayed as the organizational leadership may not feel equipped to make informed choices.

For example, one of my clients, a cable TV sales executive (let's call him Jose) joined a telephone communications company and launched an advertising revenue stream that generated millions of dollars. He mined the data from set top boxes (that track what channels you watch) to create "addressable advertising"—ads that can be sold for less money and to more companies because marketers can target the households that receive them. The revenues are impressive, the team he built is respected, and yet the reporting lines continually shift. Does this initiative sit in the product or marketing division? What sales commission would Jose receive? There were no previous models. Jose had to coach his boss on how to pay him. Jose went to Washington, DC, to discuss regulations as the privacy protection laws weren't keeping pace with the innovations he was pioneering.

Another client of mine (let's call him Paulo), a banker, joined a multinational insurance company with the mandate to build an investment fund that would back "disruptive technologies" in the industry. But management understood insurance, not technology or early stage investing. Paulo told me he was going to write a book called *I Told You So* to reflect the number of deals missed because the speed of decision-making required was at odds with the insurance company's culture.

Jose and Paulo both had a strong vision of what was possible and required the apparatus of a large company to achieve their goals. With no assigned resources, both men had to use their influencing skills to recruit talent from existing teams to work for them. Other managers saw them as a threat. Figuring out which meetings they should attend to align with larger company objectives was a challenge. Efforts to get press coverage to grow their campaigns were squashed.

I've counseled many clients like Jose and Paulo. Their ability to see into the future and drive change before others even know it's needed is their key asset. It's also their greatest pain point. Almost by definition, the intrapreneur will not be fully understood or adequately valued by the organization. Sometimes the system isn't ready for your ideas. Success requires that you make every effort to bring people along on your journey recognizing that there will be many times when you will feel alone. To maintain energy and conviction, it's critical to remember that it's not personal—it's part of the process. I coach my clients to rejoice in not being understood (or properly managed) as that means you get to work the gray zones (the spaces between job roles that no one owns) to your advantage.

THIS IS FOR YOU IF

- You need the backing and infrastructure of a major organization to launch your great idea, and they think they want to support you but aren't sure how.

- You have a restless leg. The way it is is not the way you think it should or could be.

- You are solving a problem that may not even be on most people's radars.

- There are no metrics or compensation formulas to evaluate your performance.

- It's not clear who should be your supervisor or even what division you should be part of.

TAKE ACTION

▶ Make people backers rather than blockers. Manage the ego of potential critics. Keep colleagues informed on the progress of your work and invite their expertise. Offer your telescope to see into the future and help assuage your underminers' fears by showing them new ways to apply their skills. Don't get discouraged if it takes several tries to get in the door. You may have to try a few different examples of how your colleagues' talents can contribute to your initiative.

▶ Help potential supporters look smart (and forward-thinking) by giving them bullet points and buzzwords to help promote your ideas.

▶ Provide the framework for colleagues to appreciate the value of your initiatives. Keep the language simple, with examples relevant to their work.

▶ Have patience with others. Help your audience get comfortable with your concepts. Speak slowly, avoid jargon, and synthesize complex or new ideas ahead of time so that you can present information as clearly as possible. Practice at home. If your teenage child doesn't understand your message, keep refining it.

▶ Stay happily below the radar. Being recognized while your ideas are in formation can be overrated. Publicity triggers corporate antibodies.

▶ Find support beyond your office walls. Attend conferences with other innovators, even if they are not in your field.

▶ Accepting you won't be understood does not mean that you give up. It means sharing a smile with yourself (knowing that as soon as your initiatives become core to the company, you are likely going to explore the next horizon).

KEEP IN MIND

• There are times when fostering the differences within the "we" is necessary to collectively advance.

• Sometimes you'll find the most energizing connections with people outside your organization.

CASE STUDIES

Incubate on the Outside First

"Let's open our club to nonmembers on Thursday nights, and invite them to join conversations we curate on a given topic, hosted by a rotating master of ceremonies we select from our loyal customer base. That way, we expose a select group to the benefits of our club, offer new programing for existing members, and still maintain some of the mystery that has surrounded our establishment." It seemed pretty straightforward to Silas, but when he first presented the idea, his bosses balked. They were afraid of diminishing the exclusivity that gave them an edge in the market. Silas was frustrated but excited by the concept, so he decided to test it with friends. He started hosting salons in his home. He invited some members of the press, with whom the idea resonated, so they ran a few pieces in the society pages. A year later, his bosses offered him the opportunity to bring the program into the club. The buzz was appealing, and the publicity helped boost their dwindling returns as dues-paying members were opting to spend time in places that felt more modern.

Create an Internal Brand

In 2005, Lisa Sherman and Kristin Frank co-led the Viacom launch of Logo, the first advertiser-supported commercial television channel in the United States geared toward the LGBT audience. They weren't simply creating entertainment; they were building a community and generating social change in an inclusive and, hopefully, profitable way. It wasn't easy.

Back then, watching full episodes on computers was an emerging concept. What started as a limitation (their shows weren't carried by TV providers) became Logo's unique niche. They developed and promoted content with the online viewer in mind. By starting with computer-based viewers and then developing demand for traditional TV, the Logo team reversed the conventional order. As their advisor, I suggested that the Logo team refer to the group internally as the "R&D Center for Viacom," pioneering an industry shift from TV distribution to a multiplatform delivery strategy.

In three years, the Logo team put more than 40 original series on the air, grew ad sales, and became the number-one destination of online properties for the LGBT audience. A few years ago, as other outlets expanded their offerings to the gay community, Logo shifted its programing strategy to focus on more general cultural interests. The startup on the margins is now part of the mainstream. Lisa and Kristin have moved on. Lisa now heads the Ad Council (America's leading producer of public service communications), and Kristin is president of AdPredictive, an emerging tech company that provides market intelligence.

35

NEGOTIATE A PSYCHOLOGICAL CONTRACT

Mutually Commit to Extreme Honesty

Have you ever wanted to put your fingers in your ears and say, "Not now"? Sure, you're committed to personal development and want to be a sensitive, informed, and inspirational member of the team, but today may just not be the day to hear how you can do better. The kids crawled into your bed at 3 a.m., it's allergy season, the credit card payment is overdue, and you have a wall of meetings. You don't have the emotional bandwidth for a meaningful discussion.

How about the time you summoned up the courage to tell your coworker Kyle that he repeats the same stories over and over? The tales weren't that interesting, and your peers were starting to cringe as the "facts" weren't always the same, but Kyle was always the hero. He's a really nice guy and does good work, but his boasting was getting on people's nerves. Your goal? Save Kyle from embarrassment or criticism from a less friendly source. The experience? Kyle saw you as intrusive and now he's giving you the cold shoulder.

This book is all about building relationships that drive your success and happiness at work. To connect, you have to "get real," be a human first, responsibly give voice to emotions, and have the courage to invoke difficult discussions. Honesty is a great policy. In my experience there's honesty and then there's *extreme honesty*—the unvarnished truth, delivered with care and by mutual agreement. To avoid offending others and to free your colleagues from the fear of offending you, negotiate a psychological contract. It's not a written document. It's a stated agreement about boundaries—how much you want to know . . . and when. How candid do you want them to be with you? How far can you push a conversation about feelings (yours or theirs) before best intentions backfire?

There are two types of contracts. The immediate and the ongoing. Each involves being sensitive to giving and receiving feedback.

The immediate: "I'm really nervous about this presentation. Can you tell me afterward what I did well and what I can do to improve?" In requesting this up front you are bringing your colleague or advisor on your side, and inviting them to listen actively and provide a candid review of your performance, rather than the socially accepted, "It was great." Or, if you want to provide commentary, you can say, "You just gave a great talk. Let me know if/when you want to chat about the audience reactions I heard during the break." In this instance you are offering an invitation but not assuming the presenter who is soaking up compliments wants to hear anything but positive regard.

The ongoing contract: You seek out peers, potential mentors, your manager, or your subordinates and say, "I'm aware that I need to establish my credibility in this group. Can you please let me know when I am being effective? If I am not being bold enough or providing enough direction, send up a flare." You've owned your developmental challenges and given permission to receive potentially tough messages. Or if the tables are turned, you can say to your supervisee, "You are being considered for additional responsibilities, but there are times when your choices have been questionable. I believe you can do better with some additional training. Would you be comfortable if I point out those situations when they happen?"

You may be thinking, isn't giving feedback part of a manager's job? Ideally, yes, but it's not always that easy in practice. This chapter takes the concept one step further by setting limits on when and how much commentary is offered. In addition, the psychological contract sets boundaries around a conversation that can feel *too* personal in the work setting.

THIS IS FOR YOU IF

- You want real-time, honest feedback.

- The mandate is to make omelets! Now you have to break eggs. You want to know how much is too much when you and your team are pushing the limits of accepted behavior.

- The boundaries of what's OK to say aren't clear. Not everyone seems to appreciate your candid commentary.

- Blunders unfold in front of you, and no one has asked your opinion—but you want to help.

- Some members of you team are comfortable with open discussions of feelings; others are not.

TAKE ACTION

At the Individual Level

▶ Don't assume that your pearls of wisdom are always welcome. If your colleague is a subordinate or peer, ask, "Can I share some impressions with you? What would be a good time?" Check how comfortable the person is with criticism (human resources calls this *developmental feedback*, but let's face it, it's not exactly praise). Ask if you can be totally candid, and offer your ideas as a hypothesis for consideration. Be ready to accept "No, thank you." If you believe your observations are critical to your colleague's success, but they are not expressing interest in your gift, say, "I would like to help, so just let me know when you are ready." As the saying goes, you can lead a horse to water, but you can't make it drink.

▶ Think about your goals for the next six months. What reflections on your behavior would help you succeed? Who often sees you in action? Not sure about how smart you sound in meetings? Afraid you are too long-winded? Ask your peer who's often in those sessions with you to tug on an ear if you go on for too long or to touch their nose if you make an insightful comment. It's a great way to bond, have a laugh, and receive real-time feedback. You make yourself vulnerable when you ask for such immediate commentary while also indicating that you value your friend's opinion.

For the Group

- If you are heading a change initiative or anticipating a difficult reception to your group's work, be explicit with your team and say, "We are entering a tough period. We will likely make some people unhappy. Can we agree that our meetings are a safe space to share what we've heard in the hallways and on the streets? If there's information we need to share more broadly, or reputations we have to buttress, we will have an hour every Wednesday to decide a course of action together. This requires that we be as candid and supportive as possible. If anyone has reservations, let's discuss them now, or see me in private after this meeting."

- There will be times when tensions are high or interactions between team members are awkward and stilted. Giving voice to the many emotions will likely relieve the pressure. Before jumping into a discussion where the expectation is for people to be honest, ask for permission first. Check how comfortable people feel. Are they ready to engage in frank conversation? What are the consequences they fear (e.g., retaliation for admitting an error)? What can be done to address these concerns? A workplace isn't psychologically safe just because you say it is. There needs to be a shared effort to point out judgmental comments when they happen and shut down side conversations.

- Group discussions to align values, clear conflicts, or address difficult topics are often more successful when conducted in a circle. This allows everyone to see each other. It may lead to the expectation that participants will go around in a circle to answer a prompt. If you are facilitating the group, it's best if you let people volunteer their reflections. If everyone is expected to speak, say so in advance of the question and allow a few minutes for participants to gather their thoughts. Being passionate pulls on your right brain; articulate prose is formed on the left. It's hard to care deeply, and in the same moment deliver neatly packaged observations. Give permission for messy answers.

- Acknowledge that not everyone can emote on demand (nor should they). If the room is getting too heated, stop and ask for permission to keep the conversation going. Check on or renegotiate the contract. Has the discussion exceeded the point of safety? If so, hit the pause button. Are you involved in a discussion that's going beyond the point of comfort? Be brave. Ask the group if this is going in the intended direction, and if not, redirect or halt the conversation.

KEEP IN MIND

- If your well-meaning feedback has precipitated more of an emotional torrent than you are comfortable handling or you suspect that your colleague is oversharing (e.g., telling you too many personal details of struggles at home that may be impacting performance or feelings at work), suggest that you cap the conversation. You can revisit the topic later when that colleague has gained composure or suggest that a professional be consulted. The psychological contract doesn't mean you have to play psychologist.

- Psychological contracts aren't binding forever. Remember to revisit and recommit.

CASE STUDIES

Is It OK to Proceed?

Ike likes to think deeply. His nickname is "the guru." He's a little bit older than many on the team and has been a good source of insightful suggestions when it comes to staffing. The guru sends out suggested readings once or twice a month. Many people in the department find him charming and fun to talk to. Others move their seats when they see him coming. Why? Ike likes to probe. He asks provocative questions that initially are intriguing, but then, for some, go too far. Ike operates without a license. He goes beyond what has been "contracted." Rather than ask if you are interested in his interpretations of your behavior, he corners you and tells you. It would be a loss to ignore Ike, but through coaching, he learned that it was best to first knock on the interpersonal door before assuming he would be granted entry.

Change Happens When Courage Meets Permission

Kiki, fresh out of her MBA program, was hired to double the revenues of a successful but casually run sandwich shop that had just received a small business grant. She energetically gave (barked) out orders to the staff. "Talk less." "Carve the turkey faster." Profits were rising, and so were tempers. Steff, the cashier, had the courage to ask Kiki if she could offer some suggestions. Kiki was intrigued. Steff shared that the staff had ideas for expanding business (music nights, promotions, earlier opening hours, etc.), but they were afraid to speak. Kiki spoke loudly and over people. The refrigerator door was covered with instructions. Often Kiki's ideas weren't realistic for their community. Kiki enlisted Steff's help. She assured her that it was safe to coach the boss. They shook on it. Steff would signal Kiki when her voice got too loud and reminded her to hold the desired brainstorming sessions. Steff whispered in Kiki's ear when it was a staff member's birthday and pointed out when a new regulation might aggravate the kitchen crew unnecessarily. The mood in the shop improved. After a month, Kiki revealed her secret to success—Steff. Kiki invited the rest of the team to tell her like it is and they had the confidence to do so, seeing how respected Steff was for her honesty.

36

ADVOCATE FOR
YOURSELF

The Discomfort Will Be Worth It

" I tell the comp committee: 'Pay me the most you can. Then push and pay me even a little bit more. When you reach the height of what you can pay, dig deeper.' After all, this is how I advocate for our clients. Why wouldn't I advocate for myself?" says Brad, a lawyer.

Can you be as direct as Brad? If you're nodding yes, then perhaps I should put you and Brad together to run a workshop on asking for what you're worth. Everyone else, read on.

Repeatedly, I have clients call me, frustrated about failed salary or promotion discussions, angry (at themselves and their bosses) that they accepted offers that were underwhelming, demeaning, and, at times, disrespectful. Is this familiar? You enter the performance review with your manager feeling confident, hopeful that you will get a decent bump in pay and feeling good about all that you have accomplished this past year. And then . . . you're told you weren't as great as you'd thought, or you were awesome but the company is capping salary increases, or "Here's a great big bonus" (but it's not really that big or that great). This wasn't the way it was meant to go. Your chest tightens, you're unable to open that mental file filled with this year's wins, and you are starting to feel sick. Get me out of here! You want the tension to stop, so you acquiesce. Success. There's immediate relief. But not for long. You leave the meeting and demotivating resentment kicks in. If you don't take further action, your relationship with the manager (and others) deteriorates. Advocating *well* for yourself restores and deepens workplace connections and enhances self-respect.

True, there are situations when it's best to simply say, "Thank you," but more often than not, the necessary conversation doesn't happen because *you* wanted out of there. Don't run. Channel your connecting superhero confidence and stay put. Give voice to your discomfort, express your disappointment, and ask if your superior is willing to work through this awkwardness so that *together* you might find a more satisfying solution. Naming the tension releases some of the emotional pressure (for both of you). Not a good time to go into the details of why you are being denied what you thought you were worth? Pick a date to continue the conversation before you leave. Acknowledge that this can't be easy for your boss; underscore your commitment to the job. Remember this discussion ultimately is about what you can do for your boss—and that's why you are being paid. Ask open-ended questions—who, what, when, and why—to learn more about the company's priorities in the coming year and help your manager get excited about achieving them with your help. Speak in terms of "we."

The traits associated with the highest levels of success at work—perseverance, tenacity, and doggedness or "grit"—have been studied extensively by Angela Duckworth. Grit was a more accurate predictor of whether an incoming cadet would complete the first summer of basic training at West Point than academic GPA, Military Performance Score, and West Point's own Whole Candidate Score. Grit also predicts the success of female attorneys in major law firms. It's not enough to have talent, says Duckworth. You need to work hard, bounce back, and persevere. Next time don't get angry. Get gritty. Push through the discomfort.

THIS IS FOR YOU IF

- In the moment you opt to relieve tension rather than pursue a difficult conversation.

- It's hard to stay motivated when you feel so undervalued.

- Feeding others is easier than taking care of yourself.

TAKE ACTION

▶ Be clear about your goals. Are you asking for a raise or a bonus? Write down the number before you enter the negotiation.

▶ Ask for what you're worth. Don't apologize and devalue yourself.

▶ When your employer preempts your request by "giving" you something you "should" be thankful for, consider it the start of a negotiation, not a done deal. Rather than saying (lying), "That's so generous of you," try, "That's a good place to start, but it won't close the gap between my market value and current salary."

▶ Avoid the trap of making it easy for the person with whom you're negotiating. Stay put and don't retreat at the first hint of tension. Don't fill the silence.

▶ Focus on mutual wins. What does the other person or the enterprise need for success, and how can you uniquely contribute? Make the conversation about them, not about you and your disappointment or unpaid rent.

▶ Offer to help your manager argue on your behalf. What information would help your boss influence their manager? Prepare those materials.

▶ Create a visual tool. Chart out what you need immediate help with or support for. Put that in red to indicate urgency. Use amber to alert your audience to potential issues and green to illustrate what you have under control. The green is very important as it is a reminder of what you have contributed and validates why your requests are worthwhile. In your meeting, focus on the red to be sure that your needs are met, but leave the chart behind—in paper form (and follow up with a thank-you note and attach a soft copy that can be used by others advocating on your behalf).

▶ Getting to the right solution is often hard. If your salary is capped, be creative. Look for other forms of compensation, such as press coverage, paid meals, parking, or travel expenses. Perhaps moving your desk and shifting your hours would make work more enjoyable (that's a real value).

▶ If negotiations didn't end the way you wanted, ask if they can be revisited in three or six months.

KEEP IN MIND

• In their 1969 song, "You Can't Always Get What You Want," the Rolling Stones said it well, further suggesting that it might be possible to obtain only what is really essential.

• Our mind can play tricks when requests are met with ease; suddenly, we find ourselves dissatisfied.

CASE STUDIES

Keep Your Head in the Game

Katie was a collegiate athlete known for her fearless offense on the basketball court. A loyal employee with more than 16 years at the same advertising agency, Katie continually took on new responsibilities but frequently didn't receive the salary increases commensurate with her expanding role. We decided it was time for a reset. We identified "the number" that would reflect her worth and created several avenues to achieve it (through base pay, bonus, stock options, and perks). In anticipation of the meeting with Josh, the tough head of human resources, Katie had prepared salient examples of her recent successes and vibrant ways to communicate her vision for the future.

Her stomach was in knots entering his office. Josh greeted her warmly, complimented Katie on her accomplishments, and told her how much she was valued. She relaxed. He shared the expectation that she would have even more authority in the coming year, and she beamed. Her initial anxiety dissipated. She was having fun! Josh then told Katie that she would be paid 2 percent more than last year, and she hardly heard it. She felt a burning sensation rush through her body, and all she wanted to do was flee. She wanted immediate relief. The much needed (and practiced) determination had melted while she was basking in Josh's praise.

Preferring to feel *good* with her colleague, Katie had been quick to relinquish her fight in exchange for the warm glow. When Katie called me that evening, she was frantic, frustrated, and disappointed. We reviewed "the seduction" and revived memories of times when she felt most confident charging through opponents. We invoked the muscle memory of being an athlete when no amount of hand-waving, screaming, or fancy footwork stood in the way of a goal. Katie asked Josh for another meeting. This time she was prepared to sit with the tension and to forcefully insist on a new salary. It worked. She didn't get all that she wanted, but it came close. We were convinced that Josh could literally feel the change in her, and Katie was going to enjoy the game to get to her desired number.

We Both Win

Franco brought out the best in people, which was a huge asset as a professional photographer. He recently set up his own shop, having apprenticed with some of the top names in the field. We worked together on articulating his brand. We created brochures that listed his services and the associated prices. When potential customers called, Franco didn't give in to the temptation to quickly make a deal. The materials gave Franco the confidence to say, "These are our policies." It made it more official and less personal. When customers challenged fees, Franco was defending the company brand.

This helped at the contracting phase. It was harder to set limits once clients received the footage from their shoots and pushed for endless retouches. Franco wanted to build his reputation and often acquiesced. As a result, he was spending endless uncompensated hours in the studio. We came up with a plan. Franco would advocate for additional fees from the outset, but when that wasn't possible, he would ask for nonmonetary payment, such as photo credits and invitations to corporate-sponsored events where he came as a guest and snapped shots to post on his own social media platforms. Generating in advance a list of alternative ways for his clients to meet *his* needs reduced Franco's resentment and enabled a mutually beneficial partnership.

37

NAME THE ELEPHANT

It's Taking Up Way Too Much Room

When there's an elephant in the room, introduce him.
—RANDOLPH PAUSCH

As a consultant, I often go on safari. No jeeps or rangers needed. I'm not on a game reserve. I'm in your office, looking for a supersized mammal. "An elephant in the room" is the issue with no name. It's a term used to describe a situation, question, problem, or controversial issue that most, or all, of the people involved know about but don't discuss for fear of the potential consequences. They prefer to ignore it, hoping it will vanish. When the elephant's presence is felt but everyone is denying its existence, there's no way to resolve it. So, you learn to live with it, often with deleterious consequences.

There are plenty of high-profile, dramatic examples of the elephant in the room derailing careers and companies—Enron, the Space Shuttle disasters, Lance Armstrong, and Bernie Madoff, among others. Something didn't add up, and subsequent investigations showed that those who initially questioned what was happening (i.e., had seen the elephant in the room) were ignored.

Elephants stomp on quality dialogue; they inhibit effective decision-making. It takes courage and strong leadership to name objectionable behaviors and make sure that the tough (unspoken) issues (the elephant in the room) are surfaced and dealt with. While we can't prevent elephants from entering the corporate space, the goal is to foster a culture and create the mechanisms that quickly show the big-eared animal the door.

If this large organizational threat is hiding in plain sight, how do you know it's there? Conversations are happening in the wrong places. You call a meeting to resolve a significant matter and are met with silence. You've invited input, but nobody volunteers a useful response. Your colleagues aren't really quiet; they're just talking in unofficial gatherings that feel safer. Gossip going on in the corners? Look for the elephant. Then transform the covert conversations happening in the hall into safe, overt/explicit discussions between the relevant parties.

THIS IS FOR YOU IF

- Unaddressed issues are stunting the team's full potential.

- Change is afoot, but information is lacking. Gossip is on the rise.

- You can't quite put your finger on it, but something is wrong.

- Conversations are going in circles. People nod their heads in meetings, yet fail to act.

TAKE ACTION

▸ Be brave. Ask, "Why aren't we discussing X?" Ideally, your inquiry will prompt a more open discussion. Alternatively, putting the issue into words might stimulate an investigation outside of the immediate setting, with (*ideally*) a report at a later date.

▸ Gain as much knowledge as you can about the elephant. Don't make assumptions. If you are the manager, make it safe for your colleagues to share their impressions. Interview people individually and confidentially. Consider bringing in an outside consultant to have the conversations and present the findings back in a nonemotional way that doesn't embarrass anyone.

▸ Prepare for the unleashing of strong emotion. If the elephant wasn't such an evocative topic, it wouldn't be hiding. Some people may be hurt as the discussion unfolds. Encourage everyone to learn and support, rather than jump to judgments. The elephant didn't come out of nowhere. Inquire, "What do we think may really be going on?"

▸ If you're addressing an issue that's been simmering for a while, think about the best moment to tackle the situation. Look for a time when those involved are likely to be less frazzled, when distraction will be at a minimum, and no one outside the situation is likely to be around.

▶ Be careful that the elephant isn't you! Don't assume you can continually sneak out of work even if it's for necessary medical care or other good causes. Asking coworkers to pretend you haven't gone missing creates undue stress on everyone. Remember: you are not invisible.

▶ Make it about the issue, not the person. Issues don't have emotions, but people do. Many times, undiscussable topics are tied to individuals who are sitting right there when the delicate conversation begins. The goal is not to embarrass or humiliate.

▶ Once the issue is aired, agree on how to communicate the findings more broadly (if appropriate) and be sure to include a statement of next steps. Identifying a plan of action restores trust and can be a source of pride for the individuals who helped craft the solution.

KEEP IN MIND

• If your boss is the one with the big ears and tusks, you may want to seek guidance from your HR department before confronting the issue.

• If you find yourself around the watercooler with colleagues, delighting in scandalous office drama, do a fact-check. The big secret may be a big nothing.

CASE STUDIES

Know When You Are the Elephant

I interviewed 15 executives of a professional services firm in advance of their management offsite. The only thing they all agreed on was that trust among them was at an all-time low. Some were calling for a change in leadership, going so far as to nominate themselves. The sitting CEO was a charismatic, high-energy leader who was pushing the group to pursue new strategic alliances with boutique providers. He set ambitious financial targets. He also invested his personal money in the firm's clients' businesses. Several members of the leadership team questioned whether this was a conflict of interest.

Several actually said, "There is an elephant in the room." This was particularly amusing to me because (1) I was in the middle of writing this chapter and (2) English wasn't their first language (suggesting the great universality of this concept). I asked them to name the elephant. They all said the CEO's name, but didn't agree on what exactly the problem was. So . . . I decided to introduce the elephant at the start of their meeting. I shared my interview data, noted the distress, and then passed the microphone to the CEO who addressed each of their concerns. A slide featuring an elephant was on the screen behind him as he opened the floor to questions. We kept on talking until everyone had aired their grievances and agreed on a shared agenda for the weekend. The elephant was shown the door, but the CEO stayed—and received renewed public support for his leadership.

Think Inside the Box

Kicking the elephant out is more challenging when the hot gossip requiring cold hard discussion is about your boss. Twenty-five technologists were gathered for an offsite at which their team leader critiqued them for not thinking strategically. The company's infrastructure was at risk of becoming outmoded. Work groups were formed to review project management, skill improvement, and so on, and yet the mood was lackluster.

I decided to ask the team to submit questions anonymously and then read the queries out loud to the room, which included senior managers. The elephant jumped out of the box. The messages were consistent. The team leader and his boss were eager to please their internal clients and seldom said no to a request. As a result, the tech team was constantly responding to immediate demands with little time to be strategic. In addition, the senior leaders were inconsistent in their stated priorities. The company had recently downsized, and rumors of further reductions were rampant. The team didn't dare raise these concerns directly with their bosses for fear their heads would roll.

While direct conversation is a preferred method of communication, sometimes protecting the source allows for the discussion to begin. Once the elephant was named the meeting took on a new life. The focus shifted to establishing processes for setting and communicating clear priorities and strategies for saying no (or not now) to unscheduled demands.

38

BE A SIMPLIFIER, NOT A COMPLICATOR

Make Precision Execution Seem Easy

Complexity is your enemy. Any fool can make something complicated. It is hard to make something simple.
—Richard Branson

In our lavishly linked world, with immediate access to an array of information and opinions, it's tempting to overengineer processes, overperform, or overexplain. Do you provide superfluous jargon-laden details to convince others of your unique qualifications to deal with incredibly complex situations? Rather than coming across as supersmart, you may be experienced as alienating and exhausting. As Leonardo da Vinci said, "Simplicity is the ultimate sophistication."

Complicators reveal their insecurity by amplifying the difficulty of a situation. They are advertising, "I don't trust you to value me unless I make what I do seem hard." They generate confusion and a sense of inadequacy in their coworkers. Complicators use buzzwords and policy mumbo-jumbo and tend to be rigid in their thinking as well as risk averse. Complicators create distance between colleagues rather than connecting first.

Simplifiers take intricate situations and provide clear options for action. They are calming and clarifying, and provide focus. When working with simplifiers, people often feel energized, confident, and optimistic. You can identify who's who in a matter of seconds. Complicators take the problem side of the equation. They love drama, revel in petty details, and are disappointed or slightly annoyed when someone offers a solution. Simplifiers are the opposite. They prioritize action. They size up situations quickly, study circumstances carefully, and prefer to spend their resources on solutions. Simply put, one loves predicaments; the other loves answers.

Translating complex ideas into language that enables your audience to make informed decisions is an art. And it takes time.

THIS IS FOR YOU IF

- Your memos have so many acronyms, they look like eye exam charts filled with random letters.

- Colleagues ask you to slow down, repeat what you said, and then follow up the next day, asking for clarification.

- Coworkers leave lengthy instructions to help you cope when they are out on holiday, and you can't decide if they are invaluable or infuriating.

- Misunderstandings happen because complicated terms are used that not everyone understands.

TAKE ACTION

If You Are Working with a Complicator

▶ Don't be embarrassed. Ask for a three-line summary of the problem and a one-line solution before going into the details. If you are leading a team, encourage all members who write memos to begin with an executive summary. Keep the body of the report to as few pages as possible and put footnotes at the end. This provides a rapid understanding of the issues along with a depth of information for those who want more.

▶ Suggest that all emails be only one phone screen in length. Otherwise, pick up the phone.

If You Want to Be a Simplifier

▶ Set a clear intention. Before you set out to do something, you should be 100 percent certain about exactly what it is you want to do. Ask questions of others at the onset to avoid confusing your coworkers later.

▶ Don't overcomplicate the problem you are about to solve.

▶ Kill your darlings. It's terrific advice from the great writer William Faulkner. If you're working on something, and you write a fantastic sentence or create the perfect chart but it doesn't work with the rest of the project, get rid of it. Be ruthless.

▶ Review your material for: Must Have, Should Have, Good to Have. If it's a must-have item, keep it. Trim the should have, and consider deleting the good to have (as the latter will likely be less important).

▶ Give yourself enough time—to save your audience their time.

▶ Diversity at work comes in all forms, including how people process information. Find the relevant message for your audience, and be prepared to present it pictorially, numerically, and in direct speech. Try using analogies to build bridges between familiar and new territory.

▶ Avoid elaborate language. No jargon! If you can't avoid them, define abbreviations, acronyms (the NATO agreement on NASA rockets), and initialisms (the FBI called the CIA to find out who went MIA).

KEEP IN MIND

• Simple solutions are not simplistic; they're just easy to understand and execute.

• Your value is affirmed when you make it easy for colleagues to digest information.

CASE STUDIES

Don't Tax My Brain

Russell Makowsky was the co-head of the Goldman Sachs tax department for several years. A multivolume set of three-ring binders with the Internal Revenue Code, the Treasury regulations, and the latest tax rulings burst from the shelves in his office. Few people outside his group were tempted to dive in, yet the tax law had a massive impact on business decisions. I asked him how he served up a regulatory meal. His advice? "You have to live in the complexity of the tax law you practice, but speak in the simplicity of your audience's ability to understand." Give me an example, I asked. Here's one: Under the tax law ending in 2017, there were seven tax brackets, ranging from 10 percent to 39.6 percent, with the top bracket applying to incomes over $418,400 for single people and over $470,700 for married people filing jointly. Under the new tax law for 2018, there are still seven brackets, but the top rate is now 37 percent and applies to incomes over $500,000 for single people and over $600,000 for married people filing jointly. Or, put simply, the new tax law reduces income tax rates by about three percent for most people.

Tell Me How I Will Benefit

The management committee of an investment bank decided not to support an investment of millions for an upgraded trading platform. Gary, the director of the technology division, had gone into minute detail about the problems with the current system. He had data on processing speed, calls to the help desk, and amount of overtime for his team. The top decision-makers weren't moved.

I was hired to help Gary. We took a different approach. He altered his pitch to start with the solution and how it would impact the business. Gary said, "If you invest X dollars in a new platform, your investment will be returned in a year as deals will be processed Y times faster, yielding Z more profit." Those interested in the details could follow up after the meeting or read the footnotes. Gary got the funds he needed.

PART VI

FIGHT
FEAR

Fear. It's pervasive. I've seen you sweat and heard you cry. The organization is under pressure to innovate, and you dread being left behind. Downsizing? You might lose your job. Maybe there will be a merger or a new acquisition. The robots are coming. The company's computing platforms aren't competitive enough. You aren't keeping up with the systems.

In the face of uncertainty, we are more likely to turn inward, defaulting to fear and restricting our field of vision at the very moment when what is most needed is an eager embrace of other perspectives and a willingness to experiment with new ideas.

You can't know what you don't know if you keep on talking to the same people. It's lonely at the top. And at the bottom. And in the middle. Survival in volatile, ambiguous environments requires agility and wisdom. Here's the moment to secure a place for new voices (from inside and outside of your organization) and create true partnerships through shared experience. No matter where you sit at the office, work is more fun when you are not afraid.

Make the first move. Step outside your comfort zone, invite others in, and build bridges. Find common ground and relax into conversation by connecting first as individuals not as representatives of a cause or employees of a company. Don't underestimate the importance of a little small talk and certainly attend to the details that promote a fruitful exchange or you risk wasting everyone's time at an awkward gathering. Being an artful host is a form of diplomacy, don't leave things to chance.

This Part Is for You If

- You are ready to be courageously curious.

- You're told to be the market disrupter. Easy for the board, boss, or analyst to say. But how? The only thing disrupted is your sleep.

- You are out of ideas.

- It's not just the engineers, all of your colleagues seem to be speaking in code. What *are* they talking about?! There are so many acronyms and devices and apps.

- "They" are fast, but you are s-l-o-w.

- You don't know what you don't know, but you do know that you don't know the answers—and the questions are getting harder and your heart is pounding faster and you are in the spotlight. You can't hide. And you can't breathe.

- The invitations were accepted. The money to bring everyone together was invested. There are diverse voices in the room, but the group is afraid to talk. No one's making eye contact. It's too quiet. It's awkward and you're embarrassed (publicly).

- The competition is coming! The competition is here! And they don't look (or think) like you.

- This connected, small world sounds good in theory, but you feel suffocated, overly monitored, and exposed.

39

STEP OUTSIDE YOUR COMFORT ZONE

Being a Little Terrified Is Good for You

Fear is excitement in need of an attitude adjustment.
—A FORTUNE COOKIE

When my son was five, I strapped him to my waist and ran down the beach in Bali until a parasail lifted us into the sky. We were flying. It was exhilarating. The new vantage point was fabulous. I've pushed myself to ski off mountains (with a parachute), raft class five rapids, and rappel off a 65-story building. The adrenaline rush relaxes me. I focus only on the present. At work as in sport, I have plunged myself into potentially anxious (periodically mildly dangerous) situations. It keeps me alert and, hopefully, a touch more interesting and informed. I believe being a little terrified is good for you.

Resting in a place where stress is minimal, where you know what's coming next and can plan accordingly, may at first seem like a good plan, but the negative impacts are insidious. You didn't sign up for the coding course when it was offered by the company because no one you knew was taking the class; you opted out of the entrepreneurs support group because you prefer playing video games with your brothers online; and you didn't take the time to get to know the new hires who have now been promoted over you. You've stagnated while everyone is moving on. In an increasingly ambiguous and accelerated world, those who jump into the unknown, experiment, embarrass themselves, bruise their egos, and start again, position themselves for some of the biggest rewards. Being slightly on edge kicks your system into gear.

Have you ever noticed that you perform better when you are just a little bit nervous? Did you ever do better at an athletic event after making eye contact with your biggest opponent? Did you ever score higher on an exam when you were somewhat pressured about your result? In 1908, psychologists Robert M. Yerkes and John D. Dodson explained that maximal performance occurs when our stress levels are slightly higher than normal. This is called *optimal stress*, and it's just outside our comfort zone.

The Yerkes-Dodson Law

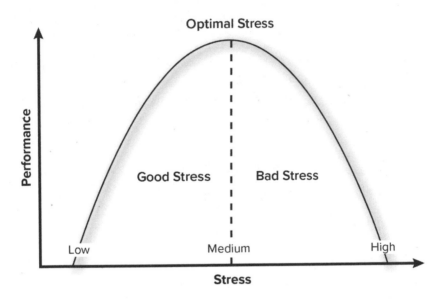

Being uncomfortable can push us to achieve goals we never thought we could.

THIS IS FOR YOU IF

- You eat the same lunch every day (often with the same group of friends).

- Mess makes you anxious.

- You like things perfect and in their place.

- You expect to be flawless, always.

TAKE ACTION

▶ Try saying yes to three things you usually say no to, and then say no to three things you usually say yes to.

▶ Take small steps, like driving a different route to work or turning your desk at an alternate angle. Pick up a magazine devoted to an interest that you never explored. Sit in a new place. Try a day offline.

▶ Create a personal mission statement about why you're stepping out of your comfort zone, such as "to build courage" or "to become more creative." Start a list on your phone, in a notebook, or on your office wall of ways you want to challenge yourself. Try putting a date beside each goal. If you have posted your list in your office, invite others to make suggestions or to join you.

▶ Make a point of visiting the communities your organization is serving. Try holding company meetings in venues that are in the center of towns you don't know (and might be a little uncomfortable entering), rather than in the usual locations.

KEEP IN MIND

• We don't need to stretch ourselves *all* the time.

• Don't judge yourself for being apprehensive.

CASE STUDY

Get Your Shoes Dirty

"We will be charging Melanie for all the psychotherapy needed to recover," exclaimed the pension fund professionals who joined me on a community visit to the South African township of Alexandra. Until that moment, the group assessed the potential of private equity investments based on spreadsheets and PowerPoints. Previous trips to Johannesburg had kept them sequestered in air-conditioned conference rooms. We were about to put a face on the emerging market.

"What do we say?" they inquired, as we entered the neighborhood, which was packed with people socializing and conducting commerce on the narrow, poorly maintained streets. We learned about the residents' lives, buying habits, and how they sourced water and electricity. We started with hello, knelt beside the kids, and with their permission, snapped digital photos and showed them their images. We took selfies together because even though they didn't have running water, most of them had a phone. We showed pictures of our families and exchanged stories of how we make choices. And then we compared how we use our devices, how we charge them, pay for them, and protect them.

We had frank discussions with local women about safety when it was observed that I had unconsciously turned my engagement ring around, so the stone wouldn't show. They speculated as to the dangers I might experience after dark. We learned about the many public services that never reached this community. On the way back to the hotel my travel companions were proud of themselves for pushing past their trepidation, enduring a few stares, and most important, getting a glimpse into someone else's life. They also realized how oversimplified their previous financial analyses had been. They had relied on secondary (and tertiary) sources to make impactful decisions devoid of the context. The chance to connect personally to the community members influenced not only the amount they were willing to invest in infrastructure building but the questions they would ask to ensure that their funds reached the intended targets.

40

INVITE OTHERS IN

Take the First Step

*Bonds of belonging redeem us from our solitude, helping us
to construct together a gracious and generous social order.*
—Jonathan Sacks, former Chief Rabbi of the
United Hebrew Congregations of the Commonwealth

Regulators. Protestors. Competitors. The new recruits. The old regime. There's the coworker who looks like me but thinks *so* differently, the guy with the faltering English, and the man who's now self-identifying as a woman. I'm sure I have something to learn from them. Or maybe they only want what they can get from me. I don't want to get to know them. I'm busy. It's awkward. There's pressure to comply, respond, automate, diversify, collaborate. *Aghhh!*

Our neurophysiological alarm system is activated. Our body responds as if we are under physical attack. We lock the doors and surround ourselves with the ever-shrinking cadre of associates we trust. Familiar instinct. Wrong response. Rather than retreat, try facing fear. Literally put a face on it. Invite the unknown in. You can't connect if you don't ever meet.

We live in a world where I win/you lose is old news. Our success and survival are interdependent.

WHEN THE UNKNOWN IS OUTSIDE

Create forums for conversation with experts external to your organization. For example, don't demure from the robot. Ask for a demonstration of its capabilities from the company that you think is looking to put you out of business. Rather than disdain the green movement brewing on your block, ask the conservationists to have lunch with your team next Tuesday.

Educate regulators about your industry concerns and learn from their experience analyzing and monitoring behavior in your market. Establish your integrity among peer institutions by organizing the panel that brings the lawmakers into your corporate homes.

Communicate confidence by inviting your competitors to explore potential partnerships. Dare to have brainstorming sessions with rivals that solve for some of the limitations you mutually experience and then divvy up ways to own and execute innovative answers (by leveraging your respective strengths).

Invite community members in to meet your staff, tour your facilities, learn about potential employment, and hear about how you source locally (and if you don't, why not and how they can help).

WHEN THE UNKNOWN IS INSIDE

Opening doors and our minds to be more inclusive is the start, but it's not enough. To fully engage the talents of diverse minds (and hearts), we need to create a sense of belonging and affirmatively invite individuals into our discussions, whether they're more junior, more senior, or from other departments. Make it easy for someone lingering on the margins to join the conversation. Avoid inside jokes, translate jargon, and don't be afraid to draw a road map illustrating how decisions have historically been made.

Bain & Company reported that more women than men aspire to top management in the first two years of their careers. However, over time, women's aspiration levels drop more than 60 percent, while men's stay the same. Their analysis shows that this is not related to marital and parental status. Women stopped vying for leadership because they didn't feel like they belonged. They didn't feel supported by supervisors (e.g., male executives were hesitant to have 1:1 meetings with junior women), and they didn't see other females in the C-suite.

New recruits and staff from diverse backgrounds, even if apparently extroverted and motivated, will air potential conflict, produce higher quality work, and stick around when they can relax in a secure environment. When the belonging quotient is high, everyone wins (that includes you).

THIS IS FOR YOU IF

- Your door is open, but nobody is coming in.

- You're not kidding yourself. The "open culture" poster in the elevator isn't necessarily enough to give staff the courage to pursue conversations with those in power.

- There are lots of ideas out there, and you want to learn.

- In the face of uncertainty, you are more likely to turn inward.

TAKE ACTION

▶ Create a "space," an emotional arena, for conversation. Don't just call the meeting to order. If the group size allows it, welcome each individual personally and say why you're looking forward to their contributions. Describe why the assembled were invited. Be sure everyone has had a chance to speak (even a sentence) before you jump into a discussion.

▶ Have seats for everyone. Invite the person who looks (or acts) the most differently to sit near you. If you have invited professionals from outside your company, pay more attention to them than the colleague you rode with on the bus to work. Before the session begins, make some quick informal introductions between newcomers and people you know, so they have a friendly face to connect to once the proceedings begin. After the meeting ends, be sure to offer your appreciation for any new entrant's comments and show interest in that person's assessment of the interactions. Wait long enough for a full answer as it sometimes takes time to articulate a response (especially if someone is new to a group and not accustomed to being asked).

▶ The attendees at your presentation can be transformed from passive listeners to sources of energy and insight if you begin by finding out about your audience, who's in the room, and why. Opening the floor immediately to the audience reduces the "you vs. them" phenomenon that happens when one person is at the podium. Set the stage for a shared discussion.

▶ Ask your colleagues at the end of a meeting, "Who could we have included from inside or outside our company who would have increased the quality of our discussion?" If you don't know the person referenced, ask for some background and possibly an introduction. Ask if that connection can be made by a specific date, put it in your calendar, and assign yourself the task of reaching out.

▶ Leave a handwritten welcome note for the new hire. Be playful in making yourself available to questions: consider leaving three little rocks on your new colleague's desk and say each of these can be traded in for answers to even the silliest inquiry.

▶ Make an in-person request that someone "come on in." Announcing your willingness to entertain impromptu visitors may not be enough for someone to cross the threshold into your office—especially if you are more senior. Get up from your desk and ask the young, alternative-thinking employee if they would like to spend a few minutes with you. Your conversation could be about work or just say, "I wanted to get to know you a little bit more. Tell me what you are reading or who you are following online." Are you sitting in an office now? Open your door and scan the cubicles. Can you recall one unique fact about each of the people working there? If you don't even know their names, better get into gear. Try offering invites to a rotating group of employees, for casual conversation each Thursday at 4 p.m. (or whatever regular time works for you).

▶ Watch out for "here vs. there" dynamics. Data suggests that nearly 40 percent of the workforce will soon be independent—freelance, contractor, or temporary employees. Keep a list of contractor workers and invite them to your strategy sessions. Their experience working with your company, as well as other similar organizations, provides a valuable perspective.

▶ A competitive athlete told me he could anticipate his rival's behavior better than he could predict his girlfriend's preferences. If your mental real estate is occupied with strategies to conquer, defeat, or defend against a person or organization, it's a good cue to pick up the phone and make a date to spend time together. That wasn't a typo. I meant "use the phone." It's so powerful when the email barrier is broken.

▶ Recently merged with or acquired by another institution? Don't wait for the boss to sponsor the get-to-know-you with the parallel group that now shares your company logo. Ask if you can hold an informal coffee for the related groups (and invite the managers to join).

▶ Create emotional connections. Strengthen a sense of belonging by promoting shared memorable experiences. At lunch today, see if someone you don't know wants to join you. Personalize interactions, look for ways to share relevant and timely information.

▶ Pitch a big tent. Individuals coming together to address what they care about, in collaboration with other like-minded people, produces extraordinary results. What's the problem? Who can you invite? Don't be afraid to hold a forum for potential solutions.

KEEP IN MIND

• Note who is included (or not) in meetings and on distribution lists. If you took the time to invite someone into the discussion, be clear about the boundaries/expectations for continuing input. When eliminating someone from communication they previously were a part of, explain why.

• Don't assume that conversation will flow just because you invited the "right" people to the meeting, dinner, or reception. Make sure to follow up.

All He Wanted Was to Belong

Hiring Zhang Wei, a Chinese national, to raise capital for an Australian hedge fund was a coup. Zhang Wei was whip smart and multilingual, and his family had strong relationships with mainland billionaires. His arrival was a relief to the head of human resources who worried about the homogeneity of the senior leadership team. Zhang Wei did not disappoint. He got investors to commit millions of dollars to the fund. He was rewarded and recognized for hitting his financial targets. For Zhang Wei that wasn't enough. He couldn't rest until he was seen as "a fellow warrior, contributing to the enterprise's success." He wanted to be invited into management meetings, to opine on the quality and focus of investments. Without the capital he raised, there would be no future. He didn't want to simply be a salesman. He frequently traveled with the founders, who shared their professional fears and vulnerabilities. Why couldn't they make Zhang Wei's role as advisor (not just fundraiser) official?

He asked twice for a seat at the table. Nothing changed. Was it his nationality? His personality? His pay continued to rise, but without an invitation in, Zhang Wei opted to leave. The partners were dismayed; they thought the bonuses and accolades were enough. What they missed was how much Zhang Wei wanted to belong, to be validated as part of the management team in the truest, most trusted, collaborative sense. As a parting "gift," Zhang Wei made clear that his reasons for finding a new job were not monetary. Although the founders expressed remorse at his departure, Zhang Wei believes that his greatest impact will be in his new role, where building an inclusive culture is at the core of the business model.

Regenerative Ecosystems

The ride to Wadi Attir straddles the dividing line between Israel and the West Bank. It's hot, dusty, and monochromatic. Arriving at the visitor center is akin to entering an oasis—of education and cooperation. Dr. Michael Ben-Eli, an ambitious architect who wanted to "redesign the world," and Muhammed Alnabari, the mayor of Hura with a PhD in chemistry, created a mission-driven sustainable farming model in the Negev desert to showcase how Bedouin traditional values combined with cutting-edge technologies can drive economic development locally, as well as in other arid areas.

In a region laced with conflict, everyone is welcome here. Scientists and students come from all backgrounds. Bedouin sheepherders, Israeli academics, and Arab entrepreneurs collaborate on initiatives for eco-tourism, waste reduction, growth of medicinal plants, dairy production, and so on. The novelty of such a cooperative project has brought researchers and funding from around the world and attention, understanding, and income to the surrounding Bedouin community. Defining a neutral space and actively recruiting and inviting neighbors has helped the desert (and its tribal communities) bloom.

41

BE A GRACIOUS HOST

Tackling the Hard Stuff Is Easier
When Everyone Is Comfortable

I can hear you thinking, *What's a chapter on hosting doing in a part called Fight Fear?* Going to each other's offices takes effort. We do it because there's an important topic to cover, a relationship to form, or a conflict to clear. Job candidates are hired and potential partnerships are often solidified once someone has been to your space. Knowing how to welcome someone is essential to establishing a quality connection. Whether your guest is eager to make a good impression or gearing up to argue their case, help attenuate anxiety and set the conditions for a successful exchange by doing away with distractions and unnecessary power plays.

It doesn't take money to be a gracious host to office visitors, but it does take awareness and a touch of class. I have seen companies spend fortunes on décor and artwork, yet forget the little behaviors that convey respect (e.g., executives who entertain lavishly in their homes don't offer water to external colleagues arriving for a meeting)—and it matters. The mood is set and an organization's personality is communicated by attention to details that contribute to your guest's basic well-being. Especially in the age of remote working and long-distance collaborations, the (often rare) moments for social interactions leave a lasting impression. If you are taking the time out of your day to welcome visitors, make it worthwhile not only by what you do but how you do it.

I was once hired to negotiate peace between warring departments at a marketing agency. Same company, two division heads, two wildly different leadership styles. My first step was to collect data from key staff members in preparation for a joint discussion. On day one, having passed security, I let myself into a conference room where I stayed for seven straight hours interviewing team members. Good thing I packed my water bottle and protein bars. It was a disembodied experience. I was provided no orientation to my surroundings, no codes to enter the toilets, no point person to answer any questions.

In contrast, the next day, when I arrived, the other division head met me (it took five minutes) and introduced me to his assistant who would be on call to help during my stay. The secretary had prepared a printout of my schedule and asked what I'd like for lunch. Twice during the day, she popped in to see if I needed anything. She delivered snacks and drinks between meetings. I received a personal escort to the front door when my eight hours of back-to-back meetings ended. The care was beyond my expectations. Did the difference in hosting skills influence how I analyzed the data obtained during my two days on site? No. But I wasn't surprised when my interviews revealed rampant complaints about the first leader's approach to management—competitive, acting from scarcity, and a disregard for fellow team members.

THIS IS FOR YOU IF

- You want people to feel welcome from the moment they enter your office.

- You've had the experience of needing a toilet, wanting to connect to Wi-Fi, and being desperately thirsty (and nobody seemed to notice) when you arrived for a meeting.

- Why behave differently at work than at home? A guest is a guest and should be treated with respect. You want to make a visitor's trip to your office a worthwhile experience.

TAKE ACTION

- Upon arrival, offer visitors a glass of water, directions to the restroom, and a place to hang their coat. Provide the Wi-Fi code where appropriate.

- Don't make your guests wait. Be ready to receive your guests on time. Clear your desk. Don't act surprised when attendees walk in.

- If your guest arrives with several subordinates, don't ignore them. Learn their names and titles; make sure they are equally comfortable. I shouldn't have to spell this out, but there are executives who pretend "unimportant" people aren't there.

▶ Stand up to greet your visitor. Ask your guest to sit down; gesture if there are choices. Try to avoid seats that position one person higher up or force them to sink down into a couch.

▶ Minimize your computer screen. Avoid flashy screensavers. Turn off your cell phone or at least turn off the notifications. Allow voicemail to pick up calls on the office phone.

▶ Have extra pens and note paper handy. Providing paper makes it easier to keep everyone's attention away from screens, and it's often helpful to draw a quick diagram to illustrate a point.

▶ If the topic of conversation is confidential, close the door. If you work in a cubicle, take the meeting in a conference room.

▶ If it looks like the session will require extra time to finish, pause 10 minutes before the scheduled end and ask if it's OK to run over. If not, plan a time to pick the conversation back up. Offer a break if a meeting is running long.

▶ If there are unscheduled gaps between meetings, show your visitor how to leave and reenter the building, where to charge electronics, and where to find available workspace so that they can make good use of the free time.

▶ Take a minute while walking the hall with your guest to make introductions to staff. Give your visitor a second to take in the view if you are lucky enough to have one (don't pretend it's "ordinary" to be on a high floor with commanding vistas of the city, wharf, or rolling fields).

KEEP IN MIND

• Just as it's important to welcome people in, we need to let them leave with grace. When hosting business colleagues in China, I have learned the importance of the closing toast, the thank you that signals you are welcome (and have permission) to leave. The guests, previously in rapt attention over the meal, suddenly clear out. After all, traffic in the city is horrid, and it's been a long night.

• Being a good host does not mean showing off.

CASE STUDIES

Be an Inclusive Host

The setting was sublime, the silent auction had raised thousands, the wine was flowing, potential donors were dressed in black tie, and the evening presentation was about to begin. Yet the honorees—the schoolteachers working in disadvantaged communities whose hard work set a record for high school graduation rates—were all standing in the hall waiting to be called on stage. And they waited. The event planners hadn't thought about the teachers' dinner, so hadn't supplied meals or drinks. The organizers had focused on the timing of the educators' speeches and ensuring they knew where to stand for pictures. Rejoicing shifted to reproach. The divide between "we" and "they" was on embarrassing display. "We" was hosting an event for people with money. "They" were there as the entertainment, the props to make the case. The teachers' pride morphed to anger. How could they get things back on track? The school's mission was to reach across divides, and the school administrators seized on this teachable moment.

The teachers invited the donors to visit the school, to share their routine—their food, their lesson plans, their joys and frustrations. The educators anticipated the potential discomfort that their affluent visitors might experience, and bookended the visit with facilitated reflections on class and opportunity. The teachers were *inclusionary hosts* and role models of making others welcome in their world.

It's Not About Financial Wealth

A group of us were meeting with Brazilian community organizers to discuss the impact of nearby business development. The *favela* (slum) overlooking Porto Digital, the high-tech hub in Recife driving disruptive innovation and entrepreneurship, didn't have running water. Hardworking women lugged barrels of liquid from the pump to their modest (yet spotless) homes. When we arrived, they put the barrels upright, dusted them off, and presented us all with an impromptu seating area and glasses of refreshment from the casks they had literally transported with their bare hands. Our local hosts conveyed a conviction and authority over our well-being that went way beyond words.

42

BE A PERSON FIRST!

Help Strangers Feel Less Strange

You don't have to be brilliant, just nice.
—BERNARDO CARDUCCI, PhD,
former director of the Shyness Research Institute

When it comes to small talk, your words may be forgotten, but how you make people feel will be remembered. Light chatter may seem trite, but it's the small talk that leads to the *big talk*. Studies show that tossing in a bit of interpersonal prattle builds bonds at the office, engenders a feeling of well-being, and creates a welcome break. The goal is not to become best friends; it's simply the enjoyment of sharing a topic of mutual interest—for a few minutes. There are painfully shy people who admit to hiding in restrooms or faking phone calls to dodge conversation, but don't let them stop you from offering up a moment of human connection.

According to an Ernst and Young study, the workplace beats neighborhoods and places of worship as sources of community. Being asked about one's personal and professional lives is more significant in fostering belonging than public recognition or invitations to office events. Do not underestimate the power of small talk.

Chinwag (a UK campaign to combat loneliness) reported that 40 percent of British workers feel isolated at work. If someone has a quick chat with them, 61 percent express positive feelings, but . . . they won't initiate conversation if they don't know their colleagues well enough. Taking the first step is hard—and appreciated.

Management by walking around (or MBWA), is the practice of wandering in an unstructured manner through the workplace to engage in unscripted, unplanned conversations. Promoted by Thomas Peters and Robert Waterman in 1982, the timeliness of this technique is ever more apparent as coworkers are communicating and being managed electronically, even when they work in the same building. Rather than being distracting, the judicious unannounced visit builds rapport and can facilitate the exchange of productive ideas.

THIS IS FOR YOU IF

- You're goal-driven, but smart enough to know you can't always just jump in and run to the target.

- It can feel lonely at times—time to connect with humans.

- Three minutes doesn't seem like that much of an investment to make things run more smoothly around here.

TAKE ACTION

▶ My Israeli colleagues assure me that a head nod is all that is needed (grunt, optional) to acknowledge one's colleagues when passing by. My Kenyan collaborators advise just the opposite in their hometowns. When passing someone you know, you must stop and inquire about the family, the sick animals, and what they had for dinner. What's a work group of mixed backgrounds to do? Assuming you can "read" if someone isn't interested and given that most people are happy if someone else instigates it, figure two minutes of connection is welcome until proven otherwise.

▶ Be pro-social in your chatter. Spread positive news about others.

▶ Research areas of potential mutual interest before you meet someone for the first time. You may uncover a shared hobby or cause. Come prepared to ask about it. Take a minute before diving into a business discussion to find that common bond.

▶ Feeling shy yourself? Don't know what to say? Ask questions! Most people like to talk about themselves. Check in on the kids, their weekend plans, or the pets. Look for clues. What pictures or trinkets adorn your colleagues' desks or cubicles? If all else fails, comment on the weather or the setting (it's something you both share).

► Offer up a compliment, about anything.

► Consider building in quick small talk rituals for your team. This is especially important when working with remote teams who only hear others' voices periodically. Start your meeting with a quick warm-up. Ask what animal reflects each person's mood today, or what piece of news caught their attention. Keep it brief. You want to ease into conversation, not overwhelm it.

► Just introduced? Don't go silent after you shake hands—continue by volunteering something about yourself. It doesn't have to be anything particularly revealing, although it doesn't hurt to have a few interesting personal tidbits to share that are front of mind. For example, do you grow tulips, love Italian grappa, or collect vintage vinyl? You never know, you might be able to work that into a conversation.

► Read up on the news and make a nonpolitical comment on current events. Subscribe to a daily digest that keeps you informed.

KEEP IN MIND

• Some people take time to warm up, while others truly aren't that interested in chatting. When in doubt, ask permission. "May I tell you a quick story?" Use humor. See if you can get a smile out of them. No? Keep walking.

• Making small talk is not an excuse to spread gossip. If you do, you'll be seen as less trustworthy, and your team will become less cooperative and more political.

CASE STUDIES

Make the Investment

The pursuit of business-only conversations (when he needed something) caused difficulty for Irv. His day started before everyone else's because of a sales meeting on another floor. By the time Irv got to his desk, he already felt behind. He rushed passed his staff. The team felt disrespected and complained about their boss. Irv was initially annoyed by the feedback, but was pleasantly surprised by how quickly he could improve his image just by investing a few minutes to say hello, share the highlights of his morning meeting, and ask others about their family, their night out, or their pets.

Helping a Healthcare Team Stay Healthy

The team of government affairs specialists for a major American health insurer gathered in Washington, DC, just before the vote on Obamacare. The company response was going to require an orchestrated effort. A lot was at stake. I was helping facilitate their offsite. This geographically dispersed group worked for a number of subsidiaries, had never met in person, and hardly knew each other. After our meeting ended, they would return to phone and email exchanges. Being together even for a few days laid a good foundation, but how would they keep the sense of community alive? The group decided that going forward, at the start of conference calls, they would simply ask, "What happened on your way to work?" This would take no more than two minutes, but would anchor them in each other's immediate reality. Over the ensuing months, some related having to cross protesters outside their urban offices, while others had to wait as the cows crossed the road in their rural settings. This quick exchange connected the (remote) team and reminded them of how varied their pressures and constituents were.

43

FOCUS ON FACILITATION

Boost the Quality of Conversations by Attending to Details

Often a sign of expertise is noticing what doesn't happen.
—Malcolm Gladwell

I almost titled this chapter "Near Misses." I've attended company retreats where we were nestled in the Swiss mountains, fed fine food, woke to the roosters, and left with a binder of corporate information, little inspiration, and a few fun facts gathered from loose-lipped attendees at the bar. Equally, I have seen underfunded hospital teams travel hours by bus, at great expense, to learn together only to have a few dominant voices overtake the sessions as the other attendees struggled to keep awake. I'd give those events a B–, maybe a C. Big corporations spend countless dollars on summits and large-scale conferences. Small enterprises struggle to find funding for training sessions. Commercial and community organizations gather colleagues for strategy meetings (colleagues travel from around the world or from across the street). In each instance the meetings are meant to educate, stimulate, and, of course, contribute to success. Much effort is exerted getting "the right people" to the "right place" and jamming the agenda with timely topics. The result is that the event is *done to us*, with speakers talking *at us*.

When setting an agenda, out of anxiety, organizers often leave little to chance. They pack the day with speakers, schedule only a few minutes for unstructured discussion, and typically underestimate the time needed to move between sessions or catch up with colleagues during a break. *More is always more* seems to be the policy. The *more* team members (or if you have the funds, the more famous folks) speaking, the *more* the attendees will get out of the session. Push the content in, squeeze the time for questioning out. Time for reflection isn't built into the agenda. The vast amount of knowledge contained in the room isn't released when participants become passive audience members.

In contrast, too much *is* left to chance when it comes to facilitating social interactions. Simply getting everyone into the same room doesn't mean people will speak to each other! Introverts retreat, staff who share the same native tongue seek refuge together after a day of listening in another language, the cliques save seats for each other, and the shy hope to sneak out of the meals unnoticed.

In order to get the most out of the investment of time, money, and human spirit, I suggest *lots* of advance attention to the details. Focus on the facilitation. This doesn't mean having a heavy hand on the day of the event. If you set things up thoughtfully, you can trust that grateful attendees will do their part.

Once the dates are set, if you work in a large company, it's not uncommon for leaders to delegate the planning to support functions that are tasked with executing an event without the authority or knowledge to address the nuances that will make the difference. Management may decide on a theme (e.g., the environment, empowerment, the future of work), which is translated into logos on apparel and welcome banners. What's missing is careful choreography of the entire experience to ensure that strategic, social, and practical goals are met. Whether you gathered 5 or 500 people, take the time to consider: *In what way do we hope to shift mindsets? Who needs to meet each other? How can we make sure that happens? What do we expect participants to do differently on Monday morning, having attended this meeting?*

Think about: *How will this event reflect the values of the organization (e.g., only use recycled materials, employ immigrant chefs, provide fuel-efficient transport)? Who is being offered a platform and whose voice is left out?* Large and small events, meant to create unity, can be undermined when latent biases are revealed through insensitive behavior. This includes whose voice is featured, whose name is continually mispronounced, or who is seated on the margins—or not given a chair in the room at all. When making the effort to bring people together, don't miss the opportunity to create meaningful connections and demonstrate what you (and your organization) value.

THIS IS FOR YOU IF

- You have more windows open on your computer than sight lines into what makes your colleagues interesting.

- You've hit your diversity hiring targets, but the views in your documents reflect the longstanding opinions of the majority.

- "Hidden" biases are on full display, and you are going to do something about it.

- You've asked your colleagues to give up part of their weekend to set a strategic plan and you don't want to blow the chance to energize the group and have some fun together.

TAKE ACTION

▶ Open the proceedings with a thought-provoking question or two that will become the connective tissue for the subsequent discussions. Revisit this question at the end of your meeting. Leave adequate time for all attendees to share their responses. If you have a large number of people, allow participants to speak in groups of two, then four, then at their table, and then appoint a representative from the table to give feedback to the entire room. This can be done in 45 minutes.

▶ Allow participants to learn from each other's expertise. Set a five-slide limit so the speaker can talk with the audience rather than focusing on getting through prepared material. Leave time for questions, and if the room is large, have a microphone for the audience. Have cards available to send anonymous questions to the speaker. Some people get insecure or self-edit, especially in a large group. Even if there is a moderator asking questions of a panel, be sure the audience gets a voice. Too often "we have run out of time for questions" protects speakers from defending their views, which diminishes mutual learning.

▶ Know that everyone speaks longer, and everything takes more time than you may think. Don't fear having some empty space in your agenda.

▶ If you are planning a conference, do your speakers represent old cronies and the usual suspects while omitting women and people from underrepresented communities? Take a risk on someone less known. If you have reservations, ask a less experienced speaker (or one from outside your sector) to practice at one of your smaller team meetings so that you can provide feedback and additional context if necessary.

▶ Members of underrepresented groups are often reluctant to declare themselves "experts" and may self-select out of the proceedings. Whether it's an in-house training session or an industry-wide convention, when you invite women and/or colleagues of color, expand on why you respect their contribution and indicate what you hope to learn from them. Make it easy for them to accept your invitation.

▶ Be aware of subtle biases. If you get a question from the audience that relates to gender, don't just turn to the women in the room or on your panel to answer it. Men can answer, too.

▶ Avoid constructing an all-male or all-white panel and then tacking on a woman or person of color as a moderator.

▶ Be careful not to refer to male experts by their titles, but to women by their first names, especially when they hold the same position. Be consistent: if you use "Doctor" or "Professor" for one person, use it for all doctors and professors.

▶ Who is in the room? Make quick verbal introductions. Is it a big group? Ask a few questions that, with a show of hands, allows people to have a sense of their fellow attendees. If possible, place name cards in front of guests so they can be addressed personally and to help participants put names to faces. This is useful even in a small group if people don't know each other. It's better to have the name cards available and then toss them aside, than be relegated to pointing a finger to encourage someone to respond.

▶ If it's a large gathering, circulate the guest list with contact details at the start of the meeting so people can seek each other out (they may recognize a name but not a face). This also allows for easier follow-up in the future.

▶ Assign seats to relieve social pressure, add an element of surprise, and ensure exposure for people who might not otherwise meet. Company meetings of even six people are enhanced by shaking up who sits with whom.

▶ If your audience is not seated at tables, consider arranging chairs in shapes that are more conducive to conversation, such as a circle or horseshoe.

▶ Don't forget to assign seats at meals. Appoint a table captain to be sure everyone is introduced and to ignite conversation. Try putting some amusing questions on the table as prompts to get the discussion going. Eyes may roll, but secretly even the most outgoing folks are often relieved to have an icebreaker.

KEEP IN MIND

- Provide sufficient notice for social events that may be attached to a conference and indicate if attendance is mandatory. This allows employees to arrange child or elder care.

- Select bonding events that will be enjoyed by staff of all ages and groups of all sizes. Past clients of mine have bristled when paintball was considered an inclusive recreational event (it ruins your hair for the rest of the day). Being carried, touched, or blindfolded doesn't sit well with everyone. Be sensitive.

CASE STUDIES

How to Get Great Ratings

Tomeka sets a very high bar when she orchestrates an out-of-town meeting for a group. A packet awaits you when you arrive. This includes a personalized welcome note (often on a local postcard), annotated one-page maps, suggested places to visit before the event officially kicks off, and a small envelope with local currency so you can get a cup of tea and a sense of your new surroundings.

In advance, Tomeka provides links to the photos, contact information, and bios of the whole group. Afterward, she sends the seating charts so attendees can follow up with "that fascinating conversationalist to my left." The event team is prepped beforehand on "who might want to meet whom," and they proactively find attendees and make the introductions. Tomeka continually scans the room for the person who is feigning disinterest by playing on his or her phone, and offers to personally escort the person to a guest who might share a common interest. By modeling such attentive behavior and creating the conditions for maximum interaction, Tomeka infuses energy and happiness into what could otherwise be dull, obligatory corporate events.

Find Joy in Sharing the Stage

Anju may run a chemical company, but he was born to inhabit the stage. He loves the limelight and frequently soaks up too much of it. Grumblings in the corridors reached his corner office. A full-day business development meeting was set for the six members of Anju's leadership team, and they were anticipating lots of PowerPoint slides, detailed analyses, and many bored looks around the table. If they pretended to take notes, maybe they could catch up on some online shopping. It was going to be the Anju show and they knew what to expect. Anju reviewed the agenda and decided to act against type. He assigned a section of the meeting to each member of the team. He asked that they take turns keeping time to ensure that no one colonized the minutes from a colleague, himself included. Presenters were instructed to use no more than five slides. At least 30 percent of their time was to be devoted to conversation.

Anju concisely framed the meeting and then sat and listened to others. He summarized and validated each speaker's message to reduce the criticism he had heard in the past about publicly playing favorites. Phones were put away, though ample time was provided between sessions to communicate with the office (or family). Anju injected some levity at lunch. In advance, he had asked everyone to bring a picture of their pets (real or imagined), and the group had a few laughs trying to match team members with make-believe dragons, real labradoodles, and fuzzy bunnies. Anju felt more a part of the team and was less pressured in the run-up to the meeting as the responsibility to present was not solely his. Well rested and more relaxed, Anju took pride in the group's work and had fun in this new format. So did his team.

44

BUILD A BRIDGE

Connect Through Nonwork Interests and Experiences

You are an accountant, nursery school teacher, or thoracic surgeon. It's easy to be defined by "your job." Working in specialized, often siloed situations, the benefit of the *other* things we do is frequently missed, yet your experience, skills, and interests (often pursued outside of work) can be a repository of relational glue. Are you the insurance executive with a degree in geology? How can you share your intellectual capital with colleagues? Would you prefer to hold an offsite in the mountains or near a volcano so that nature is experienced rather than seen in two-dimensional images in a conference room? Do you ride horses on the weekend? Can visits to the therapeutic stables replace business development dinners or your annual corporate golf outing? Chefs produce under pressure. Why not highlight the two years you spent working in a kitchen, rather than trying to gloss over them as you write your tech consulting resume. "I am an X *and* a Y" communicates an expansive, energizing identity. "I am a photographer and a corporate litigator." "I am the child of Holocaust survivors, and I am a Pilates instructor." There are several advantages to recognizing the fullness of your experience and inviting others to do the same.

Overcome overt difference. Giving expression to and valuing diverse experiences uncovers potential points of connection among people working in the same company whose outward presentation seems nothing alike. When you and your team have diplomas from different schools and radically divergent family backgrounds, the ability to bond around a love of dance, coaching kids' teams, or collecting watches helps foster a sense of belonging—the foundation for workplace success.

Establish support for the future. A.S.U. Professor of Social Psychology Robert Cialdini recommends discovering informal commonalities early on as these create a presumption of goodwill and trustworthiness in every subsequent encounter. Going forward, the people you need to persuade will already be inclined in your favor.

Create new opportunities. As you seek to expand the profitability or impact of your organization, recognizing the varied spheres you can influence will . . . grow your influence! Let's say you are an Asian woman, from a family of farmers, living in Peru, with a passion for watercolors, working . . . at a bank. Can you be a bridge between quinoa producers seeking to expand their market and your company, which is pressuring you to develop new business? Invite a few representatives from your office to meet three members from an exporting company. Friends visiting from back home? Bring them along to provide perspective on changing dietary habits in their hometowns. Hold the meeting at a local gallery where your bank president is on the board. Invite two of the artists whose works are on display. Suddenly, you are at the center of a dynamic evening, inspired by and enriched by your interests, and, hopefully, catalytic for new connections.

Quickly deepen a discussion. Sometimes a shameful past can become the basis for extraordinary new relationships. Companies are increasingly introducing a day of service or other community outreach programs. The intent is virtuous, yet the dynamic that's created can often be "I am here to do something for you." The visitors' history is hermetically sealed. Sure, you're in a suit now, but you grew up on food stamps. You're helping at Habitat for Humanity, knocking in nails with your team but not speaking to the family whose home you are helping rebuild. Resurrecting the feelings you had when your parents' home was repossessed and you lived in a shelter can be the impetus for a vibrant conversation with the recipients of your service. Don't settle for a day out with the team devoid of understanding someone else's reality. Go back in time to discover ways to enrich the current exchange.

Work more effectively with partners from different sectors. There's a growing appreciation that the answers to complex, interconnected problems require cooperation among political, community, and business leaders. That's great in theory, but to get things done, your bridge-building needs to become more tactical. Once you have built the bridge, it's easier to find ways to translate each other's shorthand, agree on measurements for success, and figure out what information needs to be communicated to your various constituents to obtain the support you need.

THIS IS FOR YOU IF

- Finding one similarity—even better, two—will provide the foundation for novel collaboration.

- The focus has been on difference. Time to dip into your treasure chest of experience and find surprising commonalities.

- Sharing a vulnerable part of your past may position you for great success in the future.

- I am X *and* Y is much more appealing than any restrictive self-definition.

TAKE ACTION

- ▶ Think beyond the office walls. Allow yourself to consider your many roles and interests. When meeting people, identify a commonality you might not have previously considered.

- ▶ Resist rapid categorization of yourself and others. Think in terms of "*and*."

- ▶ Don't be afraid to be vulnerable. Sometimes the less glamorous parts of our past are the most potent places from which to build a bridge.

- ▶ Continually ask yourself, "Who else could I bring into this conversation?" How can your relationships outside of the typical work environment provide the bridge to novel alliances?

- ▶ Facilitate impactful coalitions by creating tools that foster collaboration. Develop fact sheets that share data in clear terms. Interpret industry jargon. If you worked in government (but now have a job in industry), offer coaching on the differences in organizational culture.

KEEP IN MIND

- Sometimes the most effective way to be a bridge is to make an introduction between people or organizations that share a common interest, even if you don't.

- In an effort to build a bridge between people, it's not your place to reveal information that your colleagues would consider private.

CASE STUDIES

Climate Change Requires a Shared Language

We were in the Aravalli Hills outside Jaipur, when Nigel Topping (then the executive director of the Carbon Disclosure Project) got the call asking if he would be interested in pursuing the CEO role for We Mean Business (a coalition of seven international nonprofits working with thousands of the world's most influential companies to accelerate transition to a zero-carbon economy). We had just completed a leadership summit that provoked all participants to step up and do more. In the fall of 2014, opportunity was literally calling Nigel.

In 2015, almost every nation on the planet sent a team of negotiators to Paris to pore over pages of nuanced jargon resulting in a proclamation to limit global warming. Getting a group of friends to agree on what to do on a Saturday night can be tough; can you imagine obtaining agreement from 195 countries? Although climate change advocates understood the importance of government and business working together to reduce greenhouse emissions, at past Conference of Parties (COP), corporate sustainability officers were present but had difficulty gaining access to policymakers who had the ultimate vote.

That changed when We Mean Business brought company representatives together to create one aligned message, aggregate information, and strategically leverage the power of their individual and shared networks. We Mean Business produced a daily letter that kept all participants current. They worked as translators between business and policymakers by creating a Z card (foldable guide) with the language needed on eight points to garner corporate support. Representatives of the press received user-ready messages that delivered scientific findings in easily understood language. The result? All eight points were incorporated into the Paris Agreement, and Nigel Topping took a front-row seat alongside former US Vice President Al Gore as the historic international treaty was approved.

Our Shame Brings Us Closer

The head of a corporate foundation, Charlie was facilitating a conversation between community and business leaders at a shelter for battered women in Hyderabad, India. Charlie opted not to introduce himself by his official title. Instead, he shared a previously silent piece of his past. While he was growing up, his dad spent a number of years behind bars. Charlie spoke of his shame and the impact on his family then and now. A woman whose face was disfigured when her jealous husband hurled acid at her reached out to reassure and welcome Charlie. Her face and his heart were both scarred, yet here they were advancing their lives. Inspired by the risk Charlie took, a resonant and deep conversation began.

Butterflies in the Buffer Zones

Lieutenant Colonel Joe Knott has devoted his career to bridging military preparedness and land preservation. Many army bases are century-old biological time capsules, constructed before development guzzled up forest, beach, and prairie. The Pentagon and environmental groups have quietly joined forces to build a vast conservation network protecting entire tracts of rare ecosystems *and* America's national security.

Knott served more than 33 years in uniform, including at the Pentagon and tours in Iraq. As a civilian, he is now the Director of Military Partnerships at the Compatible Lands Foundation, creating buffer zones between residential neighborhoods and military bases. These open spaces ensure that training exercises don't shake your windows from the noise of a low-flying jet *and* protect endangered species like the monarch butterfly, which migrates through Fort Hood in Texas. Knott is working with academics, conservationists, and the military to monitor and support butterflies in these buffer zones. He speaks "Army" as well as "academia" and is continually building bridges between his areas of expertise and the people and causes he cares deeply about. When Knott explains to civilians how men and women in fatigues are helping save majestic winged insects, preconceived negative notions about the military melt away.

45

CREATE THE GROUP YOU WANT TO BE PART OF

There's Energy and Power in Numbers

The strength of the team is each individual member.
The strength of each member is the team.
—Phil Jackson

Strap on your seat belt, this chapter is about to give you superpowers. Sanity. Transformation. Sustainability. *Big* concepts require a big reveal. The primordial soup of rebirth (for individuals, organizations, and society) is simmering in the space between the individual and the group. Your actions impact and define the group, and the group will assert its influence on your beliefs and behaviors, But the key to true transformation (of yourself and the systems around you) comes from deeply appreciating and unlocking the power in the reverberating, reciprocal arena of mutual creation. You want to improve; I want to improve. We form a group that amplifies our collective voices, and it doesn't stop there. Our association (ideally) prompts personal moments of insight, courage, and joy.

Here's where it gets exciting. We've set off an ever-refreshing, interdependent cycle. As your individual experiences are processed in the group, the group dynamic starts to shift. As a collective, we gain confidence. We challenge each other—model new norms. Learning together, we get smarter. We push harder for the goals that brought us together initially. There *is* bravery and strength in numbers. And that vitality is personally metabolized as you are motivated to do even more, be more. You are changing, transforming your inner self, and through your actions, impacting the world around you. You are sustained, energized by the visible effect you are having. You no longer feel alone.

At the Core of Individual and Group Interactions Is Your Mutually Created Superpower

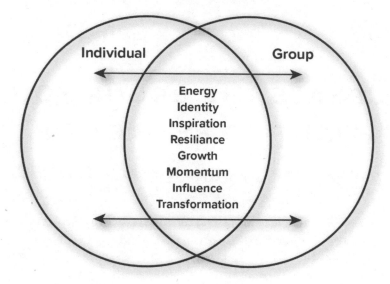

Speaking of power, you may not have heard the term, but we all have potential to exercise *convening power*. Convening power refers to the ability of a person or organization to successfully bring people together for a particular purpose. Activists deploy convening power regularly. They appreciate that a collective force is more capable of getting the attention of influential individuals and institutions.

The ability to define a compelling purpose, mobilize participation, and put structures in place to maintain meetings creates value for you, the group members, and your cause. Personally, you have a tailor-made tribe that reduces loneliness and affirms an identity that matters to you. Group members gain insights, build new networks, and experience a heightened sense of responsibility, not just to the concept but to each other. The group bonds to each other—and to you. Your reputation is enhanced. By naming the issue and creating an association, you have asserted the reality of your concept. Your shared idea starts to take on a life of its own. It's a living, breathing thing that has an identity and value of its own—in driving organizational or social policy. The group you create becomes your platform. And platforms can continue to be expanded to raise others up. Creating a meaningful group is a great act of generosity and a wonderful example of finding abundance.

THIS IS FOR YOU IF

- It's exhausting and lonely being a pioneer, and you're looking for the energy and creativity that only a group can provide.

- You want to belong, but there's no obvious group to join.

- It would be more cost-effective to share resources and learn from each other's mistakes, but who's like you? It's time to go beyond your company walls and find out.

- You want to solidify a new identity and appreciate that being part of a group will strengthen your sense of self and clarity of purpose.

TAKE ACTION

▶ Form the band you want to play with. Define the mission. What are you *trying to achieve*? Is it internal to your company—a program to promote minority candidates? What's the issue or challenge that excites, irks, or terrifies you? Ready to combat noise pollution around your office? Are you looking for general support as you transition into a new role or community? Are there other retirees teaching English to new immigrants in your community? Are there other recent college graduates getting ready to launch a new product? Or are you gearing up to fight for a cause? Are you concerned about safety at your chemical plant? Ask around. Try to find like minds. Social media may help you cast a broad net. Personal invitations allow you to target your desired group members.

▶ Sharing similar experiences that may not be common to the majority of people around you creates a more immediate bond. Five thousand people graduate from your Midwestern college each year, but how many are living in Shanghai, and of those how many are working on cultural arts exchanges? Send a personal email; dare to make a phone call. Point out the unique characteristics you share. Explain your desire to form a group to compare experiences working in China, test the limits of artistic expression, and potentially share exhibition space. If your invitee declines, ask if they can suggest someone else. Once two or three people have accepted (and they have agreed you can share their names), you're ready to invite others. State your goals, list the growing group of members, and propose an initial meeting date and place. It's OK to start small.

▶ Not all groups have to be large. In fact, six to eight people is a very effective size. Employ Amazon CEO Jeff Bezos's two-pizza rule. He suggests limiting all meetings to the number of people who could be fed by two pizzas. This allows room for everyone to speak.

▶ Define success. Be clear and realistic about your goal. Consider setting a time limit. You can always extend; however, setting targets and timelines will mobilize action. "We want to reduce the sound decibels by X percent by December." Potential participants are more willing to say yes when they know the length of their commitment (even if they renew their vows as time goes on).

▶ You convened the group, so at the start you are the leader. This doesn't mean you have to do everything. Share responsibilities like setting up the venue, confirming attendance, and planning the agenda.

▶ Define expectations. Review and commit to confidentiality. Agree how new members will be chosen and oriented. How many meetings can a person miss and still be considered a member of the group? What's the frequency and mode of communication between meetings?

▶ Your group is made up of individuals. Start each gathering by connecting to the why. "Why are you excited to be here today?" "What's bubbled up for you since we last met?" "Any frustrations you want to surface?" As your group size swells, continually recommit to the mission by stating your personal why.

▶ You are together to achieve a shared goal. How does each person want to contribute? This may include sharing contacts or getting press coverage. Alternatively, a member may contribute by flexing their curiosity or actively challenging assumptions.

▶ Form, storm, norm, perform, adjourn—these are the stages of group development. Form: you got the group together. Storm: time to argue about what was left unsaid or unrealized when you began. Norm: affirm expectations. Perform: ready for action. Adjourn: know when you are done.

▶ Act like a genius. Thomas Edison, Henry Ford, and Alexander Graham Bell were all members of Mastermind Groups that provided feedback and accountability. It's a peer-to-peer mentoring approach. You meet weekly, monthly, daily even, if it makes sense, to tackle challenges and problems together. It's an opportunity to give advice, share connections, and do business with each other when appropriate.

▶ Transformative organizational change is accelerated and sustained by groups that incubate and then disseminate new practices and beliefs. Gather the people who can influence attitudes, and give them the tools and support to connect to, inform, and model desired behaviors. Remember that culture carriers do not always have the biggest office or esteemed title. Mixing up employees from different levels provides energy and insight for the individuals and the enterprise.

▶ Your organizational affiliation can be a platform to drive larger change in your community, especially when you join forces with other institutions. Community reform is accelerated when the educators, shopkeepers, police, and parents all come together. Want to see a change outside the walls of your company? Can you convene a group with representation from various constituents? You don't have to know the people you approach for membership. You just have to be able to make a compelling pitch that draws the connection between your idea and their participation.

▶ Share your vision. Convening stakeholder groups around a shared purpose drives meaning for your staff, customers, and you.

▶ Use your organizational heft to create movements. Companies are flexing their convening muscles to orchestrate events that promote a cause while also building their brand. What can your organization do to spark social change?

KEEP IN MIND

• Stay authentic. Convening events purely for marketing or branding purposes can undermine your reputation.

• Extend invitations, but be ready to graciously accept a no.

CASE STUDIES

Understanding and Regulating the Invisible

Justin wanted recognition, more stimulation, a new job, and some advice. He was the chief compliance officer at a hedge fund that was leading the way in cryptocurrencies. Justin wanted to make sure the company was following the rules as they forayed into this new domain. The firm's lawyer didn't have any answers. Neither did the outside attorneys. There were no rules . . . yet. The industry was moving faster than the legislation. Justin was nervous. His boss seldom even made eye contact with him, but when he wanted information he was "in my face." Justin said, "We are dealing with high-frequency trading, a cryptocurrency, and operating out of Germany. That combo has no precedent."

Justin formed the group he needed to get the answers. He invited lawyers, fellow compliance officers, and traders. He limited invitations to 12 people so it felt special while optimizing the chance that at least 8 people would attend. Once established, they shared experiences, invited guest speakers, and visited regulators. Justin went from being the one who didn't know to being the one with an informed perspective. His company got the advice it needed and the distinction of being associated with what became an important council. Justin's peers (and competitors) had a place to learn together and influence emerging policy. It was a triple win.

Justin's exposure outside the office impressed his boss, who suddenly had more time for him. Having raised his profile and extended his network, Justin was approached with an offer from another firm. Work was now more stimulating. Justin got a raise and felt appreciated.

Transformation at Scale

Following the 2008 financial crisis, Andrew Bailey, deputy governor of the Bank of England, observed, "The financial crisis was a painful reminder that commercial banks should operate for the good of the public, their customers. Now we must tackle the question of what banking system we do want?"

To explore how to build a healthier, more resilient, and inclusive banking sector, Leaders' Quest and Meteos (a British think-tank and strategy company) convened an in-depth dialogue, "Banking Futures," for a group of senior bankers and investors in the United Kingdom. Anne Wade of Leaders' Quest and Sophia Tickell of Meteos, both leaders in their respective nonprofit organizations, hadn't worked together; they didn't have previous relationships with the people who were asked to attend. Being outside the industry was an advantage in securing a nonpartisan arena for candid conversations. Participants came from competitor institutions. During the course of 14 months, through interviews and open round tables, the working group heard from 200 stakeholders (including regulators, customers, and community members). This resulted in specific recommendations to create long-term value for British society. For example, banks and government agencies received a list of practical steps to finance and advise small and medium-sized businesses, which account for 60 percent of private sector employment. Bank leaders and investors also obtained concrete direction on ways to deliver long-term value and better societal outcomes. These recommendations have greater resonance as they were crafted jointly by champions in key organizations who are positioned to bring them to action.

46

BE PRACTICALLY
OPTIMISTIC

Instill Hope

*True failure is turning away from opportunity because
you don't want to face your fear.*
—TIFFANY PHAM, author of *You Are a Mogul*

Join me as a guest on the Worldview game show. As a contestant, you get to pick which door you want to walk through. Behind door number one is denial, conflict avoidance, and clinging to what could have been but isn't. Behind door number two is experimentation, ambition, and possibility. Deciding to adopt an optimistic perspective will have positive effects on your mood and the people around you, increase motivation and engagement, and promote innovation. Do you want to take a few more minutes before you choose? Really, it's up to you. And it *is* a choice. Even if you default naturally to more dire assumptions, you can train your mind to see opportunity.

Israeli artist Paz Perlman explained to me that the Hebrew word for *reality* is מְצִיאוּת (meh-tsee-OOT)—"that which is found." It shares the same root as the word להמציא (Lhamtzi), which means "to invent." It's a dynamic, changing view of what is. In contrast, in the Western vernacular, the "real" in *reality* is static, fixed. You can't argue with it. When someone says, "The reality of the situation is . . ." they are asserting an immutable state of affairs.

I believe you can make a clear-eyed, reasoned assessment of a situation, no matter how grim, *and* identify paths toward a positive outcome. We wake up every morning knowing lots of stuff is broken, and more stuff is about to break. Stuff that can make life glum. The glaciers are melting, people are starving, politicians are acting in their own interest. There's been a fire, an earthquake, another mass shooting. A chain of disappointments awaits at work. Yet a practical optimist knows that, despite how broken things can be around them, if you can survive the day-to-day fractures, the arc of growth will bend in the right direction. The aim is to keep going and maintain faith in what's possible.

I'm not taken by the con that everything is great, but I do believe that people and groups are capable of great things. I called this chapter "Be Practically Optimistic," playing on the double meaning of *practically*: "almost" (not fully, but mostly optimistic) and "pragmatic" (not blind to the facts). When you walk through door number two, you see life's realities *and* possibilities, you choose hope rather than fear.

Many managers and employees focus primarily on what isn't working. Studs Terkel interviewed workers from all walks of life for his book *Working*. He opens with a brutal observation, "This book, being about work, is by its very nature about violence—to the spirit as well as the body." Does it have to be this way? The most productive professionals incorporate the right amount of optimism, nurturing a belief among employees that something good will come out of their work. This doesn't mean you are shiny and happy all day, but it does mean that you don't bow to the shrine of problems and retreat when things get tough.

"Being optimistic goes far deeper than just positive thinking," warns Dr. Gabriele Oettingen, a professor of psychology. She tells a joke about a guy who dreams of winning the lottery. After years of desperate fantasizing, he cries out for God's help. Down from heaven comes God's advice: "Would you buy a ticket already?!" Dr. Oettingen dispels the notion that dreams will inspire us to act. Her research demonstrates that wishing alone (blind optimism) doesn't lead to success. Instead, it tricks our minds intro believing we have attained the desired goal, and we become complacent. Dr. Oettingen and her colleagues developed a technique called *mental contrasting* or WOOP (see the Take Action section below). Rather than simply fantasizing about success, you imagine your desired result and conjure up the ways your own behaviors will get in the way. And then you make a plan to conquer the obstacles. Sorry to burst your bubble, but a "you can do it" attitude only goes so far. Dreaming big is great, but you must also take the practical steps to turn it into a reality. Want to experience success and joy at work? Set ambitious targets, have the courage to consider the obstacles, and remember to rejoice when you conquer them.

THIS IS FOR YOU IF

- You prefer a warm glow to being frozen with fear.

- Opening vistas has greater appeal than cranky cynicism.

TAKE ACTION

▶ Pessimism is an explanatory style, not a genetically determined condition. The field of positive psychology is bursting with evidence indicating that more optimistic mindsets are formed when you see negative experiences as temporary, specific to a situation, and not indicative of some fatal flaw of yours. Did your new product fail the safety test? You can make the necessary adjustments and pass next time. Were you passed over for promotion? Next year you will have more experience and a chance to cultivate additional committed sponsors. Check out the book *Learned Optimism* by Martin E. P. Seligman. It's a classic.

▶ Practice active-constructive responding. When your colleagues share good news, listen in a way that encourages them to savor the positive emotion. Rather than responding, "That's nice" when a coworker tells you about their latest success, say, "Tell me more. How did you accomplish that?" It's an infectious injection of possibility. As an active-constructive responder, you share in the emotional high, and your coworker with the good news develops an even greater opinion of you.

▶ Break big goals into manageable, tangible actions that can be accomplished and celebrated. Opening a restaurant is a huge goal. What are the steps? Did you find a location? Sign your lease? Hire your first employee? Be sure to "show off" your incremental successes with friends and coworkers. Invite them to a drink in your soon-to-be operational venue.

▶ WOOP: Wish. Outcome. Obstacle. Plan. Think of a wish. Imagine for a few minutes it comes true. Shift gears. Imagine the obstacles that stand in the way of realizing your wish. This helps you decide and plan for which goals to pursue and which can be discarded as unrealistic (for the time being).

▶ Reimagine your goals. Don't get stuck in the problem at hand. What can be fixed? With how much effort? Do you need to pivot? Share the shift with your colleagues. "We have not been able to succeed at X, so we are now going after Y." It's demoralizing for your team to fail. Not knowing the change in direction will alienate them further.

▶ Be honest. Openly review obstacles you anticipate, and ask others to make suggestions. Pretending everything will work out won't lead you to success, and will likely undermine your reputation. It's OK not to know the answers. Ask for help.

▶ Offer a tour of duty. In *The Alliance*, cofounder of LinkedIn, Reid Hoffman, explains the concept: "[They] focus on honorably accomplishing a specific, finite mission." Employees go to different company departments and contribute their talents to the success of a specific measurable goal. They deepen their understanding of the business while showcasing their skills and strengths.

▶ Envision the future. Bring together the dreamers, the analysts, the self-proclaimed pessimists, and those in between. Ask, "What if?" Don't give in to the urge to find a solution or shut down wacky ideas. Air all perspectives, capture the quotes, and post them where they can be seen. Let conversation unfold naturally in the hallways. Reconvene the group in a few weeks and see if the chance to live with what may have seemed to be polar opposite realities has prompted new thinking.

▶ Examine time from a nonlinear perspective. Professional futurist Bill Sharpe created a technique called Three Horizons to help individuals and organizations build shared hope and commitment as they navigate from the familiar to the new. The core idea is that time is not one-dimensional. For example, the university administrator is making sure professors have the traditional resources they need in their classrooms. They keep business running as usual (inhabiting horizon one). The professors work for the same entity as the engineer who is developing a chip that will implant knowledge in your brain (that's the third horizon). In this mix is horizon two, the pockets of the future that already exist today (university buildings remain standing, but many students are attending virtual classes instead). By default, many people inhabit just one horizon in their work, and view other horizons with misunderstanding or hostility. When people appreciate the positive contribution of each horizon, they can release the grip on "their" horizon and travel together on a more flexible and empathetic path to the future.

KEEP IN MIND

- Overly optimistic colleagues can be annoying if they lack information or choose to ignore important data. Don't make fun of them. Instead, share what you know and why it impacts decision-making.

- You can't force another person to be optimistic, but you can be a positive role model.

CASE STUDIES

We Are Hospitalarians

Leo ran the in-house events team for a very successful business-woman and the philanthropies she supported. Well paid and highly respected, he craved independence. He wanted to start his own company, possibly open an events space of his own or maybe launch a new restaurant. Recently married and trying hard to adopt a child with his husband, many of Leo's friends urged him not to leave a sure thing. He thanked them for their concern and proceeded with his plan. Several past clients offered to invest. He declined. A friend offered him a desk at her office. He accepted.

Not knowing which of his ideas would take hold, Leo opted to leverage his core competency: corporate event planning. He set realistic revenue targets and hired two part-time employees. Leo also created a personal board of directors composed of friends who had been successful entrepreneurs, a former client, and a well-known decorator. He hired young freelancers who worked at a discount in exchange for gaining experience. He got certified by the LGBT chamber of commerce. He hired graduates of a job-training program for people living with HIV/AIDS to oversee the pickup and delivery of decorative materials. Leo committed to a year of monthly coaching appointments. Five years later, Leo has built a multimillion-dollar business and employs nine people full-time. He's the proud father of a four-year-old son.

Leo had a vision and surrounded himself with people who could support and challenge him. He remained optimistic about his success, but he refrained from being overconfident or from taking too big a risk.

Winning Isn't the Only Form of Success

In an open letter to her children, Halla Tomasdottir wrote, "In a complex world, where many things are broken, it may seem easier to stand on the sidelines. I ask you not to do that. It is too crowded there already. Step onto the field and actively participate in creating the community you dream of." Halla has modeled resilience throughout her career, which included working in consumer goods, being on the founding team of Reykjavík University, and co-founding Auður Capital, an investment firm that incorporates feminine values into finance (the only Icelandic investment firm to survive the financial meltdown in 2008). Through the years, Halla and I have had a chance to talk about strategies for accomplishing the seemingly impossible. She's never short of ideas. Halla is now CEO of The B Team, a global nonprofit dedicated to catalyzing a better way of doing business. But that's not all. She ran for president of Iceland in 2016.

Halla had no prior political experience and was reluctant to subject herself and her family to the scrutiny and loss of freedom associated with a high political position. She did it anyway. Running for president was a platform to promote her vision and values for the nation. More than 20 candidates entered the race, but by Election Day, the race was among 4 candidates, 3 men and Halla. It wasn't easy. Halla explains, "When I finally got access to mainstream media, I was repeatedly asked if I was going to quit. During the TV debates I typically got less airtime, and more than once moderators forgot to ask me a question asked of all the other candidates. I was the only candidate of the final four that never got a front-page interview."

Despite that, Halla won nearly 30 percent of the national vote, outperforming the polls to finish second by an unprecedented and surprising margin. "Even if I did not win this election, I can truly say the journey was successful." Halla received a photo of preschool girls kissing her picture as it was displayed on a bus stop. "That picture alone was really enough of a win for me. What we see, we can be. So screw fear and challenges. It matters that women run for office, be it the CEO office or the office of the President."

PART VII

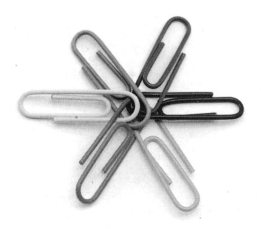

HAVE A
BIG IMPACT

You took the time to listen, to praise, and to include others; you've stood in someone else's shoes. You've learned that when you're paralyzed by an issue, strength and wisdom will emerge by connecting first on a human level. You've seen how you can act with intention to accomplish your goals without withering your soul. You've cultivated your curiosity. Now what? Time to be joyfully courageous.

Don't let your level of seniority or organizational role define you. Find ways to leverage your platform. No matter your position, there are ways to create meaning and drive positive impact by the choices you make and the expansiveness of your ideas.

Most of us want to make a difference but get overwhelmed when confronted with the enormity of the problems before us. This part provides the tools to broaden your definition of success, to work across generations, to consider how you want to leave a mark, to be significant.

This Part Is for You If

- You want to be remembered—with admiration.

- You've identified new, better, or different ways of doing things and you want to lead the change.

- You're fed up with business as usual.

- You want to live your values at home *and at work*.

- Succession planning is, or should be, on the radar.

- Employees are pushing for more responsibility (and meaning).

- The roots of your organization aren't known but could be inspirational to the newer members of your enterprise.

- Recruiting talent is a challenge.

- Experienced executives (yourself included) are uninspired and thinking of finding a new job to make a difference.

47

EXPLORE THE UNKNOWN
The Future Depends on It

It is not the answer that enlightens, but the question.
—EUGENE IONESCO

Ajit Rangnekar, the former dean of the Indian School of Business, welcomed me to his Hyderabad campus saying, "This is a place of inquiry, not answers. I am interested in what you are bringing into this building." I've never forgotten that invitation.

The opportunity to explore, debate, take an idea and turn it inside out is a luxurious necessity. Luxurious because active contemplation without the pressure for immediate answers is a rare indulgence in corporations, and a necessity because in our rush to action we expose ourselves to several pitfalls:

- We leap at obvious (though potentially incorrect) conclusions.

- We don't stop to consider if we are even asking the right question.

- We don't fully assess the complexity of a situation.

- We focus on what we know and let seemingly intractable issues simmer beneath the surface.

- We ask questions to confirm our conclusions rather than obtain new information.

- We give the illusion that we are interested in other views, but all we are after is support of a predetermined idea.

- A conceptual emergency becomes submerged as action overtakes attention. We miss the big picture (or the intricacy of the details).

Why does this happen? It takes courage to say, "I don't know." or "We don't know." When employees are paid to perform, competency is too often equated with having the answer—on demand. We fear that not knowing will make us appear weak. Even more anxiety-inducing, sometimes we don't know how to formulate the question. We just know something is wrong—or we anticipate it will be. And for extra tension, it's possible that the emergent answer may threaten the status quo. How uncomfortable can you get?

Be brave. Be messy. Luxuriate in the not knowing. At the root of innovation is the courage to ask a beautiful question. Sometimes it's as simple as, "Why isn't someone doing this?" or "What if I tried to do that?"

THIS IS FOR YOU IF

- The future excites you.

- Opening the window for wisdom to flow in is more important than shutting the door to any idea that isn't already proven.

TAKE ACTION

▶ Run toward, not away, from the question without an obvious answer. As you read the latest memo or sit in yet another meeting, stop to ask, "What are we avoiding because we don't know?" Bring people together to explore, not solve the dilemma. Your gathering can be immediate: grab a few of your colleagues and ask them for 30 minutes this afternoon at 4 p.m. to share in the fun of not knowing (bring snacks). Or plan ahead, and make it interesting for yourself and others. Pose the question, send an invite, and make it clear that this is a chance to swap ideas on a topic without judgment or pressure. Brainstorming? Have plenty of paper (whiteboards if you have access to them), markers, and Post-its so you can colorfully *play* with ideas.

▶ Don't get lost in the details of execution while you're still toying with concepts. Examine your question from a distance. What patterns can you recognize?

- ▶ Play doctor; make a good diagnosis. We don't know what's wrong, but the patient (organization, product) doesn't look well. Consider several possibilities simultaneously. What's needed to test your hypothesis? Don't settle for three possibilities. Push yourself to generate at least 10, no matter how wacky. Now what? Will you reconvene after your colleagues have had a chance to get more data? In person? By phone? Agree on a date now. Is the metaphorical patient on life support? If not, don't rush the answer, but don't delay by adding greater depth to the exploration. Agree to a timeline to reach a considered conclusion.

- ▶ Don't let the Internet define your search. Your keyboard isn't always a reliable tour guide. Don't outsource problem-solving to an algorithm. You may have to have a conversation—with real people.

- ▶ Invert the problem; see it as the solution. The costume jewelry market is taking off and your gem stone business is faltering. The women flying in first class are wearing diamonds made of paste. Rather than seeing your customer's choice to wear fakes as the problem, ask, what are they solving for?

- ▶ Each Friday, Flipboard, the online news aggregator, invites employees from all levels to a one-hour demo called "mock o'clock." The staff gather around a large table, and anyone can share their latest projects and get ideas from colleagues who work outside their functional teams.

- ▶ Whether you are pulling together an impromptu group or planning a session next month to envision the future, think across age groups. By nature of how they consume and share information, millennials and Gen Z staffers are likely to see different interconnections than their baby boomer counterparts.

- ▶ Hold an exploration session at the library. It's cheaper than renting a conference room, and libraries are now more than a place that lends books. They are becoming maker spaces set up for tantalizing tinkering.

- ▶ Explore the online, free tool box from Stanford's D School that encourages you to question everything. Even (and especially) the things you think you already understand. You will learn a lot, including how to write "how might we" (HMW) questions (https://dschool.stanford.edu/resources/design-thinking-bootleg).

KEEP IN MIND

- While there are no *bad* questions, don't be lazy; challenge yourself to search for even better ones.

- Don't disguise an attack on a person or concept as a question.

CASE STUDIES

How to Fill an Empty Head

What do you do when you are the chief innovation officer, but you've run out of fresh ideas? Richard pioneered the use of social media for marketing campaigns. He rose to lead innovation at his agency and landed in my office with "an empty head" and a panic attack. Richard felt dated relative to the new, nimble startups and disconnected from his former tech colleagues. Many of the entrepreneurs he wanted to learn from were interested in exposure to his well-respected organization. The chief innovation officer became chief host for a monthly innovation lunch. He invited two outside speakers and six internal colleagues of different generations and perspectives. Richard presented a challenge in advance so everyone could prepare. His unanswered questions transformed from aspirin-inducing to brain-activating opportunities. The sessions sparked new ideas for Richard, and the exposure to a wider community of strategic partners meant he could deliver novel products more quickly and often with lower overhead.

Pushing Past Politeness

A network of senior black executives at a major investment bank invited me to facilitate their first workshop on race relations. There were 30 black professionals and 30 white managers. The white managers anticipated that the conversation would focus on career tips for getting ahead, how to select a mentor, get on the right deals, and so on. But that's not what unfolded. We began with participants working in pairs, taking turns answering the question, "When did I first become aware of my race, and why did that matter?" The conversation between two people grew to a discussion among four, and then eight at each table.

When I opened the floor to the assembled, it became clear that the question of "How do I advance at the firm?" was not the right prompt. What the group wanted to address was "How do we become color brave, not color blind?" The white participants shared how, in their effort to see everyone as equal, they had shied away from conversations that drew attention to racial differences. Several black executives said they welcomed being asked, "Are you worried for your son's safety?" after the news reported yet another police shooting of an unarmed black teen. A Nigerian woman with a striking headdress lamented that no one ever complimented her on her style. The white managers' polite, cautious behavior reinforced a sense of otherness. The firm had invested in recruiting diverse candidates; they had set targets for promotions, but until our workshop, there hadn't been a forum to address the difficult question of "How do we recognize our differences daily while striving to achieve greater unity in the future?" There were no easy answers. But we started to shape the question.

Discovery Is Fundamental to Our Humanity

NASA scientist Dr. Lindy Elkins-Tanton is teaching all of us to be explorers seeking novel solutions today, and into the future—on earth and in space. Dr. Elkins-Tanton and her team at the Arizona State University School of Earth and Space Exploration are providing answers to questions many of us didn't even know to ask, such as:

- How will we extract drinkable water from the lunar polar deposits?

- How best do we train NASA administrators to communicate with extraterrestrial life?

- What policies are needed to govern future interplanetary settlement?

Her team is also maximizing the workplace potential of students by providing a process to respond to opportunities we have yet to imagine. The focus is on learning how to learn and to do so collaboratively. Education doesn't stop in the classroom. Dr. Elkins-Tanton and her team demonstrate that contemplating the celestial is an opportunity to reflect on what it means to be human. Innovative pilot programs are engaging the public with prompts like, "What Would You Pack for Mars?" Participants are asked to imagine a scenario where 100 people are going to another planet in our solar system. They are taking a box with them that contains all the knowledge they will need to build a vibrant and sustainable community—a kick-starter "Community-in-a-Box." What are the three things you would put in that box, and why?

Dr. Elkins-Tanton's fearless pursuit of knowledge is palpable, as is her commitment to collaboration. Soon after we were introduced, she invited me to join meetings and contribute curriculum ideas. Inclusion was her first response.

48

HONOR HISTORY

Let the Past Propel You Forward

*The past is a kind of screen upon which
we project our vision of the future.*
—Carl Becker

Where have we been? Where are we going? Where am I? Your Google Map isn't equipped for navigating existential dilemmas, but your company history can help. A shared past knits an individual into a community and imbues the group with a distinct identity. The history of your organization can be a source of pride that helps you see events and yourself as part of a larger, still-unfolding story. History connects you to meaning.

Whether you are re-envisioning your brand or wondering, *Why do we do things this way?* the past can provide rich insights. Has your company survived turbulent economies or lasted for centuries? Find the energy (and confidence) to reinvigorate the future by tapping into your organizational roots.

Learn from those who came before you. Innovating for tomorrow doesn't mean forgetting all the acumen acquired in the preceding eras. As companies merge, leadership shifts, and employees depart, institutional knowledge offers pragmatic insights.

We all want to be remembered when we are gone (and while we are still around). As an employee, hearing your name called out at the company meeting of 200 people recognizes the risk you took in believing before there was something to believe in. The new staff is reminded to tap your experience.

Recalling the personnel who traveled thousands of miles (in the middle seat of often delayed airplanes) and the late-night teams that loaded trucks in the rain humanizes your company and reminds employees that they, too, have a chance to earn their place in history.

THIS IS FOR YOU IF

- The inspiring "why" of your company has been forgotten.

- You want to be remembered, and would like to do the same for the people on whose shoulders you are now standing.

- Less glamorous roles have been filled by staff who have been invisible but highly impactful. You want to inspire the organization by telling their stories.

- You're new in the job and appreciate that learning about the organization's history may help you better adopt the culture.

TAKE ACTION

▶ Think and talk about the past in living color in the present. Tell stories about charismatic leaders, long-tenured but less famous workers, breakthrough innovations, involvement in notable social movements—and what it says about the company you are today or want to become.

▶ Create your own organizational "museum" with artifacts like the receipt for your first desk or ideas for a logo. Start with a corner of your shelf: the prototype for a new ski boot that never gained market share, the kitchen sponge that inspired you to make a cartoon series. You'll honor the past and have great conversational prompts in the present.

▶ Agree on the founders. In the absence of money, entrepreneurs, keen to involve other talent, may offer the title of cofounder. As the company expands or gains fame, the initial founder may be less comfortable sharing the credit, believing that the cofounder isn't pushing growth, taking risks, raising capital, or working as hard. Resentment kicks in. Meanwhile, the cofounder believes he or she earned the title, given the sacrifices made. It can get ugly. Best to be abundantly clear from the outset about how you want to write your organizational history in the future.

▶ Decorate the office walls with employees' pictures. Use obstetric doctors as a model. They often have poster boards with pictures of all the babies they delivered. What kind of new life has your team brought into the world? Start a collage of your product advertisements—and have the staff that worked on its launch sign the picture.

▶ Include a company history in the employee manual to connect new hires with the organization's DNA. List the names of people who worked at the company even if they no longer do. You may surprise or make a new hire proud when they discover an unknown family connection. And you will demonstrate that you are an organization that doesn't forget its people.

▶ Create an internal database of past blunders, the conditions that led to them, and how they were solved. That's it, three lines. Keep it simple. During brainstorming sessions, encourage risk. Read these examples as a reminder that the organization has survived mistakes in the past.

▶ Include alumni. Your former colleague knows your company's system and has now been trained at a new enterprise. She is in a great position to challenge your assumptions. When putting together strategy sessions, don't forget to invite the outside expert who used to be inside.

▶ Establish an annual award. Keep a visible record of the winners. Mount a wooden plaque on the side of the conference room, and add an engraved plate with each year's winner. If you move offices, don't forget to pack and rehang it!

▶ Let history speak for itself. StoryCorps (www.storycorps.org) and Brazilian Museum Museu da Pessoa (www.museudapessoa.net/pt/home) have methodologies to capture the oral histories of individuals and institutions.

▶ If you are part of the new regime responsible for ushering out loyal, long-time employees be sure to help plan or attend their farewell dinners.

KEEP IN MIND

● History can be subjective. Be sensitive.

● Don't let disagreements about the past prevent you from documenting history. It's OK to share a few alternative perspectives.

CASE STUDIES

Send a Really Big Thank-You Note

In February 2016, Delta Air Lines employees received their portion of the largest payout in the history of corporate profit-sharing programs ($1.5 billion profit), and the airline thanked employees with a Guinness World Record–setting 50-foot greeting card. It included the name of every Delta employee, all 80,000 of them, recorded for posterity.

The Positive Power of Capital

Actis Private Equity was established in 2004 after it was spun out from CDC Group, the UK government's development finance institution, which promotes private sector investment in former British territories. Many members of the Actis management and investment teams previously worked at CDC in Asia, Africa, and Latin America. As Actis grew and new partners joined, the connection to the initial vision attenuated. The focus was less on the why of infrastructure building and more on the profit to be made in the market. Paul Fletcher, founding CEO, decided to reconnect his firm to its roots. He arranged for the partners, their spouses, and their board members to visit China, South Africa, Nigeria, and Brazil to experience firsthand the potential social impact of their capital.

In each country, they met with innovators at the grassroots and leadership levels in finance, energy, agribusiness, education, transportation, retail, and media. Each night they gathered to review the effect their experiences were having on them as investment professionals and family members. What did they want to be known for going forward? There was a breakthrough. In Paul's words, "They shifted from a group of people who thought that the only thing that mattered was financial returns, to a group of people who now run a balanced business between financial returns and nonfinancial outcomes." Actis has become a leader in establishing funds that focus on the environment, sustainability, and good governance.

Locate Yourself in Time

At a Leaders' Quest retreat, we created a belt around all four walls of our meeting room with butcher block paper. A line was drawn through the middle of the sheets. Notable events in world history were inserted for orientation. Above the line the founders drew key positive moments, and less glorified experiences below. Then each person grabbed a different color marker and added their historical highs and lows to the sheets. As the paper rounded each corner of the room, the explosion of color and energy grew ever stronger. You could literally see the impact of each new staff member. Eight years later, our team was 67 people strong, and we once again "exhibited" our organization's art. New members of the team received an immediate visual orientation to our organization's highs (and lows) and an invitation to add themselves to the ever-enlarging story. As our group set future goals, it was all the more dynamic in a room that hugged us with history.

49

EMBRACE AGING
AT WORK

60 Is the New 30

I'm 60 years old. I will be 61 when this book is published. I gave a talk about *Connect First* and mentioned "the number." (Why not? It seemed to flow from one of the stories I was sharing.) An audience member thanked me for being a role model of women remaining active as they age. It took me a beat to process. I don't think of myself as *old*. My kids think I have an energy disorder. I work all day and go out with friends at night. At dawn I meet my 30-year-old son for an exercise class. I'm in my prime. I'm healthy and strong. I'm confident in what I know (that's why I am writing this book), and astute enough to know that there's no end to what I can learn. I'm not afraid to speak my mind. I've acquired enough experience that it's hard to rattle me. My relationships are decades deep, tested and trusted. I'm in a position to open my network to help others achieve their goals. Why would I stop?

The world's older population is growing at an unprecedented rate. A quarter of the US workforce is over 55 years old. If people are living and working longer, then young and old, we're going to be stuck with each other for a long time, so let's make the most of it. Let's have honest conversations about age.

How long is too long, or not enough in a position? As employees mature in their roles, should the focus be on severance packages or retention bonuses? While many older workers continue to work for economic or social purposes, others are considering a transition but find themselves in a conversational vacuum. Employers don't initiate the discussion for fear of being seen as discriminating, and employees don't raise the topic for fear of being pushed out before they're ready. The inverse is also true, top (senior) talent is left out of development programs because they are considered too old to learn, on the way out, or disinterested.

Rather than pretend you (or your colleagues) are Peter Pan, recognize that growing older isn't an assault on reason, it's a ripening of wisdom. Contrary to popular lore that innovative ideas spring only from young minds wearing hoodies and working in a garage, scientific data suggests that most successful entrepreneurs tend to be middle-aged—even in the tech sector. A 60-year-old startup founder is three times more likely to launch a successful company than a 30-year-old. Nobel Prize winners are having their breakthrough successes later and later in life. Accumulated experience leads to smart tactical decisions. Cognitive studies reveal that while younger adults may excel in the speed and flexibility of information processing, older adults make more adjustments after a mistake.

And there's more good news! Across the lifespan, there's a U-shaped positivity effect. Happiness starts out high in late adolescence and bottoms out in middle age (think middle managers angling for advancement, with unpaid mortgages, searching for a mate, caring for kids, struggling to pay taxes—or all of the above). At old age, there's a second zenith. From Armenia to Zaire, people around the world tend to be happier as they mature—regardless of their nationality.

Stay with me, I'm on a roll. Pattern recognition, the ability to read emotional cues, and self-regulation also increase through the years, leading to greater empathy, intuition, and informed judgments. But don't worry, the grey hairs aren't showing off because, guess what? Egos mellow with age (usually). Rather than seek fame and recognition, as the years go by, we're likely to become more focused on helping others than promoting our own agendas. When seeking ways to connect first, tap into the generosity and experience of people born in the twentieth century.

THIS IS FOR YOU IF

- The "success" in succession planning is prompting you to look for ways in which everyone wins.

- It's been easy for you to see older executives as the barrier between you and the promotion you crave.

- You appreciate that shiny and new isn't always the smartest and best.

TAKE ACTION

▶ You *can* teach an old dog new tricks. Review career development plans at least annually with people of all ages. Don't assume that someone older than 60 isn't interested in growing.

• Take the tension out of the team by openly inquiring about intentions and crafting a plan together. Succession planning stalls and junior people get restless (and consider leaving) when there's no road map for the future. Organizations run the risk of having a talent canyon (not just a gap) if the senior leader (finally) retires and the designated replacement left months before, tired of waiting for a promotion.

• Don't let your high potential seniors slip away. Just because someone has been with the company for decades, doesn't mean they will stay forever. If the feisty septuagenarian believes he is going to live until 120, there's a chance he's looking for a second act at a different institution. What would keep him engaged? Is it a change in hours, structure of the day, assignments, better lighting, or an ergonomic desk chair? Explore part-time arrangements that benefit you both.

• Openly discuss the age structure of teams. How can different personal or health demands across the decades be deployed as an asset? If an older team member is rising with the sun, have them take the early shift and let the young mother drop off her daughter at school before coming to the office. Can you keep a roster of retired employees who can work as temps to cover workers on leave?

• Plan for, rather than be surprised by, succession. Create training initiatives that allow younger employees to walk with, not in the shadow of, their elders. Devise clear plans to transfer knowledge, both technical and cultural. Have a "crossover" period where young and old employees appear in public meetings together, showcasing and affirming each other's skill set. Honor the retiring employee by connecting their replacement's success to the foundation the retiree laid.

KEEP IN MIND

• Tone and timing matter when raising questions about age. Prepare. Find a calm time to initiate the conversation.

- When setting up learning experiences across age groups, make sure everyone is familiar with the technology needed to share information.

CASE STUDIES

Can't You Just Talk to Me?

One of my clients experienced a doubly awkward moment. Holly got a call from human resources to explain why David, her direct report, would not be promoted—"No more room at the top." Holly was surprised and disappointed, as she had focused a great deal of attention on David's career development, and he had been taking on increasing responsibilities with great success. As the call was ending, the HR representative asked, "Have you given any thought to when you might leave? That would create the space for David to move up." After 32 years with the company, Holly was thinking about retiring but felt insulted by the question, however relevant it might have been. Wounding rather than collaborative, it seemed to come out of left field. Although Holly had been in extensive talent reviews and succession planning meetings throughout her tenure, there was no process to ask executives overtly about their potential retirement plans. Holly, the HR manager, and David all would have benefited from a more intentional and structured discussion that recognized Holly's ability (and desire) to help ensure her team's future while also planning for her own departure.

Holly had to make a choice. She could stew silently, or she could seize the opportunity to use her respected leadership to drive change in the company procedures. Along with HR, Holly helped institute a proactive review of retirement benefits with all eligible executives. The process equipped older staff to evaluate their personal timelines for continued employment and paved the way for more open conversations at the corporate level.

Do I Still Belong Here?

Systemizing the links between the old and new guard seems so obvious, yet it happens so infrequently. When Paul was transferred to the Paris office, he and his family received all kinds of relocation support. There was no question that this was going to be a major change. In contrast, when Paul retired years later, there were celebrations and heartfelt toasts, but no other preparation. Neither Paul nor the company had fully considered the personal and organizational impacts of his departure. Paul had chosen and mentored his successor, Sasha. But what were the expectations for contact once Paul left the firm? Would Sasha be seen as weak if she asked for his guidance? Would Paul be viewed as lost if he returned too often to the building?

Paul and I identified that his greatest fears were losing the relationships he worked so hard to build and not sharing his vast repository of institutional knowledge. Paul and Sasha made a plan. During the course of his first year of "freedom," there would be six formal mentoring meetings. While at the office, Paul got to see and solidify friendships with colleagues. He was able to shed the self-consciousness around "What are you doing here?"; the company was able to utilize his institutional knowledge and experience for a year longer.

Calling on History

It was a very emotional moment for everyone when Tyler took over as executive director of a community services organization. The previous leader had been in the post for 16 years, and had seen the organization through a major capital campaign and the construction of a new facility. But it was time to usher in the new era! Tyler's profile and style were quite different from his predecessor, Judy, and both respectfully wished each other well. Interactions between the two were infrequent until 18 months later, when Tyler called Judy and asked for advice. He found the role more challenging than he'd anticipated, and relations with the board required some deciphering. Judy was positively "tickled" and "thoroughly impressed with the lack of ego Tyler had in picking up the phone." With a bit of distance, some time on her hands, and deep knowledge of the organization, Judy was delighted to further contribute to a mission she cared so deeply about. As word got around, Tyler's reputation was further enhanced. How could you not respect a guy who knows what he doesn't know and knows where to find the answer?

50

LEVERAGE YOUR PLATFORM

Make a Difference

To the world you may be one person;
but to one person you may be the world.
—Dr. Seuss

The future of work is being drawn with lighter border lines. Professional and personal identities are fusing as a result of social media. Organizations no longer choose between social impact or profit. Governments *and* businesses are being called on to shape society. And it's easier than ever to collaborate across geographic regions. Businesses will increasingly be judged not only by the value they bring to their shareholders but also by their positive impact on society.

Larry Fink, chairman and CEO of BlackRock, one of the world's largest asset managers, delivered a call to action in his annual letter to CEOs, stating, "Your company's strategy must articulate a path to achieve financial performance. To sustain that performance, however, you must also understand the societal impact of your business as well as the ways that broad, structural trends—from slow wage growth to rising automation to climate change—affect your potential for growth."

The confluence of societal and organizational needs has led to this moment. Displaying different values at home and at work is falling out of fashion.

And that's really good news. Interconnectivity, transparency, and greater accountability. Grab your career ladder, climb onto your platform, and take a stand.

Did you race out of the office to meet with a nonprofit agency about establishing a job-training program for underprivileged youth, but veto the budget for staff development at your office? That's not a good look for you. If you are truly passionate about equal access to education, how about creating corporate training programs that have spaces for community members to attend? By doing so, you are endorsing an educational initiative that serves your business *and* the community. You can actively facilitate mission-driven, personal connections across sectors that create change.

Think of your life as an atom. Each time you make a split, energy is released. In contrast, integrating personal, organizational, and community goals expands personal and corporate capacity.

Integrating Your Many Roles in the World Produces the Most Powerful Effect for Yourself and Others

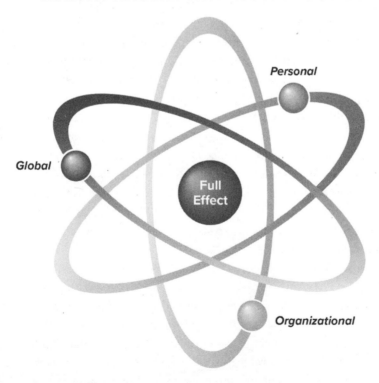

Whether you are a CEO or the newest associate, consider how your position provides you a chance to make a big decision or perform small tasks that will alter the world around you (for the better). This is not necessarily about investing more money, it's about investing attentional capital.

It's becoming increasingly popular for companies to establish Corporate Social Responsibility programs. However, recognizing how to leverage your platform is more than a campaign carried out at the institutional level. It's a state of mind in which you ask yourself, "How does my position allow me to help others?" It begins with a desire to act with intention and an inventorying of your nonmaterial assets, such as the ability to speak up, share access, and be generous with your relationships. Our choices can have inadvertent negative or purposely positive civic, environmental, and financial consequences.

Sometimes your power comes from asking the right questions (that leads to a more informed decision): "What are the community and workforce impacts if we build the factory in this town verses another?" "Will any families have to be moved?" Working in China, where many employees are from one-child families, the responsibility to care for parents and grandparents can be great, and the stress is multiplied when families are relocated far from the only offspring. After working long hours, will your employees spend their energies traveling far distances to care for relatives? How will they cope in the absence of family support nearby? Official presentations may not paint the full picture. The choice you make in a conference room in Madrid will reverberate for the factory supervisor, worker, and grandparents in Asia.

Have you earned enough respect that you can invite a dissenting voice to your organizational meetings? Can you advocate for others? A little experience may enable you to say what others can't. My client Marc, three years into his role, asked the senior managers at his firm to make a point of dismissing the newest employees in the evening because he observed that they were afraid to leave even though their work was done. That small intervention had a huge ripple effect, as the junior analysts got to spend their evenings with family, head to the gym, or go on a date.

India is a country of more than 60–70 percent functionally illiterate people. Osama Manzar, founder of the Digital Empowerment Foundation, is on a mission to "eradicate informational poverty" for India's poor and rural population who are deprived of access to information and rights. He has traveled to more than 5,000 villages, established in excess of 700 digital resource centers, fought for net neutrality, and advocated for investment to connect the unconnected. He has digitally empowered more than 7 million poor tribal members, aborigines, and minorities. Through amazingly creative means, his team taught people throughout the country to leverage their positions. For example, Osama constructed cubes with different symbols on each side and used these to teach illiterate communities to access the Internet not by learning the alphabet, but by memorizing pictures that could lead them to information they could consume aurally.

THIS IS FOR YOU IF

- You want to live your values—in everything you do.

- Increasing capacity is the goal, as there aren't any more hours in the day.

- Your company has resources that cost you nothing to share and are invaluable to others.

- Triple wins excite you. You're ready to benefit yourself, your organization, and your community.

TAKE ACTION

▶ Make sure your choices are aligned with the person you want to be and what you want to achieve. Whether your company is big or just getting started, include a "social cost" when evaluating your financial budgets.

▶ Review your supply chain, including vendors of consultancy services. Hire a firm owned or led by women, veterans, immigrants, or members of the LGBTQ community. A few keyboard strokes can connect you to lists of certified minority-owned businesses. Identify the decision-makers in your company. Share your research and ideas with them to make it easier to request proposals from more diverse companies.

▶ Make reading the news an active exercise. What's getting you excited or frustrated? How can you support people working for causes you care about? Look around the office with a widened peripheral lens. Think about practical offerings: a desk to work at, a closet to store flyers, a place to plug one's phone, even access to restrooms.

▶ Remember that your company may have resources that cost you nothing to share and are invaluable to others. Brazilian cosmetic company Natura sends vans to pick up employees living far from public transportation.

Empty seats on the van are offered to students who live along the corporate bus route but far from their schools.

▶ Dare to ask the second and the third questions—because you can.

▶ Your presence can be an asset no matter your place in the hierarchy. Show up and honor a person or program.

▶ Talk to your colleagues about the issues that you care about, and see who else shares your passions. Worried about rising obesity rates? Do you work at a kid's TV channel? Are you on the marketing team? Perhaps you can opt not to advertise sugary food, thus stimulating candy and fast-food companies to offer healthy alternatives.

▶ Professor Adam Grant refers to the sharing of our knowledge, skills, and connections as "microloans." Become a lender.

KEEP IN MIND

• You can delegate tasks, but you have to do the personal work first. Who do you want to be in the world?

• Be sure your initiative has true heart. People see through branding and marketing opportunities masked as community service.

CASE STUDIES

Turning Trash into Opportunity

"What is my role in the world, and what do I want to do with it?" was the prompt for a program I co-led in India. For inspiration, we met Milind Arondekar, founder of Aakar, along with the "waste pickers" he helped organize. Waste pickers earn a living by collecting recyclable materials dumped by India's burgeoning middle class. The women's saris flowed elegantly as they separated discarded plastic cups from paper products. We chatted while we worked. We began talking about families, and then moved into a discussion about gender roles and domestic responsibilities (for our children and our parents). As the exchange progressed, the Indian women asked for advice on retirement savings. People who not long before didn't have enough money to get through the day were inquiring about financial planning!

How did the waste pickers' circumstance improve? In 1993, Milind Arondekar and his wife, Sharada, realized that the success of their small store depended on their neighborhood's appeal. Buckets of refuse rotted in the sun. Official sanitation trucks didn't service the area. Waste pickers decanted the trash onto the street to see and sort the recyclables. They were an eyesore to the community and were frequently chased away by the police, leaving carpets of garbage behind. Milind worked with the local government. He obtained permission for the women to use a vacant lot to sift through the rubbish before taking it to recycling centers. Hauling the trash to the yard was hard. Milind asked the municipality for a truck to transport the refuse. The women would drive the vehicles. The waste pickers became part of the sanitation system. As city employees, they were eligible for identification cards. Now the women could apply for social benefits, register their children in school, and even open a bank account. Today, with very modest resources, Aakar assists up to 7,000 families in Mumbai, organizing small collectives to help the previously destitute women save money and receive small but important loans.

Pulling the Levers of Social Change from the C-Suite

Fábio aspires to build a better society based on strong values. He initially made his name as a Brazilian financier and later shifted sectors to lead a media conglomerate. Why? "Because banking and journalism are both levers of social change," he told me, providing a platform to execute on strong personal convictions. When he was president of Banco Real, Fábio introduced a sustainability program that included social and environmental risk analysis, ethical investment funding, microcredit operations, and tailored banking for disabled customers. Fábio later became CEO of the Abril Group, one of Latin America's most influential media enterprises. He believes the development of Brazil, like many other countries around the world depends on transparency. Fábio remarked that once you "turn on the lights, there's no on and off." He said he works every day to build better companies, better markets, and a better country. He reminds us: "Society and the world are made out of our attitudes."

Beauty Contests Become a Microphone for Female Advancement

A highly motivated teenager, Kiah Duggins won a scholarship to study business. She enrolled at Wichita State University, where she founded "The Princess Project" to help high school girls from disadvantaged groups prepare college applications. She received a young social entrepreneur fellowship (and seed funding) through The Resolution Project and was recognized at the Clinton Global Initiative University (CGIU). I asked Kiah how she managed to gain so much notice for her work. A fervent feminist, she leveraged an unlikely platform when she entered a beauty contest through a fraternity to raise money for charity—and won. She advanced through various competitions, ultimately competing for Ms. Kansas. Kiah used her media coverage to speak about diversity issues and the importance of providing quality education to often unseen young women. One of the judges at CGIU confessed that Kiah's bright pink booth covered in sparkles certainly caught her eye. Kiah knows how to get a response, and she's not afraid to get positive attention for issues that matter deeply to her.

51

CHALLENGE
THE STATUS QUO

Unleash Intergenerational Energy

*It is not your responsibility to finish the work of perfecting
the world, but you are not free to desist from it either.*
—Rabbi Tarfon, Pirke Avot 2:21

Audacious ambition, sector-shifting initiatives, work imbued with meaning while responding to market forces—it's not youthful folly. It's the opportunity for experienced executives to leverage their platforms for enhanced personal and professional impact. With greater experience, influence, and access, baby boomers can now drive the systemic change they could only dream of when bell bottoms were first in style and they were raging against "The Man."

The numbers are in. Gallup's recent 155-country study on the State of the Global Workplace reveals that only 15 percent of employees worldwide are actively engaged at work, and more than twice that number are so disengaged they are likely to spread negativity to others. Recent graduates are rejecting organizations that are unable to connect profit and purpose. There's a growing expectation for companies to assume a larger role in responding to social issues. Corporate leaders have a mandate. Yet rather than step up, many business leaders are stepping down, just when they have the most influence and are at the height of their abilities. I encourage staying put.

"What should I do with my life?" My 25-year-old and 55-year-old clients ask the same question. With a career ahead of them, the pressure is on new entrants to the workforce to "make it meaningful." Facing the prospect of retirement, the boomers' refrain is, "Am I doing anything worthwhile? What will be my legacy?" In my experience, the two ends of the occupational work spectrum are best suited to drive change, and to do so from a place of passion and meaning. Senior leaders, no longer stimulated by the status quo, contemplate leaving their posts to make a difference—to give back—through board memberships and nonprofit work. Once "on the outside," there's often less scaffolding for their idea; money and administrative support are constrained. Partnering with and empowering shared stakeholders can be far more efficient and motivating than leaving to create a new nonprofit, and then lobbying companies for support.

With greater confidence and credibility, seasoned change agents can cascade their wisdom within their existing companies, challenging their enterprises to effect changes in their communities by doing business differently. Having reached the institutional summit, they now have the opportunity to integrate a personal sense of purpose with the goals of the profit-driven organizations they lead. By reconnecting to and expressing a point of view that matters both to themselves and to others, executives can personally reenergize their careers and inspire the workforce they lead.

This is the chance for older colleagues to cash in on their experience dividend and make use of the respect they command, the resources they can access, and the public platforms they inhabit to integrate what they care about and what they do. Rather than fear the impending grey tsunami, we should harness its force and drive change from within the enterprises that are lucky enough to still benefit from these leaders. Why not consider teaming up millennials and boomers with the express purpose of bringing social impact to the core of the business? At a time when there is great trepidation about managing across the age divide, why not match up these dynamic duos of social change?

The mature leader concerned about income or gender inequality can have a sweeping effect by altering their company's recruitment policy, supply chain expectations, and governance of their own and investee companies, as well as by creating products that respond to (rather than create) social need. The list goes on. Driving social impact as a core corporate strategy requires the gravitas that a senior professional has earned and responds to the younger generation's expressed expectation of its employer.

You're nearing the end of *Connect First*. Earlier chapters encouraged you to develop a point of view, cultivate an identity that fosters meaning for yourself and others, convene groups, invite others in, and bravely tackle questions with no obvious answers. This entry combines these skills, demonstrating how you can embrace aging, leverage your platform, and work across generations.

In *Aging Well*, George Vaillant asserts that "biology flows downhill." We are naturally inclined to serve those who come after, and thrive when doing so. Working together in pursuit of similar values, silver-haired veterans and fresh-faced recruits have the opportunity to achieve exponential impact.

THIS IS FOR YOU IF

- You're ready to leave your job to make a difference.

- Corporate responsibility is more than a department; it's a strategy.

TAKE ACTION

▶ Seek out purpose on the job. If you are currently in a position of power (but losing interest in business as usual), before you declare boredom and leave, stop to think: *What issue would you dedicate time to if you had all the hours in your day to do so? How does your interest intersect with your company's activities? Are you bothered by the fact that neighbors go hungry while your company wastes food?* Call the manager in charge of the kitchen, and speak to your facilities supervisor. Tell them you want to understand the process of dealing with leftovers. Explain that you are gathering information because their work is connected to a cause you care about and not because you are looking to displace their authority. Share a personal story to express why this matters to you. Are they also concerned about how much healthful food is being discarded? How would they improve the situation? What are the obstacles? It's possible there's an archaic organizational regulation on how long you can store food, or there's no overtime allowed for staff to pack up donations to a shelter. What may seem like impossible constraints for the person in charge is a matter of a few calls for someone with your clout.

▶ Hold workshops to clear the air and align values. Don't be afraid if initially the generations are less than complimentary with each other. I conducted a session with representatives from multiple insurance companies. When asked to describe challenging aspects of their youthful colleagues, people age 45–65 listed "entitled, impatient, disrespectful, and high maintenance." The 25- to 35-year-olds referred to the senior staff as "judgmental, scared, and closed-minded." While the millennials aspired to hold positions of responsibility, they wanted to do things differently. The stress they observed in their superiors was not an ideal model. Many of the older participants agreed. They wished they had better work/life balance, freedom from relentless requests, and more opportunity to learn new things. Once the frustrations were aired, the mood shifted. There were remarkable similarities in their desired work environments. We paired millennials from one company with boomers in another. This set the stage for mutual mentoring, with the added benefit of providing an outsider's perspective.

▶ Experiment with reverse mentoring. Pair interns or new recruits with colleagues twice or three times their age, with the instruction that the younger person's role is to expose the older executive to social platforms, technology, and emerging business ideas that they might not have discovered on their own. Encourage the pair to compare how they consume and store information. Discuss who influences their decisions and to whom they go for advice.

▶ Include millennials in forums to explore questions that don't yet have answers. Respect their creativity. Seasoned managers can model the importance of leading into the unknown. The younger generation, coming of age in an era of social entrepreneurship, may see links between business, social, and environmental sectors that are not readily apparent to their more senior coworkers. As potential action plans unfold, the elders may be able to call colleagues in positions of power at other institutions, creating (and funding) more impactful collaborations.

▶ With the ability to direct resources and navigate organizational terrain, the C-suite veteran can use their platform to free oxygen pockets of innovation, convening groups that might not otherwise work together. The senior executive can more readily establish special interest committees within the firm or sign off on sponsoring a summit of industry leaders from different sectors. With more name recognition, the elder statesperson may be able to attract greater attendance. The millennials may be able to shape the agenda by crowdsourcing diverse perspectives from within and outside of the company using social media.

▶ Join forces to communicate your message. Compare notes on influencers. What's the best way to reach them? Shape public discourse by deploying social and traditional media.

▶ Too often the CEO articulates a vision for social impact and then delegates its execution to junior staff in brand-building or community service departments who lack the power to effect strategic decisions and create programs. The result is cosmetic. Working together, the millennial in marketing and the senior manager in the boardroom can bring the organization's stated mission to life.

▶ Innovations in artificial intelligence will significantly impact workers at all stages of their careers, in white-collar and blue-collar jobs. This will demand continual lifelong learning and re-skilling. Create learning groups of all ages.

KEEP IN MIND

• Recruitment of new talent may depend on retaining the wise veterans as inspiration—and a source of energy for the future.

• Be careful not to create "age ghettos" with your office seating arrangements. Allow for organic exchanges.

CASE STUDIES

Tying It All Together

"I got to go," said Sandrine on the first day of coaching. She had risen from receptionist to human resources professional and was now the COO of a Connecticut-based private equity company. She'd made and saved more money than she ever imagined. Her hometown in Florida was battered during two recent hurricanes, and Sandrine was ready to turn her attention to rebuilding the community. The folks reliant on fishing for their income needed new docks. The local workforce wasn't able to meet the demand. I asked Sandrine whether she saw synergies between her current role and community development goals. "No, they're not interested in anything but a quick profit. I've done my best to encourage caring for others, but it's not happening. I go to work like a zombie. I come alive when I'm doing things that matter."

I asked Sandrine if she shared her vision for the community with the company. She hadn't. She thought it was too personal. What if she tried? She wrote an article for her company newsletter about her plans to help the Florida community. The staff *were* interested in what she was doing. We started to make more links between her business and civic interests. When Sandrine asked the local government for funding to establish a jobs training program, she pointed to her experience as a COO, which gave her greater credibility. "I wasn't going to use my job in Connecticut in my pitch," she said. "I was going to make the appeal as a concerned Florida citizen."

Now the benefit of integrating her two worlds was becoming more apparent. Sandrine continued with her bold vision. She recruited recently released ex-convicts and unemployed veterans to train as dock builders. She hired a retired school principal and a former army lieutenant as supervisors. She had amassed quite a group of characters, and the results of their work were immediately apparent. No longer committed to keeping her worlds separate, Sandrine asked her Connecticut-based colleagues to hold the company planning meeting in Florida, so that they could meet the people rebuilding her community. She closed the session with an impassioned request that the firm expand their definition of adding value to the companies they invest in. The CEO was impressed with the energy Sandrine sparked in others. He offered her the opportunity to redefine her role. People of all ages in the firm volunteered to help Sandrine with the new strategy to put community improvement at the core of their business planning.

Breaking the Art World Rules

"I'm done hiding *my* canvases," exclaimed Alon, co-owner of an esteemed art gallery in Manhattan. "I am tired of living a fractured life. I am a gallerist and an artist myself. I am a gay man and a trusted businessman. I wasn't afraid to tell my parents I was a homosexual, but if I tell the artists I represent that I am also a painter, they'll think I'm not pure. I won't be seen as representing their interests." Although Alon had spent decades building a strong reputation in the art world, he was ready to leave his dealing days behind in order to assert another part of his identity that meant so much to him.

What was driving Alon's readiness to make such a dramatic departure? "I'm tired of paying such high rent, and the insurance rates are killing me." "The second half of my life needs to have fewer rules." We chose two rules to break. Alon could still be a gallerist, but without a permanent venue. He could curate shows in pop-up spaces, most likely downtown, which would expand his clientele, while offering a new destination to his established customers. He would challenge the assumed division between dealer and maker, and invite the artists he represented to not only be part of his exhibitions, but to take a more active role in the curation. Since the rents were lower, Alon could take more risk on whose work he showed. New artists could benefit from Alon's reputation and gain more exposure to collectors who were accustomed to investing in talent.

"They can build their reputations with mine." Alon was reinvigorated. "I am not paralyzed with fear. My ego isn't as involved as it once was. I am freer to experiment." Alon shuttered his gallery but expanded his reach. He created an online platform for buyers to see and purchase art. He used a portion of the money he saved on rent and insurance to hire newly minted professionals to launch social media campaigns about the artists and their shows. Alon now holds about four exhibitions a year and devotes the rest of the time to painting. He's launching the careers of young artists, while modeling a new way of doing business, *and* working on his own art.

52

DREAM
AUDACIOUSLY

Move Beyond Success
to Significance

I had a dream. Now I can't sleep anymore.
—BRAZILIAN BUMPER STICKER

"I don't want to lead a little life," declared Taddy Blecher, as he described the motivation behind creating CIDA City Campus and then later the Maharishi Institute, both business schools in South Africa for students with limited resources and few job skills. In the beginning, and in the absence of funding, Taddy taught typing using photocopies of a keyboard; the students' fingers danced over the paper while they sat on the floor. The curriculum developed, as did the proof of concept, and over time, backing came from philanthropists like Oprah Winfrey and Richard Branson.

How big a life do you want to live? This is not a prompt to consider how many acres of land you will own or parties with celebrities you will attend. It's a chance to take stock in what journalist David Brooks terms our *resume virtues* and our *eulogy virtues*. Resume virtues are what we write about ourselves to measure up to the world's expectations. Promotions and positions with grand titles communicate our success. In contrast, eulogy virtues are what others say about us at our funeral: what kind of person we were, how we led our life, and how significant a role we played in caring for others. Dr. Aravind

Srinivasan, head of the purpose-led and profitable Aravind Eye Hospitals in India, put it well: "Success is what happens to you. Significance is what happens through you. Success is what comes to you. Significance is what you give away to others."

No matter what stage or position you are in life (as captured in the musical *South Pacific*) ". . . if you don't have a dream, how you gonna have a dream come true?" This book ultimately is about dreaming; dreaming that *joyful work* won't be an oxymoron for you or your coworkers. *Connect First* started with a smile, and now we end with a dream. Close your eyes or open them wide (whichever suits you). Treat yourself to some space and silence. Go for a walk, take a long shower, or linger in bed a few moments longer. Unshackle your mind from the day-to-day lists, for just a few minutes. How do you want to be in the world? What do you want to be known for? Legacies are not the province of the rich. We all have a chance to leave our mark through small daily actions that do make a difference. By being intentional in who we choose to look at, listen to, eat with, and invite in, we solve problems and shift mindsets. Our jobs can be the source of community and pride; they can provide a platform for personal growth and social change.

Success, meaning, and joy are minted at the office in the interactions among people, by people just like you and me. We all have the power to significantly impact the future of work.

THIS IS FOR YOU IF

- You don't want to live a little life.

- You want to leave a legacy.

- You're not embarrassed to make a wish—and make it come true.

TAKE ACTION

▶ Entertain the dream. It will give you energy. Think big. You can always crop the picture to fit reality.

▶ Trust yourself and others. Don't be afraid to share your dream. Saying it out loud starts to make it real.

▶ Don't linger with those who deflate you.

▶ Remember that "a journey of a thousand miles begins with a single step" (Lao Tzu). Think about the smallest, easiest actions you can take to get started, to test your idea, and to build momentum.

▶ Don't be embarrassed! I told a colleague about my plan to write *Connect First*. "You are so ambitious," she said. I was taken aback, a little ashamed. I hadn't thought of my efforts as ambitious, and once labeled as such, I blushed. It's not always easy to dream big. It can feel self-aggrandizing, but hey, "If you don't have a dream, how you gonna have a dream come true?"

KEEP IN MIND

● Negative self-talk can undermine your confidence: you don't have to have all the answers, but you do need the determination.

● Dreams take time.

CASE STUDY

Connect First

I had a dream to write this book. I indulged my inner middle-school self and bought neon-hued index cards, poster boards, and Post-it notes in various sizes. The bright, jelly-bean collage of supplies made me smile. I reviewed old notebooks and computer files. I storyboarded different concepts and the examples to back them up. What emerged was a temple to my obsessive-compulsive qualities, as well as the framework for a book. For years, every Thursday I set a writing target. As I completed an entry, I affixed a sticker to the index card bearing the chapter's name. What can I say? I'm not above a little positive self-reinforcement.

I sought feedback. My first round of readers were 15 people—ranging in age from 24 to 61 years old, from five different countries and multiple American states, and almost equal numbers of males and females. The group's work experience included opera, policy, personal training, labor law, spiritual guidance, academia, sports business, board leadership, banking, neurobiology, and global campaigns to teach empathy. Not one person I asked to participate in this project said no!

Everyone contributed multiple enhancements. I listened to many but not all of them. I wrote and revised and rewrote and edited. Over and over. I continued to ask for help. I drafted the book, but I wasn't clear on how to frame the problem I was solving or why I was in the unique position to do so. Unable to answer my own questions, I convened the group I needed. One weekend morning I turned my dining room into a writer's room and invited a half-dozen participants. The group had a balance of men and women and reflected a diversity of ages and races. I offered generous introductions honoring everyone's experience. We made sure each participant had multiple opportunities to contribute their ideas. They were assigned seats and given name cards at the start. I served food. We told stories. We started and ended on time.

To achieve my *Connect First* dream, I followed the advice I have shared in this book. That included challenging my negative thoughts and showing lots of appreciation. Now's my chance to say, *"Thank you!"* for sharing the journey and daring to be more human at work!

ACKNOWLEDGMENTS

Modeling the courage, commitment, and curiosity to change, my patients and clients have taught me the lessons you read in this book. I have had the good fortune to always love my work. Thank you to all the people who trusted me with their deepest secrets and most exciting ambitions. *Connect First* comes to life (at least I hope you think so) through the case studies. I am so appreciative of the clients and colleagues from around the world who gave me permission to share their stories and, more important, welcomed me into their lives.

This book took form over several years, generating thousands of emails, hundreds of conversations, and multiple advice sessions over coffees and cocktails. The concept seemed so simple, but the execution, well, that took lots of input and encouragement. Although I hid away every Thursday to write, I was never alone. Thank you to my immediate and extended family, friends, and colleagues who responded to impromptu polls as I tested ideas, images, and positioning for *Connect First*. You offered to host book parties from the moment my fingers first hit the keyboard. Extraordinary!

Ron Beller, Mike Clancy Jr., Philip DerMargosian, Debbie Evangelakos, Chip Fournier, John Gartner, Julia Mart, Eric Messenger, Kerri Kwinter, Kenzie Kwong, Daniel Newman, Anamaria Schindler, Steve Schwartzberg, Gary Simon, Helen Strnad, and Sharlene Wolchik turned their big brains and huge hearts to my manuscript and found ways to express my ideas more effectively than I would have. Thank you for your suggestions to stay positive, reduce density, increase specificity, drop jargon, and keep my ego in check. Members of my writers' room morning—Stephen Fenichell, Leah Johnson, Deepa Lakshmin, Harper Makowsky, John Paul Newport, Jacob Tugendrajch, and our intrepid facilitator, Marcy Gregory—helped articulate the unique contribution *Connect First* could make and brought the importance of my clinical experience into sharper focus.

John Gerzema told me he wanted to read a book about my experience as a coach and therapist. His prompt set off the torrent of ideas that filled these pages. Karin Forseke's astute reading of early drafts and powerful belief in me electrified my synapses and gave me energy. Emily Greenberg dazzled me with her conceptual comments, refined my grammar, and encouraged me to incorporate more of my own voice. After endless hours at my desk, meeting Mike Clancy at the gym kept me in physical and psychic shape through the entirety of this project. Adam Brooks is a real writer, and he made sure I felt like one at every stage of this process. Thank you for your writer-to-writer motivational texts. Peter Rose was unremittingly gracious in sharing his vast wisdom, informing the focus and title of *Connect First*. If you find joy in the book, join me in thanking Peter; he insisted that linking joy and work was critical, and I believe he is right. I am grateful to Jayne Jamison and Cevin Bryerman for decades of friendship and their professional support as my book met the world. Special appreciation goes out to Adam Grant, a generous colleague for many years.

Lindsay Levin has shown so many people how to shift what's possible. When I asked her advice about bringing on a writing partner, she encouraged me to look in the mirror. She knows me so well—it was just the boost I needed. Thank you for thinking and feeling with me through every step. My Leaders' Quest (LQ) family cocreated and practiced many of the methodologies described in *Connect First*. We've traveled many miles together, survived and thrived in complicated situations. No matter what the universe throws at us, there's peace and calm when we return to *the circle*. The energy Leaders' Quest radiated after my initial *Connect First* talk lifted my feet and soul off the ground. Thank you for providing such a safe and loving professional home. Extra gratitude goes to our "other Mel," Melanie Jamieson, and her team for making sure *Connect First* reaches the widest audiences.

Julie Kantor kept this doctor sane by stepping in at all the right times to ensure that Katzman Consulting clients had the coverage they needed when my days could stretch no further. Larry and Claire Aidem deployed their relational charm, making connections to people who share my vision. Suzanne Gowler is a talented thinking partner . . . about everything. Viviane Barreto de Azevedo Lamego continually models commitment to personal and organizational growth on a global scale. Lori Zabar and I have shared so many milestones, including the joys (and a few miseries) of authorship. Amy Wolf, Helen Gitelson, Jen Moses, Jill Kristal, Judy Bernstein, Lainey Fallek, Sandy Rokoff, and Susan Newman have provided the emotional trampoline to bounce back from life's challenges. I work like crazy, racing around the world, and they nourish me when it's time to play.

Jill Grinberg is more than an agent. She's the midwife of *Connect First*. With the most elegant touch, she calmly, wisely, and with relentless patience pulled this book out of me. Jill responded instantly to my ideas about work and naturally practices so many of this book's suggestions. Thank you doesn't capture the heaps of gratitude and mountains of respect I have for Jill and her exceptional counsel. Jill can speak shrink, analyze a market, manage multiple relationships, and be tons of fun. I could not have written *Connect First* without her. Jill's colleagues at Grinberg Literary Management were equally supportive. In particular, Denise Page was unflaggingly dedicated to doing whatever was needed, reading multiple versions of the proposal, testing titles and covers, and guaranteeing that everyone was always in sync. Sophia Seidner totally had my back.

Casey Ebro, my editor at McGraw-Hill, understood me, my message, and my mission immediately. I am grateful that she felt the connection as strongly as I did when we first met. In less than a year, Casey signed, named, and championed *Connect First* to print. Acting promptly and with precision, Casey always listened to my concerns, and then delivered a better solution than I could have imagined.

Through late nights and weekends Jill and Casey sent me "Got It" emails and made sure *Connect First* was headed in the right direction. They orchestrated a dream team. Nora Hennick and Amanda Muller of McGraw-Hill brought their marketing prowess and wonderful spirit of collaboration. Jeff Weeks created a cover that communicates the universality of connecting, no matter the color of your skin (or paperclip). Andrew Mauney performed magic with the author photo. A book that appeals to everyone at the office runs the risk that no one thinks it's uniquely for them. Mark Fortier and Lisa Barnes are virtuosos of communication and trusted advisors who expertly targeted my conversations. Alona Beloussova was my literary angel—appearing at just the right moment—making sure *Connect First* launched smoothly. Gregg Sullivan lit up the internet and never grew tired of my endless inquiries.

Many people have wondered if Gerry Sanseviero is a real person or how many people make up this one phenomenon. She's everywhere doing everything, seemingly effortlessly, with great humor, purpose, and compassion. Gerry runs Katzman Consulting, managing the relationships, schedules, and finances. When I said I wanted to write a book, she snapped into gear and cleared my calendar on Thursdays. She critiqued ideas, researched, and fact-checked. She restructured sentences, formatted prose, and mocked-up covers. She obtained all of the case study permissions. Press? She helped organize that, too. Web design, camera angles, voice coaching, making sure I eat—Gerry does it all. Actor, editor, intellectual muse, Gerry diligently and passionately anticipates my needs and those of Katzman Consulting's associates and clients. She's made sure we follow the *Connect First* principles in our office. Thanks to Gerry, so many of us have achieved success, meaning, and joy at work.

Amanda Roman Makowsky and Trey Brademan slipped into our loud, opinionated, excessively social family, flexing their smarts and wickedly fast sense of humor, at a time when *the book* occupied its own seat at the table. Focus groups at dinner weren't part of their job descriptions when our kids brought them home, but they rose to the challenge with panache.

My children grew up with a mother who couldn't sit still, didn't believe in jet lag, and never stopped hugging and kissing them (when I was around). They taught me, tolerated me, and teased me. Nobody can point out my fault lines like Wyndam and Harper, and for this I am deeply grateful. They are both active in the workforce now, and I couldn't be prouder of the professionals they have become.

Wyndam contributed his expert editorial skills, reviewed passage after passage, called out missing or extra commas, modified the title and subtitle countless times, sharpened the applicability of my advice, and kept me going with his belief that companies of the future would benefit from my work. I knew I was onto something when Wyndam told his whole executive MBA class about my book. I'm biased of course, but Wyndam is and will be the kind of boss for whom you want to work.

Harper unleashed the multitude of her superpowers to bring *Connect First* to market. She reviewed positioning documents, participated in strategy discussions, built my first YouTube channel, did my makeup for filmed sessions, and edited the book and chapter titles. During multiple difficult projects she wrote me (and my team) motivational messages. She sends clips and keeps me laughing. Harper's magnetic and a maestro at decoding emotional messages. There's nothing she can't do, and she holds me to the same standard.

Russell Makowsky is the consummate executive—and spouse. He combines deep technical knowledge and strong interpersonal savvy. Russell read the manuscript with an English major's eye. He was attentive while I processed (out loud) the latest book updates and didn't take it personally when I needed to disappear for yet another rewrite. He's been this coach's coach. And cook. And best friend. He's my rock. His steadfastness is the reason I can pursue my entrepreneurial adventures. His strong moral compass always points me in the right direction. Russ has provided the continued confidence throughout my career that I can and will achieve my dreams.

REFERENCES

For a more comprehensive list of reference material, please visit: https://www.melaniekatzman.com/connectfirst/references.

CHAPTER 1

Achor, S. (2012, Jan–Feb). Positive Intelligence. Retrieved from Harvard Business Review: https://hbr.org/2012/01/positive-intelligence

Cromie, W. J. (2003, January 23). Faking happiness for fun and profit. Retrieved from Harvard University Gazette: http://news.harvard.edu/gazette/2003/01.23/13-smile.html

Grandey, A., Fisk, G., Mattila, A., Jansen, K., & Sideman, L. (2005). Is "service with a smile" enough? Authenticity of positive displays during service encounters. *Organizational Behavior and Human Decision Processes*, 96(1), 38-55.

Keltner, D. (2009). *Born to Be Good: The Science of a Meaningful Life*. New York: W.W. Norton & Co.

CHAPTER 2

Murphy, M. L. (2012, August 18). Separated by a common language. Retrieved from Lynneguist: http://separatedbyacommonlanguage.blogspot.com/2012/08/saying-please-in-restaurants.html

Porath, C. (2016). *Mastering Civility: A Manifesto for the Workplace*. New York: Hachette Book Group.

CHAPTER 3

Glassdoor for Employers. (2013, November 13). Employers to retain half of their employees longer if bosses showed more appreciation; Glassdoor Survey. Retrieved from Glassdoor: https://www.glassdoor.com/employers/blog/employers-to-retain-half-of-their-employees-longer-if-bosses-showed-more-appreciation-glassdoor-survey/

McGregor, J. (2014, February 5). A thank-you note from Mark Zuckerberg. Retrieved from The Washington Post: https://www.washingtonpost.com/news/on-leadership/wp/2014/02/05/a-thank-you-note-from-mark-zuckerberg/

The London School of Economics. (2011, May 20). When performance-related pay backfires. Retrieved from The London School of Economics and Political Science: http://www.lse.ac.uk/newsAndMedia/news/archives/2009/06/performancepay.aspx

CHAPTER 4

Carmody, D., & Lewis, M. (2006). Brain activation when hearing one's own and others' names. *Brain Research*, 1116(1), 153-158.

Carnegie, D. (1964). *How to Win Friends and Influence People*. New York: Simon & Schuster.

CHAPTER 5

Cialdini, R. (2006). *Influence: The Psychology of Persuasion*. New York: Harper Business.

Zenger, J., & Folkman, J. (2013, March 15). The Ideal Praise-to-Criticism Ratio. Retrieved from Harvard Business Review: https://hbr.org/2013/03/the-ideal-praise-to-criticism

CHAPTER 6

Kooti, F., Aiello, L., Grbovic, M., Lerman, K., & Mantrach, A. (2015). *Evolution of Conversations in the Age of Email Overload*. Florence: 24th International World Wide Web Conference Committee.

CHAPTER 7

Aartrijk. (2013, March 19). Mayor Ed Koch's "How Am I Doing? question opened the loop we're still running around. Retrieved from Aartrijk: http://www.aartrijk.com/how-am-i-doing-ed-koch-opened-the-loop-were-still-running-around/

Stone, D., & Heen, S. (2014). *Thanks for the Feedback: The Science and Art of Receiving Feedback Well*. New York: Penguin Group.

CHAPTER 9

Cain, S. (2012). *Quiet: The Power of Introverts in a World That Can't Stop Talking*. New York: Crown Publishing Group.

Covey, S. R. (2004). *The 7 Habits of Highly Effective People: Restoring the Character Ethic*. New York: Free Press.

Epley, N. (2015). *Mindwise: Why We Misunderstand What Others Think, Believe, Feel and Want*. New York: Vintage Books.

CHAPTER 10

Levin, M. (2017, June 12). Why Google, Nike, and Apple love mindfulness training, and how you can easily love it too. Retrieved from Inc.: https://www.inc.com/marissa-levin/why-google-nike-and-apple-love-mindfulness-training-and-how-you-can-easily-love-.html

CHAPTER 11

Erceau, D., & Gueguen, N. (2007). Tactile Contact and Evaluation of the Toucher. *The Journal of Social Psychology*, 147(4), 441-444.

Hertenstein, M. J., Holmes, R., McCullough, M., & Keltner, D. (2009). The communication of emotion via touch. *Emotion* (APA), 9(4), 566-573.

10 Psychological effects of non-sexual touch. (2011). Retrieved from PsyBlog: https://www.spring.org.uk/2011/04/10-psychological-effects-of-nonsexual-touch.php

Willis, F. N., & Hamm, H. K. (1980). The use of interpersonal touch in securing compliance. *Journal of Nonverbal Behavior*, 5(1), 49-55.

CHAPTER 12

Gallup. (2017). State of the American Workplace. Washington, DC: Gallup, Inc.

Kniffin, K., Wansink, B., Devine, C., & Sobal, J. (2015). Eating together at the firehouse: How workplace commensality relates to the performance of firefighters. *Human Performance*, 28(4), 281-306.

Wollan, M. (2016, February 25). Failure to lunch: The lamentable rise of desktop dining. Retrieved from The New York Times: http://www.nytimes.com/2016/02/28/magazine/failure-to-lunch.html

CHAPTER 13

Senge, P., Scharmer, C., Jaworski, J., & Flowers, B. (2004). *Presence: Human Purpose and the Field of the Future*. New York: Doubleday.

CHAPTER 14

Peterson, C., Maier, S. F., & Seligman, M. (1993). *Learned Helplessness: A Theory for the Age of Personal Control*. New York: Oxford University Press.

CHAPTER 15

Brezsny, R. (2009). *Pronoia Is the Antidote for Paranoia: How the Whole World Is Conspiring to Shower You with Blessings*. Berkeley, CA: North Atlantic Books.

Lannon, R., Amini, F., & Lewis, T. (2000). *A General Theory of Love*. New York: Random House.

CHAPTER 16

Ambady, N., & Rosenthal, R. (1993). Half a minute: Predicting teacher evaluations from thin slices of nonverbal behavior and physical attractiveness. *Journal of Personality and Social Psychology*, 64(3), 431-441.

Demarais, A., & White, V. (2007). *First Impressions: What You Don't Know About How Others See You*. New York: Bantam Books.

Ifould, R. (2009, March 6). Acting on impulse. Retrieved from The Guardian: https://www.theguardian.com/lifeandstyle/2009/mar/07/first-impressions-snap-decisions-impulse

Kahneman, D. (2011). *Thinking, Fast and Slow*. New York: Farrar, Straus and Giroux.

CHAPTER 17

Monarth, H. (2014, March 11). The irresistible power of storytelling as a strategic business tool. Retrieved from Harvard Business Review: https://hbr.org/2014/03/the-irresistible-power-of-storytelling-as-a-strategic-business-tool

Pink, D. (2009). *Drive: The Surprising Truth About What Motivates Us*. New York: Riverhead Books.

Vernon, R. J., Sutherland, C. A., Young, A. W., & Hartley, T. (2014). Modeling First Impressions from Highly Variable Facial Images. Proceedings of the National Academy of Science. DOI.

Zak, P. J. (2014, October 28). Communication. Retrieved from Harvard Business Review: https://hbr.org/2014/10/why-your-brain-loves-good-storytelling/

CHAPTER 18

Waitzkin, J. (2007). *The Art of Learning: An Inner Journey to Optimal Performance*. New York: Free Press.

CHAPTER 19

Beck, J. S. (2011). *Cognitive Behavior Therapy: Basics and Beyond*. 2nd ed. New York: The Guilford Press.

CHAPTER 20

Nish, C. (2012, July 26). How hobbies can help you get hired. Retrieved from The Wall Street Journal: http://blogs.wsj.com/atwork/2012/07/26/jobseeking-101-you-have-outside-interests-so-what/

Rosling, H. (2018). *Factfulness: Ten Reasons We're Wrong About the World—and Why Things Are Better Than You Think*. New York: Flatiron Books.

CHAPTER 22

Blanchard, K., & Johnson, S. (2015). *The New One Minute Manager*. New York: Harper Collins.

Gallup. (2017). State of the American manager. Retrieved from Gallup: https://www.gallup.com/services/182138/state-american-manager.aspx?ays=n#aspnetForm

CHAPTER 23

Ashoka. (1998). *Wellington Nogueira Santos Junior*. Retrieved from Ashoka: https://www.ashoka.org/en-US/fellow/wellington-nogueira-santos-junior

Cable, D. M. (2018). *Alive at Work: The Neuroscience of Helping Your People Love What They Do*. Boston, MA: Harvard Business Review Press.

Garton, E., & Mankins, M. (2015, December 9). Engaging your employees is good, but don't stop there. Retrieved from Harvard Business Review: https://hbr.org/2015/12/engaging-your-employees-is-good-but-dont-stop-there

Grant, A. (2014). Outsource Inspiration. In J. E. Dutton, & G. M. Spreitzer, *How to Be a Positive Leader: Small Actions, Big Impact* (pp. 22-31). San Francisco: Berrett-Koehler Publishers, Inc.

Michaels, E., Handfield-Jones, H., & Axelrod, B. (2001). *The War for Talent*. Boston, MA: McKinsey & Company, Inc.

Pfeffer, J. (1998). The Human Equation: Building Profits by Putting People First. In: *Building Profits by Putting People First*. Cambridge, MA: Harvard Business School Press.

CHAPTER 24

Goetz, K. (2011, February 1). How 3M gave everyone days off and created an innovation dynamo. Retrieved from Fast Co Design: http://www.fastcodesign.com/1663137/how-3m -gave-everyone-days-off-and-created-an-innovation-dynamo

Kaplan, D. (2014, November 14). The cult of busy. Retrieved from Medium: https://medium .com/thelist/the-cult-of-busy-bbb124caed51#.ylkxnsb0l

Levine, R. (1997). *A Geography of Time: The Temporal Misadventures of a Social Psychologist*. New York: Basic Books.

Shen, L. (2016, March 7). These 19 Great Employers Offer Paid Sabbaticals. Retrieved from Fortune: https://fortune.com/2016/03/07/best-companies-to-work-for-sabbaticals/

Whillans, A. (2019, January). Time for happiness: Why the pursuit of money isn't bringing you joy—and what will. Retrieved from Harvard Business Review: https://hbr.org/cover -story/2019/01/time-for-happiness

White, J. (2017, October 19). Ineffective meetings cost companies up to $283 billion a year (streamline collaboration with these tips). Retrieved from Inc.: https://www.inc.com /john-white/ineffective-meetings-cost-companies-up-to-283-billion-a-year-streamline -collaboration-with-these-tips.html

CHAPTER 25"

Schwartz, B. E. (2002). Maximizing versus satisficing: Happiness is a matter of choice. *Journal of Personality and Social Psychology*, 83(5), 1178-1197.

CHAPTER 26

Becker, D. (2014). *Abundance Mindset: Quick Ways to Remove "Scarcity" from Your Stinkin' Thinkin' for Small Business Owners*. Dennis Becker.

Covey, S. R. (1989). *The 7 Habits of Highly Effective People: Powerful Lessons in Personal Change*. New York: Simon & Schuster.

Diamandis, P., & Kotler, S. (2014). *Abundance: The Future Is Better Than You Think*. New York: Free Press.

Mogilner, C., Chance, Z., & Norton, M. I. (2012). Giving time gives you time. *Association for Psychological Science*, 23(10), 1233-1238.

CHAPTER 27

Buderi, R., & Huang, G. (2006). *Guanxi (The Art of Relationships): Microsoft, China, and the Plan to Win the Road Ahead*. New York: Simon & Schuster.

Grant, A. (2014). *Give and Take: Why Helping Others Drives Our Success*. New York: Penguin Books.

CHAPTER 28

Knight, R. (2016, April 1). How to work for a narcissistic boss. Retrieved from Harvard Business Review: https://hbr.org/2016/04/how-to-work-for-a-narcissistic-boss

Seltzer, L. F. (2018, August 13). The gullibility of the narcissist: What you need to know. Retrieved from Psychology Today: https://www.psychologytoday.com/us/blog/evolution -the-self/201808/the-gullibility-the-narcissist-what-you-need-know

CHAPTER 29

Cascio, C., O'Donnell, M., Tinney Jr., F., Lieberman, M., Taylor, S., Strecher, V., & Falk, E. (2015). Self-affirmation activates brain systems associated with self-related processing and reward and is reinforced by future orientation. *Social Cognitive and Affective Neuroscience*, 11(4), 621-629.

CHAPTER 30

Barsade, S. (2011, February). For better results, emotional contagion matters. Retrieved from Wharton@Work: Executive Education: http://executiveeducation.wharton.upenn.edu /thought-leadership/wharton-at-work/2011/02/emotional-contagion

Coleman, D. (2018). *Emotional Intelligence: Improve Your EQ for Business and Relationships.* Dan Coleman.

Fazio, R. (2018, August 10). Lead with laughter: How humor can positively transform a work environment. Retrieved from Forbes: https://www.forbes.com/sites/forbescoaches-council/2018/08/10/lead-with-laughter-how-humor-can-positively-transform-a-work -enviroment/#6e38a2535c94

Kerr, M. (2015). *The Humor Advantage: Why Some Businesses Are Laughing All the Way to the Bank.* Michael Kerr.

CHAPTER 31

Levin, L. (2013). *Invisible Giants: Changing the World One Step at a Time.* New Delhi: Rupa Publications India, Pvt. Ltd.

CHAPTER 32

Acharya, S., & Shukla, S. (2012). Mirror neurons: Enigma of the metaphysical modular brain. *The Journal of Natural Science, Biology and Medicine, 3*(2), 118-124.

Early, G. (2014). *3 Keys to Transforming Your Potential (An Accelerator's Guide to the CEO Within).* Harrisonburg, VA: Noble News and Books.

CHAPTER 33

Kassam, K., Markey, A. R., Cherkassky, V., Loewenstein, G., & Just, M. (2013, June 19). Identifying emotions on the basis of neural activation. Retrieved from PLOS One: https:// journals.plos.org/plosone/article?id=10.1371/journal.pone.0066032

Lerner, H. (2017). *Why Won't You Apologize? Healing Big Betrayals and Everyday Hurts.* New York: Simon & Schuster, Inc.

Sutton, R. (2010). *Good Boss, Bad Boss: How to Be the Best . . . And Learn from the Worst.* New York: Hachette Book Group.

CHAPTER 34

Altringer, B. (2013, November 19). A new model for innovation in big companies. Retrieved from Harvard Business Review: https://hbr.org/2013/11/a-new-model-for-innovation -in-big-companies/

Grant, A. (2016). *Originals: How Non-conformists Move the World.* New York: Penguin Random House LLC.

CHAPTER 35

Dalio, R. (2017). *Principles.* New York: Simon & Schuster.

Delizonna, L. (2017, August 24). High-performing teams need psychological safety. Here's how to create it. Retrieved from Harvard Business Review: https://hbr.org/2017/08/high -performing-teams-need-psychological-safety-heres-how-to-create-it

CHAPTER 36

Duckworth, A. L. (2013, April). Inventology: How we dream up things that change the world. Retrieved from TED: http://www.ted.com/talks/angela_lee_duckworth_the_key_to _success_grit

CHAPTER 37

Duncan, R. (2014, October 14). Is there an elephant in the room? Name it and tame it. Retrieved from Forbes: http://www.forbes.com/sites/rodgerdeanduncan/2014/10/14 /is-there-an-elephant-in-the-room-name-it-and-tame-it/#17e0877526dc

CHAPTER 38
Morieux, Y. (2014, January). Yves Morieux: As work gets more complex, 6 rules to simplify [Video file]. Retrieved from TED Talks: https://www.ted.com/talks/yves_morieux_as _work_gets_more_complex_6_rules_to_simplify/transcript?language=en

CHAPTER 39
Yerkes, R. M., & Dodson, J. D. (1908), The relation of strength of stimulus to rapidity of habit-formation. *Journal of Comparative Neurology and Psychology*, 18, 459-482. doi:10.1002/cne.920180503

CHAPTER 40
Coffman, J., & Neuenfeldt, B. (2014, June 17). Everyday moments of truth: Frontline managers are key to women's career aspirations. Retrieved from Bain & Company: http://www.bain.com/publications/articles/everyday-moments-of-truth.aspx
Fosslien, L., & West-Duffy, M. (2019, February 8). *How to create belonging for remote workers*. Retrieved from MIT Sloan Management Review: https://sloanreview.mit.edu/article /how-to-create-belonging-for-remote-workers/
Sacks, J. (2015). *Not in God's Name: Confronting Religious Violence*. New York: Schocken Books.
Wadi Attir. (2019). Project Wadi Attir. Retrieved from Sustainability Labs: http://www.sustainabilitylabs.org/wadiattir/home/

CHAPTER 41
Randall, R. (2015, July 16). 13 ways to make any office guest feel welcome. Retrieved from The Business Journals: http://www.bizjournals.com/bizjournals/how-to/growth-strategies /2015/07/13-ways-to-make-any-office-guest-feel-welcome.html

CHAPTER 42
EY Press Release. (2018, November 1). EY explores belonging in the workplace, with new Belonging Barometer study. Retrieved from EY: https://www.ey.com/us/en/newsroom/news-releases /news-ey-explores-belonging-in-the-workplace-with-new-belonging-barometer-study
Peters, T. J., & Waterman Jr, R. (2004). *In Search of Excellence: Lessons from America's Best Run Companies*. New York: HarperCollins Publishers.
Wilkes, D. (2015, May 14). Make small talk at work? We'd rather go and hide in the loo: Six in ten admit dodging conversations with their colleagues. Retrieved from Daily Mail: http:// www.dailymail.co.uk/news/article-3082502/Make-small-talk-work-d-hide-loo-Six-ten -admit-dodging-conversations-colleagues.html

CHAPTER 44
Cialdini, R. (2006). *Influence: The Psychology of Persuasion*. New York: Harper Business.
Military Bases Serve as Safe Haven for Endangered Species. (2016). [Radio]. J. Price. Retrieved from https://www.npr.org/2016/09/15/494127912/military-bases-serve-as-safe -haven-for-endangered-species
We Mean Business Coalition. (n.d.). COP 21 Engagement opportunities for business. Retrieved from We Mean Business Coalition: http://www.wemeanbusinesscoalition.org /content/cop-21-engagement-opportunities-business

CHAPTER 45
Leaders' Quest. (2016). Banking futures. Retrieved from Leaders' Quest: https://leadersquest. org/banking-futures
Tuckman, B. (1965). Development sequence in small groups. *Psychological Bulletin*, 63, 384-399.
Zak Borgman, S. (2016, March 9). The power of convening for social impact. Retrieved from Stanford Social Innovation Review: https://ssir.org/articles/entry/the_power_of_convening _for_social_impact#

CHAPTER 46

Hoffman, R., Casnocha, B., & Yeh, C. (2014). *The Alliance: Managing Talent in the Networked Age*. Boston, MA: Harvard Business Review Press.

Oettingen, G. (2014). *Rethinking Positive Thinking: Inside the New Science of Motivation*. New York: Current.

Phan, T. (2018). *You Are a Mogul*. New York: Simon & Schuster.

Seligman, M. P. (2006). *Learned Optimism: How to Change Your Mind and Your Life*. New York: Vintage Books.

Sharpe, B. (2013). *Three Horizons: The Patterning of Hope*. Charmouth: Triarchy Press Ltd.

Terkel, S. (1974). *Working: People Talk About What They Do All Day and How They Feel About What They Do*. New York: Pantheon/Random House.

Tomasdottir, H. (2016, November 6). My Story from TED. Retrieved from Halla Tomasdottir: http://hallatomasdottir.is/en/2016/11/06/my-ted-talk/

Tomasdottir, H. (2018, December 21). *Holiday letter 2018*. Retrieved from Halla Tomasdottir: http://hallatomasdottir.is/en/2018/12/21/holiday-letter-2018/

CHAPTER 47

Arizona State University. (2018). Interplanetary initiative. Retrieved from Arizona State University: https://interplanetary.asu.edu/about

Big Think. (n.d.). Want to lead? Learn to ask the right questions. Retrieved from Big Think: http://bigthink.com/think-tank/want-to-lead-learn-to-ask-the-right-questions

Stanford d-School. (2018). Design thinking bootleg. Retrieved from Square Space: https://static1.squarespace.com/static/57c6b79629687fde090a0fdd/t/5b19b2f2aa4a99e99b26b6bb/1528410876119/dschool_bootleg_deck_2018_final_sm+perecent282perecent29.pdf

CHAPTER 48

Delta Airlines. (2016, February 12). Delta employees take home their piece of largest profit sharing payout in U.S. history. Retrieved from PR Newswire: http://www.prnewswire.com/news-releases/delta-employees-take-home-their-piece-of-largest-profit-sharing-payout-in-us-history-300219327.html

Leaders' Quest. (2016, June 8). The positive power of capital: Integrating profit with purpose. Retrieved from Leaders' Quest: https://leadersquest.org/blog/the-positive-power-of-capital-integrating-profit-with-purpose

Seaman Jr., J., & Smith, G. D. (2012, December). Your company's history as a leadership tool. Retrieved from Harvard Business Review: https://hbr.org/2012/12/your-companys-history-as-a-leadership-tool

CHAPTER 49

Agan, T. (2013, March 30). Why innovators get better with age. Retrieved from The New York Times: http://www.nytimes.com/2013/03/31/jobs/why-innovators-get-better-with-age.html

Azoulay, P., Jones, B. F., Kim, J. D., & Miranda, J. (April 2018). Age and High-Growth Entrepreneurship. NBER Working Paper No. w24489. Available at SSRN: https://ssrn.com/abstract=3158929

Brooks, D. (2010, February 1). The geezers' crusade. Retrieved from The New York Times: http://www.nytimes.com/2010/02/02/opinion/02brooks.html?_r=0

Goldberg, E. (2005). *The Wisdom Paradox: How Your Mind Can Grow Stronger as Your Brain Grows Older*. Great Britain: Free Press.

Klaus, P. (2013, September 14). Embrace your age, and conquer the world. Retrieved from The New York Times: http://www.nytimes.com/2013/09/15/jobs/embrace-your-age-and-conquer-the-world.html?_r=0

McBride, S. (2013, February 28). Most new U.S. businesses founded by people 40 and older: survey. Retrieved from Reuters: http://www.reuters.com/article/us-startups-survey-idUSBRE91R0PO20130228

Michel, A. (2017, February). The cognitive upside of aging. Retrieved from Association for Psychological Science: https://www.psychologicalscience.org/observer/the-cognitive-upside-of-aging

Tamburo, J. (n.d.). Issues, impacts and implications of an aging workforce. Retrieved from American Society on Aging: https://www.asaging.org/blog/issues-impacts-and-implications-aging-workforce

United States Department of Health and Human Services. (2016, March 28). World's older population grows dramatically. Retrieved from National Institutes of Health: https://www.nih.gov/news-events/news-releases/worlds-older-population-grows-dramatically

United States Department of Labor. (2014). Employee tenure summary. Bureau of Labor Statistics.

CHAPTER 50

CRY: Child Rights and You. (n.d.). *Visit to Aakar—CRY project in Mumbai.* Retrieved from CRY: http://america.cry.org/site/lp/visittoaakar.html

Fink, L. (2018, January). 2018 Annual letter to CEOs: A sense of purpose. Retrieved from Blackrock: https://www.blackrock.com/corporate/investor-relations/2018-larry-fink-ceo-letter

First Global Strategic Workshop of Waste Pickers. (2012, April). *Inclusive Solid Waste Management.* Retrieved from Global Alliance of Waste Pickers: https://globalrec.org/wp-content/uploads/2012/04/report_waste-pickers-workshop_pune2012.pdf

Natura. (2013, July 24). Retrieved from www.slideshare.net: http://www.slideshare.net/romulozamberlan/apresentacao-institucional-editada-ing-jun13-24576841

Timmons, H., & Gill, N. (2012, April 6). How to help Durga and girls like her. Retrieved from New York Times:

WIEGO. (n.d.). *Empowering Informal Workers, Securing Informal Livelihoods.* Retrieved from Women in Informal Employment: Globalizing and Organizing: https://www.wiego.org/informal_economy_law/waste-pickers-india

GlobalLeadership.TV. (n.d.). Retrieved from Global Leadership: http://globalleadership.tv/fabio-barbosa-towards-ethical-banking-transcript/

CHAPTER 51

Gallup. (2017). *State of the Global Workplace.* Washington, DC: Gallup Press.

Katzman, M. A. (2015, August 7). You're the man now, dog: Grey-haired execs and millennials collaborate to change the world. Retrieved from Medium: https://medium.com/@DrKatzman/you-re-the-man-now-dog-grey-haired-execs-and-millennials-collaborate-to-change-the-world-def87afd63bb

Roose, K. (2017, October 15). Executive mentors wanted. Only millennials need apply. Retrieved from The New York Times: https://mobile.nytimes.com/2017/10/15/technology/millennial-mentors-executives.html?_r=0&referer

Toossi, M., & Torpey, E. (2017, May). Older workers: Labor force trends and career options. Retrieved from U.S. Bureau of Labor Statistics: https://www.bls.gov/careeroutlook/2017/article/older-workers.html

Vaillant, G. (2002). *Aging Well: Surprising Guideposts to a Happier Life from the Landmark Harvard Study of Adult Development.* Boston, MA: Little Brown & Company.

CHAPTER 52

Brooks, D. (2015). *The Road to Character.* New York: Random House.

Rodgers, R., & Hammerstein Jr., O. (1949). "Happy Talk." *South Pacific.*

Wavelength. (n.d.). On leadership success and significance. Retrieved from The Same Wavelength: https://thesamewavelength.com/on-leadership-success-and-significance/

INDEX

ABOUT THE AUTHOR

Melanie Katzman, PhD, is a business psychologist, advisor, and consultant to the world's top public and private companies, as well as governmental and nonprofit institutions. A sought-after expert in executive development, group dynamics, and leadership diversity, she founded Katzman Consulting in 1999 and has worked with businesses—including Accenture, Bain Consulting, Goldman Sachs, MTV, PwC, and Viacom—in 31 countries. A busy speaker, Katzman is also a founding partner of the global social enterprise Leaders' Quest, which serves a community of 12,000 members and facilitates cross-sector strategic discussions on pressing economic and social problems.

Katzman has held faculty positions in psychiatry at Weill Cornell Medical Center and the University of London, was a senior fellow at Wharton Business School's Center for Leadership and Change Management, and was a visiting professor at Bocconi Business School in Milan, the Henley School of Management in Henley-on-Thames, England, and the Chinese University of Hong Kong. She's also on the international advisory board of Fundação Dom Cabral, South America's largest business school. She cocreated and was cohost of the radio show *Women@Work* on Business Radio Powered by the Wharton School on SiriusXM Satellite Radio, channel 132. She has been featured in the *New York Times*, *Financial Times*, *South China Morning Post*, *Vanity Fair*, and *O Magazine*, as well as on ABC, CBS, and Lifetime.